Praise for *Ninete*

"A deeply personal and consistently engaging remembrance of a difficult young adulthood."
—*Kirkus Reviews*

"Nack's prose is candid and lyrical, blending sensory detail with sharp emotional insight. . . . Readers drawn to coming-of-age memoirs that explore the impact of family trauma and the long road to self-empowerment will not want to miss this sequel."
—*Readers' Favorite*, 5-star review

"Readers will be drawn in by this moving tale of childhood trauma and healing, as Nack grants them an intimate perspective on the conflicting inner battles of a young girl desperately crying out for love."
—BookLife Reviews

"Readers that choose *Nineteen* . . . should be prepared for a powerful survey of regret, remorse, reaction, and recovery analysis . . . a hard-hitting read that will lead them to question their own pasts and the foundations they've rested upon for survival."
—*Midwest Book Review*

"Leslie Nack's absorbing new memoir *Nineteen* takes us further into the stormy waters of her family dynamics. That Leslie survived and grew up to become a mother and a wife and a fantastic writer is a miracle. Her memoir reminds us all that we have an inner self, and when it's nurtured, there's all manner of beautiful blossoming."
—Linda Joy Myers, founder of the National Association of Memoir Writers and author of *Don't Call Me Mother*, *Song of the Plains*, and *The Forger of Marseille*

"Fierce, searching, and incredibly engaging—I couldn't put *Nineteen* down. A propulsive coming-of-age story about how we survive when we can't escape the wreckage of our family history and yet need the very people we are trying to flee from. Nack's memoir is a reckoning and a reclamation of self."

—Ronit Plank, author of *When She Comes Back* and host of the *Let's Talk Memoir* podcast

"Rarely is a writer as courageous, honest, and vulnerable on the page as Leslie Johansen Nack is in *Nineteen*. In her compelling narrative, Leslie never looks away from the raw truth of her unsettling teenage life. Written with a storyteller's attention to detail and a voice that draws readers into intimate confession, *Nineteen* is a memoir that reaches into the heart where compassion resides."

—Judy Reeves, author of *When Your Heart Says Go*

"*Nineteen* combines a shockingly intimate, fast-paced adventure with a heartbreaking tale of abuse, neglect, addiction, and recovery. Prepare to weep and applaud Leslie Johansen Nack for this remarkably well-written, heart-pounding memoir."

—Gina Simmons Schneider, PhD, author of *Frazzlebrain: Break Free from Anxiety, Anger, and Stress Using Advanced Discoveries in Neuropsychology*

"*Nineteen* is an intimate account of overcoming family trauma and drama. This detailed narrative evokes striking imagery that brings the reader into the experience. May it inspire all those facing challenges and foster compassion for those finding their way."

—CH Stern, LMFT, psychotherapist

"*Nineteen* is a raw, inspiring story of survival filled with resilience, self-discovery, and ultimate triumph."

—Sophia Kouidou-Giles, author of *Sophia's Return: Uncovering My Mother's Past*

"*Nineteen* is a heartfelt and sobering memoir. Written with courage and honesty, it reveals the consequences of family dysfunction and the redemption and healing that are possible in the aftermath of trauma."

—Leslie Ferguson, author of *When I Was Her Daughter*

"The author recounts her traumatic coming of age in an honest, compelling voice, exposing her family's dysfunction and her own poor choices with fascinating candor and evocative sensory details."

—Jennifer Silva Redmond, author of *Honeymoon at Sea*

"A fierce, unapologetic narrative about complicated family systems and addiction. *Nineteen* follows Leslie's memoir *Fourteen: A Daughter's Memoir of Adventure, Sailing, and Survival*. Leslie pours her heart and soul in this page-turning memoir. At times, *Nineteen* reads like a *Mission Impossible* screenplay. This memoir will stay with you well past putting the book down."

—Stephanie Maley, author of *No Longer That Girl: Retracing the Scars of the Past and Present*

nineteen

*A Daughter's Memoir of
Reckoning and Recovery*

Leslie Johansen Nack

SWP

SHE WRITES PRESS

Copyright © 2025 Leslie Johansen Nack

All rights reserved. No part of this publication may be reproduced, stored in a retrieval system, or transmitted in any form or by any means, electronic, mechanical, photocopying, recording, or otherwise, except for brief quotations in reviews, educational works, or other uses permitted by copyright law.

Published in 2025 by
She Writes Press, an imprint of The Stable Book Group

32 Court Street, Suite 2109
Brooklyn, NY 11201
https://shewritespress.com
Library of Congress Control Number: 2025908963
ISBN: 978-1-64742-996-6
eISBN: 978-1-64742-997-3

Interior Designer: Kiran Spees

Printed in the United States

Names and identifying characteristics have been changed to protect the privacy of certain individuals.

No part of this publication may be used to train generative artificial intelligence (AI) models. The publisher and author reserve all rights related to the use of this content in machine learning.

All company and product names mentioned in this book may be trademarks or registered trademarks of their respective owners. They are used for identification purposes only and do not imply endorsement or affiliation.

Author's Note

Since I published my first memoir in 2015, *Fourteen: A Daughter's Memoir of Adventure, Sailing, and Survival,* many people have written to ask me for the rest of my story. "What happened next?" they all say.

Before I give you the rest of the story, there are some things I want to say. After publishing *Fourteen,* nothing was ever the same for me, making me reluctant to keep writing. Giving the whole truth left me feeling exposed, naked, scared, and, at times, ashamed while at the same time making me feel proud, understood, loved, and healed. All of my tender truths were out in the world, living independently, being judged and praised by strangers, and I folded in on myself. My older sister, Monica, and my mother didn't make things easy. Thankfully, my younger sister supported me.

Eight months after *Fourteen* was published, Monica died from an overdose. She had helped me write *Fourteen,* remembering and reminiscing with me. It brought us closer than we'd been in years. But as the book launch approached, she recanted and refused to come. My heart broke. She got so mad she threatened to sue if I didn't take her out of the book entirely.

My mother also disavowed *Fourteen* and refused to attend the launch unless I removed her scenes. She had ducked and weaved away from her maternal responsibility her entire life. It was my mistake to be sentimental about some dream mother who would show up and support me. I must have been a masochist to cleave to such a dream. No, Mom, I can't change the book. My truth was finally being heard, and it would not be edited. She screamed and yelled, but I held firm. A few days before the launch, I tried again and invited her to stand beside me and be proud that we had both survived my father. She couldn't do it and made me promise not to publish anything more about her until after her death. I have honored that request.

After *Fourteen* came out, people I'd known for years looked at me differently, exclaiming they had no idea I had been raised that way. Some looked amazed and proud of me, while others looked cautious and unsure. The most rewarding part was having teenage girls share their stories with me. I was honored. I also had many women, and a few men, encourage me at the various events I did to promote *Fourteen*. Thank you for hearing my story.

All these things have changed me—for better and for worse. That's why it's taken me ten years to write *Nineteen*. But I have done it now. I'm proud of myself, and if things change more in the future with family and friends, I will at least be prepared.

Thank you for prodding me along with your emails and requests. Know that I have changed the names of some people, but it doesn't affect the outcome of anything. I offer you the rest of my story with a tender, open heart.

Bjorn Erling Johansen, 1979

"If five people in a family were to write the story of that family, we would end up with five very different stories. These are truths of a sort—the truth of adhering to what one remembers . . . but the intention of your father, the inner life of your mother, at these we can only hazard our best guess."

Inheritance by Dani Shapiro

Prologue

October 16, 1975 (age fourteen)
Somewhere in the North Pacific Ocean

From my diary:

Wonderful, beautiful, starless night
Thank you, whoever, for such a misty night.
The wind was strong, chilly, and cold.
And the course eighty degrees I could not hold!

The mountains lift us up with the breeze,
And set us back down with such great ease.
We all have a friend while out on the sea,
She's big, white, and free as can be.

We sat in the doldrums for 164 hours
It seemed like a year, but just 164 hours.
But Patricia's been hauling since yesterday
And supposedly we only have ten more days.

Winds, waves, and currents are with us,
We'll make it to San Diego
With just a little luck.

Part One
Before

1

It was October 22, 1975, and we were three days from San Diego in the cold, North Pacific Ocean when I looked behind me as a wall of water three stories high rose. Bending my head back to find the top of the wave, I let out an involuntary scream. The wind blew in angry gusts as the top of the wave blew off and slammed down on my head with a thud. I shivered, tasted the salt, and wiped my eyes. My hair was drenched and clinging to my face. I yelled, "Dad!" into the crashing spray. I could barely hear my own voice.

I steered as best I could down the face of the next wave, spearing the bottom of the trough with our ten-foot bowsprit, when the boat seemed to fall off a cliff, and we free-fell several feet. The cracking sound as we hit the concrete floor of water reverberated through the ship. I could feel the vibration in the wheel, through the deck on my rear end, and on my feet, which were planted between the wheel's spokes.

For days we had been taking on water from the separating planks below deck, and the water was constantly above the floorboards. The electric pump had quit, and our captain—my father—had started us on manual pumping shifts. We were also taking on water from above through a hole in the main cabin, where an air vent had been ripped off and lost in previous days. Water was everywhere, and it looked like we would sink.

The hatch opened, and Dad appeared dressed in his foul-weather gear. "What the hell was that noise?" he yelled as he made his way to me.

"I don't know!" I shouted. "The wave just disappeared, and we fell!" I could almost see my words being carried away on the wind before they reached his ears.

Frantic and shivering, I looked up into Dad's eyes. He was calm.

"I can't do this. I'm scared. Take the helm," I begged.

"You can do it! It's going to be fine," he said, patting my leg. "Use the strength in your legs to keep the wheel from turning. Steer her down the wave at a forty-five-degree angle."

I held on with both hands, my arms and legs quivering slightly at the strain. I didn't let the wheel turn. We reached the bottom of the wave, and *Patricia* began to climb the next mountain. He coached me for thirty minutes, eyeing the storm in every direction. When my watch was over, I was exhausted but proud. I hadn't crumbled. I hadn't given up and turned into a crying ball.

Dad was affectionately nicknamed the Voice of America by the crew, and I had to admit he was a great teacher and captain, always calm in an emergency. Besides him, two other inexperienced crew members were aboard the boat: Roland from Switzerland, Gibus from France, and our third crewmember, a woman who had sailed from Hawaii to Tahiti months earlier, Annie from San Diego.

I was the fourteen-year-old middle daughter of the Voice of America and the de facto first mate on board, although Dad would never admit it out loud to anyone. This was my second ocean crossing with him in the past year. He had taught me everything I knew—how to navigate with a sextant, plot our course, and sail expertly so that I could handle the entire boat. Sometimes I was proud to be his daughter, especially when he was the wise mentor or incomprehensibly generous with less fortunate people. But more often, the converse was true. He shamed and humiliated me frequently and was sexually, mentally, and emotionally abusive. His abuse started when I was nine, but there are times when I'm sure it began earlier and I can't remember.

Never a traditional dad, like the ones who mow the lawn and take out the trash, he was an adventurer. Born in Oslo in 1935, he emigrated to Ontario, Canada, in 1957 with only $50 in his pocket, unable to speak English. That's where he met my mother, and our family began. He made a success of himself without much help from anyone, becoming the single parent most of the time, raising my two sisters and me to be "Europeans." He had different ideas about how girls should be raised. We were commanded to sleep naked, not wear bras, not shave our legs or armpits, and never to complain, because we were luckier than most in the world.

Living with our mom wasn't an option very often. She drank too much, was mentally unstable, and had been in and out of mental health hospitals since I was six.

Growing up unconventionally, I loved my father desperately, as any little girl loves her hero father, but I also hated him fiercely. I would have done almost anything to escape him. He was the best and the worst father in the world. The line between protector and predator forever blurred.

The storm built every hour, but now I was off watch and ready to sleep. I waded through the ankle-deep water in the cabin and crawled into my wet bunk, trying to think positively about our current fate, hoping the ocean loved me enough to spare us, hoping the storm ended soon, and hoping we wouldn't die at sea. Everything below deck was wet, and the layers of clothes on my body, my long johns, jeans, sweater, hoodie, and ski jacket, were all damp. I pulled the wet blanket over myself, shook, and shivered, feeling salt crystals on my arms as I wrapped them around myself. I swished my bare feet back and forth, trying to find warmth.

As I lay frozen cold, Dad climbed into the bunk with me. He kissed my cheek, whispering, "You did a great job on the wheel." It was pitch black, and my eyes flew open wide. I faced away from him as he pulled the covers over himself and snuggled in. Visions of past encounters with him in the dark, in a bed, flashed through my head. Almost immediately, his rhythmic breathing and snoring filled the space.

My mind wandered as images of gigantic waves and howling wind flew by, then me at the helm trying to fight my way down the face of a massive wave so *Patricia* didn't pitchpole. Next, I saw Dad's face with that proud expression, and I knew I had succeeded at the newest challenge he'd given me. His admiration and pride were the only treasures I longed for in my heart. All of this played in my head like a movie as Dad lay sleeping beside me.

The force 8 storm ended the following day, and three long and wet days later, *Patricia* was safely tied to the Customs and Immigration dock in San Diego. We were survivors of the most desperate kind: survivors of the sea.

I longed to kiss the dry ground, but we were immediately quarantined until each crew member cleared immigration. I'm sure we deserved quarantine. I hadn't had a shower in over five days, and I couldn't remember the last time I had brushed my hair or teeth.

The officers boarded *Patricia* and went below to see if we were stashing anything illegal. The smell of moldy bedding, cushions, and clothing had them pinching their noses as they waded through the bilgewater. The disgust on their faces at the state of the boat embarrassed me. At that moment, I felt protective of *Patricia* and self-conscious about how bad she looked.

Patricia was an older lady, a 1940s sixty-foot bugeye ketch originally built in the Chesapeake Bay to fish oysters but retrofitted to sail around the world. In her original 1800s design, the two wooden masts leaned back to lift heavy nets of oysters from the bay, but to California sailors, they were a curiosity. Her maintenance had been neglected. The paint was peeling from the hull, and the varnish cracked on the deck. She looked beaten up and was now gravely injured and taking on water. I'm sure she looked homeless, but I assert she was never more loved. She had earned our respect and, in our hearts, would always be known as "The Valiant and Brave Mighty Bugeyed Ketch."

Of course, that's not how I had felt about her when we boarded her in Papeete, Tahiti, forty-two days earlier. I didn't want any part of her, but Dad had insisted she was seaworthy. I knew he mostly needed to make the dollar-a-mile to deliver her the four thousand miles to San Diego.

I had ended up in Tahiti with my dad and two sisters after sailing there on our own forty-five-foot sailboat, *Aegir*; our stay on the island came to a crashing halt when my younger sister was hit by a car. Mom was visiting at the time and took Karen with her back to Canada to heal. My older sister, Monica, opted to join Karen in Canada with our mom, having been seasick for almost the past year. While waiting for Karen to heal, Dad accepted the job of delivering *Patricia* to San Diego for a man who was too old to continue his trip.

Now, in San Diego, Immigration informed us we were free to go. We moved the boat to Driscoll's Boat Works on Shelter Island and docked in front of a slew of hauled-out ships in the yard. We said our emotional farewells as the crew disembarked and headed in separate directions, leaving only Dad and me aboard *Patricia*.

With dreams of a soft, dry bed, a hot shower, and a hamburger, I asked, "Where are we going to stay?"

"Here," Dad said, the sun reflecting off his bald head. "We're staying on the boat. The owner comes down tomorrow to inspect her."

"Dad! We can't stay on this boat. She's a drowned rat, ready to sink!"

He stared at me without saying a word, squinting his eyes in warning.

"Do we have to continue the pumping shifts—just the two of us? And do we have to sleep on those wet bunks?"

"Leslie, I am warning you. Hold your tongue, or I will hold it for you."

I stomped off the boat and off the dock to stand on solid ground, staring him down, incredulous, hands on my hips.

Dad's gruff voice followed me. "But I will take you to dinner at Boll Weevil and buy you a hamburger even though you don't deserve it with that attitude."

I twirled around slowly, smiling. "Can I have french fries and a chocolate shake, too?" A hint of a smile appeared at the corner of his mouth.

I dropped to my knees and kissed the ground beneath my feet. But it wasn't long before fear and dread set in. Soon, I'd be alone with him on the boat.

2

My dilemma was this: Where would I sleep that would be far enough away from my father that I'd feel safe? Thankfully, he solved that problem by claiming the bunk in the main cabin by the navigation station, leaving me the entire forward hold and the six bunks to choose from. The first mate's bunk had a door, and I moved in quickly, making plans to wedge a stick under the door for safety. Dad found an electric pump in the boatyard, so neither of us had to pump out the water to keep it below the floorboards.

My fear of my father had started when I was nine when he French-kissed me in the dark one night. After many indiscretions and abuses over the years, at fourteen an incident at sea on our way to Tahiti had me screaming at him in the middle of the night, and I set a boundary I was willing to fight for with my life. He backed off and hadn't encroached on my space since that day, but there were no guarantees the line would hold. Like prey being hunted, my fear lay just below the surface as I constantly tracked his presence.

The next morning, our first back in San Diego in nine months, *Patricia*'s feisty eighty-year-old owner, Ollie Olufsen, arrived. Wrinkled, thin, and hunched over, he looked genuinely happy to see his boat again, even in her battered state. While Ollie and Dad made a list of repairs, I cleaned and organized. Ollie hired Dad to fix the boat, so we'd be stuck with her for another few months. I could have screamed.

She was hauled out the following day, and we found the dry-rotted wood planks below the waterline that had leaked nonstop and nearly sunk us. The other obvious repairs were the gaping hole in the main cabin from the ripped-off air vent and the cracked boom from when we had sustained a nighttime gybe when the distracted helmsman accidentally let the boom slam from one side of the boat to the other. The shortwave radio needed replacing after it burst into flames halfway through our trip. We had ripped sails to repair and a wind vane to replace after it disappeared during a different gybe.

I worked below deck, grumbling about my terrible misfortune at being born to a father who didn't even celebrate our arrival in San Diego with a few days of holiday after the epic and near-death journey we had survived.

He commanded that I begin in the forward bunk and work my way back to the galley in the aft cabin, throwing out moldy bedding and cushions. I hauled the rest of the heap to the laundromat day after day until everything was clean and dry again. That's when I learned the value of bleach.

One evening, after many long days of work, we ate our soup and cheese sandwiches in silence, high up on the deck of the boat in the dry dock. I was itching to see my friends up the coast in Oceanside but was afraid to ask for time off. Together, we ate and stared at the spectacular view of the harbor.

"Am I getting paid for this slave labor?"

He studied me with piercing blue eyes, then slurped his minestrone, staring off to the horizon.

"I want to see my friends! I want some new clothes."

After another week of hard work scrubbing, washing, and cleaning, he allowed me a new pair of jeans and a top to visit my friends at a Friday night football game at Oceanside High School.

He dropped me off in a borrowed car in front of the school, where the reality of being there did not equate with the dream of it. Hundreds of kids sat in the bleachers, huddled in friend groups screaming at the boys on the field. No longer eighth graders, all my friends were freshmen now. I scanned the crowd for my best friend, Raine, when that old familiar feeling of being an outsider overcame me.

Raine and I had become fast friends early in seventh grade when she saved me from a crowd of ogling boys. We both had the same physical traits, meaning we were big-chested, and the boys made fun of us. Raine was called "balloons," and I was called "baby balloons." It didn't help that Dad refused to let me wear a bra, so at school, I was hassled by the boys often. Raine saved me one day from total and complete embarrassment by swooping in, grabbing my arm, and leading me down the hall away from the taunting. We'd been best friends ever since.

At the football game, Raine found me and ran up screaming with her arms out wide. Her long brown hair swayed, and her big brown eyes gushed with tears. We hugged and laughed like I hadn't been gone for almost a year.

My eighth-grade boyfriend, John De La Cruz, the boy I had idolized and dedicated my diary entries to for the past year, stood on the sidelines of the game. His long, straight black hair fell around his face, and his eyes widened when he saw me like he didn't believe them. He had hardly changed at all.

"Why are you back?" he said almost accusingly, as if I'd tricked him. His gorgeous smile disappeared and his eyes searched me for something. Surprised, I scowled at him while his group of guy friends stared at me. No words came out of my mouth. I looked around at the other kids in his circle and didn't recognize them.

"Karen got hit by a car," I blurted out, feeling off-balance and grasping at the first thing that came to my mind. It was true after all. If Karen hadn't been hit by a car we'd be on our way to Fiji now, which was strange to think about standing at a high school football game.

I had imagined this reunion a million times. In my dream we hugged and walked off together to talk and reconnect. Instead, we awkwardly stared at each other for a long moment, neither of us knowing what to say next. The other boys stared at me like a bug under their microscope. I looked around at the bright lights and all the kids and wanted to run.

"Leslie," Raine called from a distance away.

Shrugging, I turned and walked away.

In the ten months I'd been gone, I had experienced far-flung cultures and had near-death experiences multiple times. These things had changed me, but I couldn't begin to articulate them.

When all the work was done on *Patricia*, we handed her over to Ollie. The holidays were upon us and Dad had plans to return to our boat in Tahiti. On Christmas Eve, he put me on a plane to join my sisters and Mom in Windsor, Ontario.

"I'll send for you girls soon," he explained as we drove to the airport. He was already planning the next leg of our around-the-world journey.

I nodded. "You'll sail by yourself to Fiji?"

"I've dreamed of single-handling *Aegir* for as long as we've owned her. I'll fly you girls to Fiji in the spring."

He walked me to my gate, gave me a peck on the cheek, and showed me that special smile he saved just for me. It was so wide and smooth that his mouth made his eyes squint from how big it was. I could feel he loved me and cared for me, and I always wanted more of this Dad.

"See you soon," I said. I had mixed feelings about leaving him to sail to Fiji alone, even though I didn't want to sail with him. Angst also consumed me about heading to my least favorite place on earth: Windsor with Mom.

3

I arrived in wintry Windsor on Christmas Eve, 1975, and found Mom, Monica, and Karen living in a sparsely furnished two-bedroom apartment on Rooney Street, only half a step up from musty old *Patricia*. On the boat, we never had money, but we were seeing so many fascinating places that money didn't matter. We felt rich. Windsor was proof we were poor.

The sidewalks were knee-deep in snow and the dull, thick clouds covered the sky in complete contrast to California's sunny days. My sisters were home to me no matter where we were in the world, and I eagerly hugged them, Monica standing several inches taller than me with straight blonde hair down her back. "Hey, Lez," she said.

Petite, freckle-faced Karen smiled brightly and wrapped her arms around my waist. "I've missed you. How was the trip?" She was fully healed from the deep cut in her leg, cracked pelvic bone, torn Achilles tendon, and concussion she'd sustained in Tahiti when she had been hit by the car five months earlier.

"Good, I guess. Scary. I'll tell you all about it."

Mom wore an apron and stood in the kitchen, attending to our Christmas dinner. "Welcome. Are you hungry?"

"Starving," I said. She never cooked much when we were growing up but always made a big deal about Thanksgiving and Christmas dinner. When I leaned in to hug her, she shrank away, as fragile as ever. Touching was never her favorite thing, like hugging would crush her or something.

"Come sit down over here," Monica said, patting the old brown couch.

A small Christmas tree and a few presents filled a corner of the living room. I reunited with my sisters while Mom put the finishing touches on dinner, sipping her drink and watching us. She loved observing from afar, whether we were opening presents on Christmas morning or jumping waves in the ocean.

The turkey, mashed potatoes, green beans, and Mom's delicious brown gravy never tasted so good. I couldn't remember the last time we had had a traditional Christmas dinner. I regaled them with stories from the sail from Tahiti to San Diego and the massive storm we had hit. "We almost died when the boat started taking on water and we couldn't find the hole."

"Your father scares me with all the chances he takes," Mom slurred as she picked at her food, raising her newly made cocktail for another sip.

"It wasn't Dad's fault we hit a storm, or that Roland gybed the boat, causing the lines to rip the air vent off the cabin, or that the planks pulled apart underwater while we were being bashed in the storm."

She rolled her eyes. "It's never your father's fault." The ice cubes clinked together as she sipped her highball.

Here I was again, defending Dad to Mom. Those things weren't his fault, but there were plenty of things that were his fault, which I wasn't discussing with anybody. I told them we were meeting Dad in Fiji in the spring. Mom perked up at that. I knew she hoped she would be included this time.

Mom went to work at the hospital the next day, and the three of us enjoyed the apartment alone. Splayed out on the couch and rocking chair, eating Captain Crunch cereal, Karen told me about arriving in

Windsor injured a few months ago. "Mom dumped me off with her friend Diane so I could care for her newborn baby while she worked the night shift."

"With your injured leg? What a lame ass deal," I said.

"Yeah, I was still on crutches, and Diane and her husband couldn't have cared less," Karen said. "When I asked where Mom was after not seeing her for a week, I was told she was 'living with her boyfriend Alan,' like that was an excuse for dumping me off like that."

Monica sat up from her place on the couch, hugging a pillow. "When I arrived a few weeks after Karen, I was also dumped off there to help with the baby."

"Wow, Mom sucks."

"Yeah," Monica said, heading to the fridge for a Coke.

"When did you guys get this place?" The stack of unpacked boxes filled the corners of the living room.

"Two weeks ago, in preparation for the favorite child's arrival," Karen said.

I sighed. "Stop it. At least we have our own place now."

Winter was in full swing, with snowdrifts and freezing temperatures. One of the first things I did was find the secondhand store and buy a bra, a winter coat, and boots. I thought about Dad in tropical Tahiti aboard *Aegir*, preparing to sail to Fiji. We spent the rest of Christmas break playing the guitar and harmonizing to every song we knew, just like our days at sea the year before. We roller-skated on Saturday nights with the other teenagers at Wheels, the indoor skating rink. We watched a new TV show about a divorced mom and her kids called *One Day at a Time*, where I saw a commercial for Wind Song perfume by Prince Matchabelli. It intrigued me so much that I found it at the drug store and wore it religiously. We celebrated Karen's thirteenth birthday on December 29 with a chocolate cake and wishes for warm, tropical Fiji.

Once school started in the new year, Monica showed me the

routine at J. L. Forster High School, where she was in grade ten and I was playing catch-up in the second semester of grade nine. We stood in front of my locker on my very first day. "Don't leave me," I pleaded, clinging to her in the crowded narrow hallway of the two-story brick building. "Stay with me. I don't want to go to school here. Everybody looks so different."

"It's not any different from going to school in Tahiti. Those kids were different too. Besides, it's not so bad. I told my friends on the basketball team you were coming, and they're excited to meet you."

I made Monica promise to meet me at my locker between classes, and I clung to her so hard she had to peel me off. "Why are they staring at me?" I said. She shrugged.

The kids whispered and pointed, and I felt like I had two heads. The girls sneered, and I sneered back, which didn't help. Monica then admitted to telling everyone we were from California, which was like saying we were from Oz. California was legendary and notorious; nobody in that school had ever been there. It was a foreign country with Disneyland, movie stars, and surfers. Then she added that she had also told them we had sailed to Tahiti. She may as well have announced we were from Mars.

As the days progressed, I'd lock arms with Monica when we walked down the crowded hallway to our classes. Sometimes, the boys sang "I Wish They All Could Be California Girls" while the girls gave us the evil eye with their painted faces.

I had never worn makeup. Dad refused to allow it. But here, the girls wore bright blue eyeshadow, heavy eyeliner, and mascara. Their cheeks were streaked red on alabaster skin, and their hair was so heavily sprayed it never moved, not even in the wind. But the most upsetting thing was the way the girls dressed. Blousy oversize tops or patterned sweaters paired with tight, hip-hugger jeans whose huge bell-bottoms were frayed and dirty from the brown snow. What a stark contrast to how we all dressed in Southern California—in tight-fitting Ditto jeans and a snug midriff top that showed a little tanned stomach. These were the only clothes I had. What was I supposed to do? You'd have thought I was naked from the scandal it caused. If they only knew I ran around in my bikini most days and that my own father forbade me from wearing a bra. I brought my Tahitian and California style to the Canadian high school and was labeled loose.

If the clothing and makeup weren't enough to make me feel out of step, I didn't use the right words or have the proper reactions. "Don't call it soda. It's called pop here, and stop gulping it," the girls would say. "Damn!" I'd say if I couldn't remember the combination for my locker. Kids nearby would stop and stare. I tried to change, but it was hopeless. I was not a meek girl cowering in the corner. The list of things I needed to change about myself felt overwhelming.

One day, in the locker room, changing back into our street clothes, a crowd stood around the most popular girl in class. I couldn't see Beth, but I could hear her. "If you can put a pencil under your boob and it stays, then you have saggy boobs." Beth had small, perky breasts, of course. I shrunk back, knowing that a pencil would stay under my breasts if I put it there. There was no fighting gravity. Nothing about me fit. I was too loud, too boisterous, and outspoken. I didn't wear the right clothes or have the "right" look. I was a flamboyant parrot among blackbirds. Their stares wore on me. *Make yourself smaller*, I thought. *Blend in.* But it was impossible.

I wanted to shout that I was a sailor who had just survived forty-two days at sea and a near-death experience, but no one would have cared. Everything about me was just wrong in Windsor. I became depressed, withdrawn, and isolated. Even Monica eventually forgot me. I dreamed of being at sea again, where I could yell and be myself. I missed the ocean, the sunrises and sunsets, the stillness and wickedness of it. I didn't fit in on land.

When I was on the way to the store to buy milk and bread for Mom one day, a stinky old man with no teeth and sunken lips approached me with a $20 bill. "Did you drop this, pretty girl?" I shook my head and kept walking, but he caught up to me. "How'd you like to earn it? It'll only take a few minutes." I ran to the busy corner of Wyandotte and Ouellette and lost him.

    I hated Windsor.

4

Mom worked as a licensed vocational nurse at a hospital in Detroit. The daily journey to work included crossing the border into Michigan instead of just driving to a local hospital in Windsor. She made more money in Michigan than she could in Ontario. The problem was that she hardly ever went to work. Some mornings, we'd find her fully clothed, passed out, drooling, and face down on the couch. Nothing could wake her—not shaking or yelling. She'd moan and roll over and we'd leave for school.

"She resents us being here. She wants to be with her boyfriend, Alan," Monica said one morning as we trudged through the snow to the bus stop. "He's been diagnosed with cancer," she added.

"Oh, is that why she's drinking so much?" I said.

"Yes . . . no . . . I don't know. She always drinks too much," Monica said.

"Yeah," Karen mumbled as we got on the bus.

When Mom wasn't working or passed out, she was angry and resentful, maybe at having to be a mother and take care of us for the first time in three years. "Girls, clean up the kitchen, and somebody vacuum, for God's sake." It was a good day. She was getting dressed in her crisp white uniform, white pantyhose, and white shoes. She was pinning her starched hat on her head as she stood looking in the bathroom mirror, yelling instructions.

"What about the laundry? Nobody has done the laundry in a month," I said. "These sheets and towels are horrible."

"You can do the laundry. That'll be your chore." Her eyes drilled holes in me as I passed the bathroom.

"When will your chore be to clean the bathroom?" I said, entering our bedroom. "It's disgusting."

"Shut up!" she yelled, her face screwed up and distorted.

I didn't like or respect her, and I didn't hold my tongue when it came to telling her how much I hated Windsor. The snow, the kids at school, our poverty, and life in general were miserable. How could I have been diving for shells and spearfishing in tropical waters just a few months earlier?

We found Mom's booze under the kitchen sink, poured it out, and filled the vodka bottles with water. Sometimes her hands shook when she didn't have any liquor in the house. We'd laugh, run to our bedroom, and slam the door. She'd follow, screaming and yelling. We'd yell back that she needed to stop drinking and go to work. She'd say she missed Alan and start crying. She hated her life as much as I hated mine.

All of our birthdays were clumped together on the calendar. On January 17, Monica's boyfriend, Rich, threw a surprise "sweet sixteen" birthday party for her in his basement and around fifteen people came. We drank pop, and the girls scowled at me while the boys stared. "I'm Not in Love," by 10cc played, and my heart ached while I watched Monica and Rich slow dance, pushing myself into the corner of the room to make myself smaller. Maybe someday I could slow dance with my boyfriend.

My fifteenth birthday happened a week later. I'm sure Monica and

Karen baked me a cake or something, but I felt old, depressed, and desperate to leave Windsor, so nothing made an impression.

About a month later, we tried hard to make Mom's thirty-sixth birthday special and normal. Nothing said "normal family" more than going out for a steak dinner, so that's what we did. The dinner was a truce, since the fighting and yelling had gotten so bad we were barely speaking. Anything to make Mom happy on her birthday.

I had $50 Dad had given me the day I flew to Windsor, and Karen had a few dollars saved. But Monica offered to pay, since she always had lots of saved money. Karen and I never had money because, according to Dad, we were "big spenders."

At dinner, Mom picked at her food and got sloshed on too many vodka sodas, which gave Monica the courage to ask again if she was adopted. She had been asking Mom and Dad this question since we were little, convinced at various times she didn't belong to this family. Mom lowered her face to Monica in that slow, drunk way, focusing her eyes very hard, and repeated what she'd been saying for years: "No, dear, you are not adopted. Stop asking me all the time."

I jumped in. "Yeah, Monica, how could you be adopted when I'm the one who feels like a complete alien in this family?"

Karen added, "Maybe we're all adopted."

"Stop it, girls." Mom took the last swig of her drink and the ice cubes clinked.

When the bill came, Monica only paid for herself and Mom, looking at Karen and me for our contribution. We paid what we owed and hated Monica for misleading us. Mom either didn't notice or didn't care that her daughters were paying for a meal we could scarcely afford.

During January and February, two things happened: I accepted birth control pills from the school nurse when I went to see her for a headache one day. She asked if I had a boyfriend and I lied and said yes because I really wanted one. She offered birth control pills, and I accepted. The second thing was Mom started therapy at a free social services place.

She said she needed to figure out why we were always fighting. I could have told her it was her drinking, but I kept my mouth shut for once. She talked weekly to a therapist named Simon, and I imagined she told him all our family secrets, of course leaving out how much she drank. Does therapy even work when you don't tell the whole truth?

One night after a session, she came home and threw open the door to our bedroom, where we hibernated together, and announced, "We're starting family therapy next Monday."

The Newlywed Game played on our small black-and-white mini-TV. "I don't want to go to therapy," I said. "I refuse."

"You can't refuse," she said, staring at me, and then added, "We are doing this, girls!" in the most authoritative voice I had heard from her in a long time. She practically slammed the door when she left our room.

"I'm with Leslie, I don't want to do it," Monica called after her without even raising her eyes from her book.

Karen added, "Me either."

But Mom insisted, desperately pleading with us in the following days, and in the end she bribed us with fish and chips at our favorite restaurant.

The next Monday evening we all traveled together on the bus for our first therapy session. Simon's office was behind a big Catholic church, even though Mom always told us she wasn't Catholic anymore.

In his office, I slumped into one of the uncomfortable canvas chairs across the coffee table from Simon. He looked like a professor in his tan cardigan and file folder resting on his lap. Mom sat daintily on the couch, smoothing out her overly fancy dress. Monica and Karen sat beside her.

Simon gave the introduction speech with the ground rules for listening and telling the truth. "Therapy doesn't work unless we want it to. I can help you communicate better, but you have to promise to be respectful and tell the truth."

I smirked at Mom when he said that, knowing she wouldn't be telling the truth about what she did in her bedroom all alone. Simon's sparkling brown eyes held my gaze. His thick eyelashes were hooded with big, lustrous eyebrows that went up and down as he talked. He was a hairy dude with frizzy brown hair combed in place and a bushy biker mustache. I had promised myself I wouldn't speak, so I nodded my agreement to the rules, making sure Mom also nodded her agreement to tell the truth. The first session wasn't so bad.

As we continued family therapy, I got sucked in and broke my promise about not talking when Monica and Mom had a disagreement about how much time Monica was spending with her boyfriend, Rich. I had to weigh in about how much time Mom was spending with Alan. The floodgates opened, and I didn't hold back about hating our apartment and my school or the fact that we had no money to do anything. Somewhere in the middle of all that ranting and raving, I realized Simon was watching me with warm eyes. He was sort of cute for an older man.

Even though some sessions got downright loud, Mom seemed to like Simon enough, so she never really lost her cool.

We met on alternate Mondays at the apartment, where everyone became a little more comfortable. I wore my Wind Song perfume just in case Simon was interested in me. During one session, as we sat around the linoleum kitchen table, I thought I caught Simon stealing extra glances at me, but I couldn't be sure. He told us how to be better listeners by giving "Listening Feedback Responses," which my sisters and I began to call LFRs.

Mom began. "I don't like it when you girls lock your bedroom door and don't answer when I call you."

Sarcastic me jumped in with an LFR: "So you don't like the bedroom door closed and our non-replies?"

"Are you mocking me, Lezlie?" She knew I hated it when she called me Lezlie instead of Leslie, with a hard "s."

"No, Mom, I'm just giving you an LFR and trying my best here," I said in my most innocent voice. But I was really thinking that therapy was stupid while trying to catch Simon's eyes because that was way more interesting.

"Is it my turn?" I asked, and Simon nodded. "Mom, I don't like it when you drink all day and night, pass out on the couch, miss work for days and days, and we run out of food."

Mom's mouth dropped open. She looked at Simon with a reddening face. Monica kicked me under the table, and Karen said, "Leslie, don't be so mean."

"Let's all stay calm here," Simon said while his eyes slid up and down my body. *Oh, this is fun*, I thought. The session ended there on a sour note, but who cared? Not I.

With each subsequent family therapy session, Mom picked up on the signs of Simon's attraction to me with the eye glances, the side-eye, the coy smiles. She said nothing at first but began wearing low-cut blouses and red lipstick to the sessions. She acted like the concerned mother, herding us into his office like sheep, adjusting how our hair fell down our backs, and telling us to pull up our socks. She never said any of those things when Simon wasn't around. She was laying it on thick with him, giggling at inappropriate times, using her velvety voice: "Oh yes, Simon, we can have a private session on that subject." I'd roll my eyes and think, *Okay, lady, you're making a fool of yourself. Game on. Let's see who he will pick.*

5

I had been wishing for a boyfriend, but the boys at school were just that: boys. Simon was a man—a fully mature, exciting, and sexy man who seemed very interested in me. I found out just how interested he was when Monica produced tickets to see Deep Purple at Cobo Hall in Detroit. The original plan was that Monica and Rich would take me and maybe another boy from school, but when Monica and Rich broke up, this was my big chance to see if Simon's sparkling eyes really beckoned me.

After family therapy one day, I hung back while Mom and my sisters left his office.

"Simon, do you like Deep Purple? We have tickets and Mom says we need a chaperone if we go to Detroit. Will you take Monica and me?"

He was adjusting the papers on his desk and looked up with a smirk under that bushy mustache. His eyes twinkled when he said, "Yes, I would love to."

That's when I knew for sure his gooey eyes meant something.

On the night of the concert, Monica was so heartbroken over Rich she didn't want to go. Mom offered to go in Monica's place. "I'd like to see who the Deep Purple are."

"No, Mom. You can't come! I'm not taking my mother to a concert!" I nearly screamed.

"Then take Karen with you. She can be the chaperone." She lit a cigarette.

Karen as the chaperone sounded funnier than anything I'd heard in a while. I said under my breath, "As long as you don't go."

I dressed carefully in a new low-cut light-suede top with a slit down the front and tight jeans. I dabbed Wind Song behind my ears but also between my breasts like I'd seen on the commercial. Simon arrived in his red sports car, and I got to sit in the front like his date. Karen sat crammed in the tiny back seat, and she could have disappeared for all I cared. I felt so adult being driven by this man who must have been more than thirty years old. I admired his tight jeans, cowboy boots, button-down shirt, and big hands on the steering wheel.

He drove us to the Windsor bus station, where we left his car and boarded a packed bus for the ride to Detroit through the tunnel. I stood beside the driver, nearly bumping his arm as he steered. Simon stood behind me and put his hand around my waist, spreading out his fingers on my stomach. It made my insides do flip-flops. I looked up at him, and his smiling eyes were looking down my shirt. His hand tightened around my stomach, and his eyes smoldered. Karen stood beside Simon, squished between two old ladies clutching their purses. The bus took us under the Detroit River and normally I would have been claustrophobic, but my distraction was acute as Simon's hand rubbed up and down my torso. We emerged from the darkness of the tunnel on the Detroit side and walked the three blocks to Cobo Hall, Simon holding my and Karen's hands in the crush of the crowd. Whenever our eyes met, he winked, or smiled, or gave me a little air kiss.

Nazareth opened for Deep Purple and I swayed back and forth as Simon's hands explored my body in the crowded concert. Karen noticed where Simon's hands were touching and kept giving me googly eyes and sometimes squinty eyes. She was cramping my style, so I ignored her. I danced, moved, and tried to focus on something other than Simon because things were heating up. All this attention and caressing began to scare me. I didn't want to make a mistake and turn him off.

On the bus ride back to Windsor, Simon slipped a piece of paper into the front pocket of my jeans, using his index finger to push it all the way down, then he winked at me. Now I knew for sure he wanted me badly. I wanted him, too. Nothing was ever said, but things had most definitely changed. Thank God Mom was locked in her bedroom when we got home, but Monica wanted to hear all about the concert. I gave Karen a warning look, and she didn't say anything about Simon's handsy antics on the bus or at the concert. She said, "I've never seen that many people dancing. It was so loud! And the lights were flashing all over the arena, and the pot smoke choked me."

While Karen described it all, I discreetly fished the paper out of my pocket and found his address and note that said, "Meet me late afternoon tomorrow."

Wow, tomorrow? At his house? Wow! This was really happening, but then I realized I couldn't meet him and there was no way to tell him. Karen and I were going to Monica's basketball game after school. But I held the note to my chest because now I had written proof he wanted me. It was exciting and scary at the same time, like diving off the high board.

The day after the basketball game, I went to Simon's office hoping he wasn't mad at me for standing him up. His boss, Ron, was with him, so I acted like there was a crisis at home with Mom, although really there wasn't a crisis any more than normal. I became an actor and tapped into that crazy family feeling. "Mom's always drinking and today it's especially bad. She's ranting and raving about something with her boyfriend Alan."

Ron left Simon's office and I tried to keep up the ruse, telling him more generic details about Mom. "She takes these pills and then doesn't go to work. She has crazy eyes whenever I go into her bedroom." I sat on the couch, and he sat in a nearby chair. I stopped talking and fished out the paper with the address on it. "Sorry I couldn't make it yesterday," I whispered.

"Thank you for coming in today. Can we discuss all this next family therapy?" he asked. I nodded and then he put his hand on my knee and looked at me with pleading eyes. He slid onto the couch next to me, scooped me up, and kissed me hard while his hands ran up and down my body. "You are so sexy," he whispered. Sparklers went off inside and my skin tingled as I became a rag doll under his touch.

"Meet me at my house whenever you can. I can get off most days at 3 p.m."

I nodded, said, "Tomorrow," and left.

Monica had basketball practice after school the next day, so I could ride a different bus alone, and nobody would know. I went to Simon's house, a two-story brick Craftsman where I found him in a rocking chair reading the paper on his front porch. He looked every bit the professor with his sweater and glasses. He glanced at the neighbors' houses and so did I. Nobody was outside at this hour. Hopefully, they were still at work. He opened the front door and led me inside. Every nerve ending in my body was on high alert.

I put my book bag by the door on the hardwood floor, and he led me to the kitchen through a living room that looked like a grandma lived there with its high-backed couch and chairs where I couldn't imagine anybody ever sat. I wondered why his furniture was so old and stodgy, and why everything was so neat that it looked like nobody lived there.

In the pristine white linoleum kitchen, he poured each of us a glass of lemonade, and I nearly tripped while sitting down at the booth. "Whoops, sorry." The heat rose in my face as I fell into my seat. My heart beat very fast.

He sat down in one elegant move, putting the lemonade in front of me. "Did you like the concert?" he asked, sipping his lemonade. I nodded and sipped my lemonade, continuing to sip it nervously while waiting for whatever would happen next. The kitchen was just like the living room in that it looked like nobody cooked or ate there. He slid his hand across the table and the sparkle in his eyes turned warm and inviting. I put my hand on the table and touched his.

"Would you like to see the rest of the house?"

I nodded, gulping too loud on my last sip of lemonade, setting my glass back down on the table too hard. *Please don't let me fall or trip on anything again.*

He held my hand as he led me up the stairs edged with the most amazing dark wood banister, stopping at the top to kiss me tenderly. My mind went blank. "Are you okay?" he whispered when he pulled back from the kiss. I must have been standing very stiffly, even though I began to feel warm inside. I leaned into him and nodded.

When we got to his bedroom, he picked me up and laid me on his bed as if I were a china doll. "Are you on birth control?" he whispered into my ear. I nodded, relieved I had taken those birth control pills from the school nurse.

I didn't know what to do, so I froze. He kissed me and slid my shirt up and kissed my stomach, unbuttoning my jeans and sliding the zipper down. I closed my eyes and he took charge and made love to my body. He went slow, and it felt nice, and only hurt a little. When it was over, his expressive brown eyes were tender as he ran his hand over my stomach and breasts. His body was covered in soft, curly brown hairs—everywhere! My Scandinavian heritage meant I didn't have any body hair to speak of, so seeing Simon covered in it was fascinating. It grew right up to his neckline and down to his ankles and then there was a straight line where it mysteriously stopped growing.

Too nervous to just lie there, I couldn't think of what to say to him. "I should go. It's getting late."

"Okay, but let me show you my studio in the next room." His eyes twinkled as he watched me get dressed. He really liked my body. Boys at school just made fun of me for being too curvy, but he liked my curves and my thick thighs that Dad made fun of. It seemed like this was what it felt like to be with a man.

He put a robe on and took me to the next room. One large canvas stood on an easel with a half-finished painting of a lake and a mountain. A desk held all the paints and brushes.

He hugged me and kissed my neck. "Are you hungry? Or do you have to go home now?"

Feeling relaxed, I suddenly heard my stomach growl. "I can stay a while longer."

He made me fried eggs and toast in his robe, and I watched him fastidiously cook. He was practiced in his motions and only turned around once to wink at me. We ate quietly and I started to feel uncomfortable at the silence again, like now that we'd had sex, there would be nothing to talk about, but he was completely comfortable. Then, I heard the birds chirping outside, the neighbor's lawn mower, and a child's playful yells in the distance. He picked up our plates and utensils and carefully cleaned and hand-dried each item. I'd never seen a man so concerned about everything being put away perfectly.

"When can you come over again?" he asked.

"Tomorrow," I said without hesitating. He smiled and nodded. He drove me home in his red sports car, dropping me off a few blocks from the apartment. I walked through the snow feeling like the ballroom door of life had just opened and I was stepping into a new world.

We began seeing each other several times a week, and sometimes I could get away for the entire day on Saturday or Sunday. We hid out in his house. He made tomato soup and grilled cheese sandwiches, and we laughed and made love constantly. Windsor was suddenly better now that I was spending so much time with Simon. I told him all about sailing around the world, Dad's unwanted attention, and Mom's drinking. I stopped thinking about him as our family therapist and started thinking about him as my boyfriend.

We shared a big secret, which made me feel important. I was happy to continue having family therapy—playing the game. It was fun. While my sisters and Mom discussed something from our childhood, I'd stare at the tuft of brown curly hair peeking out at the top of his shirt, daydreaming about our last lovemaking. He'd catch me and the corners of his mouth would raise just a bit. I was less combative in therapy and much more compliant with everything. Mom watched me closer than ever before. I had to be stealthier and only smile at Simon when Mom wasn't looking.

She still dressed in sexy outfits, trying to get Simon's attention with her unbuttoned blouse that showed a bit of her tiny cleavage. Simon ignored her blatant advances, which made Mom irritable.

How had I been given such big breasts when Mom had such teeny tiny ones? Before Simon, I'd hated how my breasts had always brought me unwanted attention. But Simon loved them, and now maybe they were the reason for my success in winning him.

Getting ready for another therapy session after school one day, my mom and sisters and I were filing out of the apartment to the street to find the bus when Mom tucked in next to me and said, "Are you seeing Simon privately?" She continued when I didn't answer immediately, "Because I sense something different between the two of you."

"No, Mom, nothing is different," I lied.

On our next afternoon together at Simon's house, I told him about Mom's suspicions, and he confirmed that Mom had confronted him as well, but that he'd also denied it.

The adrenaline of sneaking around and not getting caught was addicting; it felt dangerous and exhilarating to dupe Mom and have a secret. I enjoyed watching her squirm while she tried to seduce Simon. He ignored her. I was winning. *Yes!*

I played the therapy game better and gave LFRs as Simon had asked, as did Monica and Karen. Mom never really got the hang of LFRs, and she especially didn't get the hang of telling the truth.

"Mom, why don't we talk about Alan and how you always go over there and spend the night on the weekends, leaving us alone?"

Mom stared at me. I looked at Simon. "She's been staying for long periods with Alan for months, but he has cancer," I said to Simon and then looked at Mom. "He's really sick, isn't he?"

Her dark-brown eyes turned black with daggers shooting out at me. "I won't talk about Alan until you and Simon admit to your affair," Mom said defiantly, sitting up taller in her chair. It irked me someplace deep that she thought she had the upper hand. I would show her, but Karen jumped in before I could say anything. "You're having an affair with Simon?"

I closed my eyes and silently shook my head in disgust at Mom for opening this can of worms.

"Leslie, that's so bad," Monica said, looking back and forth between Simon and me.

"Yes, it is very bad," Mom scolded.

We all looked at Simon, but he stared at the wall directly behind Mom and me, neither admitting nor denying anything. His eyes were glassy and unfocused. *Man, he is cool under pressure.*

Mom huffed loudly and went to the door. "Girls, are you coming?"

Monica and Karen stomped out of the room after Mom. I glided to the door in complete ecstasy, glancing back at Simon. His wink told me to stay the course. Indignant, I glared at Mom. *How dare she bring up Simon and me in family therapy. We aren't the problem. She is the problem.*

Therapy wasn't working for our family.

6

An hour later I called Simon from a pay phone in the grocery store. When he answered, "Simon Locke," I launched right in. "Can you even believe my mother? She's out of control. She's so jealous of me. She thinks we're competing for you."

Simon was quiet.

"Hello? Are you there?"

"Yes, I'm here. I have to be careful. Your mother could make my life very difficult. She doesn't understand our relationship."

"I know she doesn't! She doesn't understand anything. She lies and drinks and plays all these games. I'm sick of it. I'm sick of her!"

"Let's let this all settle. I have a client session in a few minutes. I have to run."

A lady in the grocery store walked by and furrowed her brow at me. *Am I talking too loud?* I turned my back and lowered my voice. "She can't just decide to be my mom because she's attracted to the same guy as me." I stopped and turned around to see if anybody else was staring at me. They weren't. After another long silence, Simon said, "Can you come over Sunday morning?"

"Yes, I'll be there at my usual time."

"I miss you already. See you soon," he said, and kissed into the phone.

I swooned, feeling self-righteously angry with my mother for stirring this all up and putting a dark cloud over everyone. I stomped home in the snow from the grocery store with the gallon of milk we needed.

I ignored everyone when I got home and buried myself in a book in the bedroom. My sisters looked at me funny. "What?" I yelled at them. "Leave me alone."

They peppered me with questions I didn't want to answer. "How many times have you slept with him? Do you go to his house or meet in the office? Do you love him? Is it legal?"

I rolled over and faced the wall, refusing to answer.

How could we ever go back to being the normal messed-up family we were, when now, thanks to Mom, we were an "extra special" kind of messed-up family. I hated her.

When Simon and I met at his house on Sunday, we agreed to take a break from family therapy for a few weeks and ignore Mom, thus shutting the door on that awful subject and returning to our private island of love in his house.

7

Life at home was a disaster. Since the blow-up, Mom had been sequestering herself in her room, which was fine by me. I stayed in the bedroom when I wasn't at Simon's or at school. We were still hot and heavy. Nothing could keep us apart, even though I daydreamed about getting the hell away from Windsor and going to Fiji, where I promised myself I would find a way to peacefully sail with Dad and my sisters again, far away from this nightmare with Mom in Windsor.

The phone rang and Karen answered. "Hi, Daddy." In my mind's eye I saw him in Tahiti on our forty-five-foot sailboat *Aegir* anchored in a beautiful bay, turquoise-blue water all around, pristine white sand underneath her, and palm trees dripping over the beach.

Karen's smile disappeared. "What?" She lowered the phone and said, "*Aegir* sank. She's at the bottom of the ocean."

My breath caught as I took the receiver and sucked in a chest full of air. "How can that be?" I said to Dad.

Monica's eyes grew large. "No! She did not sink." She sat next to me on the couch. We put our heads together, holding the receiver between us. "We're all here listening, Dad. Tell us what happened," I said.

It was strangely good to hear his voice, like from a previous life or time, away from the chaos we currently lived in. This was only his second call since I had arrived in Windsor three months earlier. "I can fill you in on the details later but suffice it to say that I hit a large metal water tank floating at surface level that knocked the keel off." He stopped talking but none of us said anything. He continued, "I only had a few hours to collect all of our things and abandon ship into our emergency life raft."

"Oh that's terrible, Dad," I said. He paused and then added, "I watched her sink just as the sun was rising. It was heartbreaking." His voice hitched and I was sure he had tears in his eyes.

"How long were you in the raft?" Monica asked.

"About three days . . ." He trailed off and then spoke louder. "Some local fishermen found me and saved my life."

The very next second I realized the implications of *Aegir* sinking. We would not be going to Fiji or continuing our around-the-world trip. We would not be going anywhere. We were stuck here on land, maybe stuck in Windsor. Oh God!

"Girls, I've got paperwork to do and a plan to make for us, and then I'll be in touch," Dad said.

We all whispered, "Goodbye."

When I hung up, I began to hyperventilate. I paced around the living room and ranted while Monica and Karen watched me from the couch. We were never going to get out of Windsor.

Mom came out of her room and stood at the kitchen's threshold, staring at us. "What's wrong? You girls look stunned."

"The boat sank, and Dad was at sea for three days in a life raft," Karen said in a monotone voice.

"Oh, I'm so sorry," Mom slurred. "Is your dad coming to Windsor soon?"

"I don't think so. He has a lot to handle now. He said he'd call later," Monica said, eyeing Mom and her cocktail. Damn her that she always had a cocktail in her hand.

I went to the bedroom and lay down as a huge cloud of sadness settled on me. I saw *Aegir* lying on her side, at the bottom of the dark ocean, alone, cold, and afraid. She had been our beautiful floating home for the past three years—our only home as we sailed on to Tahiti. It felt as though a family member had been killed. How could an inanimate object live like a real thing in my heart? Tears fell and I cried. She was lost, and so was I.

8

Mom's boyfriend, Alan, was very sick, and after being diagnosed with cancer the previous summer, he had a heart attack followed by open-heart surgery. Her dejected feelings about Alan were obvious when she was around the apartment. She kept to herself in the bedroom, drinking constantly.

A knock on the door startled me as I made macaroni and cheese in the kitchen one night. I had just gotten home from Simon's house, was starving, and still had homework for school the next day. I yelled for Karen to get the door. She was on the couch watching cartoons. "You get it. You're closer!" she called back.

I rolled my eyes and opened the door to find Alan bundled up in a coat and wearing a newsboy hat. I had never spoken to him before, just waved to him once on the street when he dropped Mom off.

"Hi," I said standing in the doorway.

"Hello. You're Leslie, right?" I nodded. "Is your mother home?"

I motioned for him to come inside. "I'll go and get her."

I let Mom know and then scooped up spoonfuls of mac and cheese into a bowl and went to our bedroom, closing the door behind me. I had just sat down next to Monica, who was watching TV, and taken a bite of my food when the screaming began. We ignored it for as long as we could, eyeing each other. Soon the screaming became unbearable; it sounded like Mom was really losing it.

I cracked open the door and peeked down the hall toward the kitchen. I could see Karen standing by Mom, who was yelling, and Alan backed up against the kitchen counter with his hands in front of his chest defending himself. "Paula, just calm down."

"No, I will not calm down. You promised to give me some money. I'm broke and I need it!" she hollered, her face red and ugly.

Monica peeked around me.

In a calm and quiet voice, Alan said, "Well, I don't have it for the hundredth time. I had to give it to my ex. She's very sick now, and with my surgery recently, money is tight."

Hearing that, Mom started pounding on his chest, in the very place where he had had his open-heart surgery. Alan crumbled, unable to defend himself. He tried to raise his arms, but Mom had power on her side. Monica and I ran down the hallway and grabbed each one of her arms and ushered her quickly to the couch. Alan grasped his chest and coughed.

"Stop it, Mom," Monica yelled, "or you're going to kill him!" She put her hands around Mom's neck and threw her on the couch. Mom's head bounced on the cushions a few times.

Karen yelled, "Stop!"

I couldn't move. I couldn't do anything. I just stood watching Monica slam Mom's head into the couch cushion. After what seemed forever, Monica finally got off Mom and staggered back, breathing hard. Mom touched her neck softly and sat up, staring at Monica in disbelief. Karen stopped screaming.

Quiet took over the apartment, and it was thick. We all sized each other up. Mom eyed Monica. Then she eyed Alan. Alan eyed Mom, and then the door. He inched his way toward it. Mom sat down at the kitchen table.

"Alan, get out of here. She's going to kill you if you stay," Karen warned.

Mom squinted and shot arrows at Karen, mocking her. "Yes, run Alan, or I might kill you."

Alan opened the door and backed out, pulling it closed quietly.

Monica, Karen, and I glanced at each other, wondering what would happen next. But we should have known. It was the answer to all her problems. She pulled out her bottle from under the sink and poured herself a drink as the three of us continued to shoot glances at one another, knowing we had replaced the liquid with water. I smirked at Monica and Karen.

Mom took a swig and spit it out in the sink, whirling around with fire in her eyes. "Who poured out my vodka *again*?"

"We all did," I said with my hands on my hips, legs spread apart like Dad being the King of Siam, but now I was the Queen of Siam. "You need to stop drinking."

"Don't tell me what I need to do. You need to stay away from Simon. I could report him."

"We're not in competition, Mom. Leave me alone. That whole trick you pulled unbuttoning your shirt during family therapy was embarrassing. Maybe I'll tell Alan that next time I see him." I walked over to the couch and sat next to Monica.

Mom inched toward the bathroom and pulled a small bottle of vodka out from the back of the linen closet. Monica looked at me, and I looked at Karen, astonished we had not known of this hiding place. She brought her pill bottle to the kitchen table, opened the bottle, and poured the last of the vodka into the glass.

"Mom, don't drink. That's not the answer," Monica said.

"Yeah, Mommy, please, please, don't take any pills," Karen begged.

Mom ignored them both, opening the pill container and taking one out just as Karen stepped forward and grabbed the pill bottle away. Stunned, Mom stared at Karen.

"Give it back," she said, holding out her hand.

"Dump them out," I yelled to Karen.

"Yeah, dump them all out," Monica echoed.

"You wouldn't dare," Mom said, looking back and forth between Karen, with the pill bottle in her hand, and Monica and me on the couch. She took the final swig of her drink and slowly stood up.

Karen went to the sink and poured a stream of the pills down the drain and turned on the water. She held the remaining few pills in her hand.

"No! Stop!" Mom yelled, her eyes wild and frantic.

"Choose, Mommy—the pills or me."

Mom laughed a strange guttural laugh. "It's not even a choice. Give me the pills. I can't live without them."

Karen turned her hand upside down and the five or so remaining pills landed in the sink. Mom tried to recover them as Karen skulked away, head down, staring at the ground, defeated and broken.

Monica and I followed Karen to our bedroom, making sure the door was locked, leaving Mom sitting at the kitchen table. I turned up the volume on the television and we numbly settled into some quiet time. A few minutes later, we heard the front door slam shut and knew Mom had gone out, probably to get another bottle of vodka.

"What are we going to do?" Monica asked. "Mom's sinking lower and lower every day."

"Keep pouring out her alcohol and dumping out her pills," I said.

"It won't work anymore. She loves them more than she loves us," Karen whimpered.

"Yeah, but we still need to try. Dad would be so mad if he knew she was behaving like this," I said.

"Dad would be so mad if he knew about Simon," Monica said.

"Shut up, Monica."

"Mom wants to date Simon, and she wants money from Alan," Karen announced, like we didn't already know these facts.

* *

Thirty minutes later, the front door opened and closed again. The apartment was quiet and we drifted off to sleep until Mom woke us. She was in the hallway leaning against our door, drunk and slurring her words, talking about Alan not giving her the money and about how she wanted to date Simon. We stayed quiet.

I fell asleep during one of the extended quiet times when Mom stopped whining. I woke up still in my school clothes, having to pee badly. I pushed past Mom, who was still lying against our door in the hallway and mumbled something about Simon when she saw me. "It should be me dating him, not you. You're too young."

Over the next few hours, she worked herself into a frenzy until she really scared us. She spewed horrible, hateful words toward all of us, but especially Dad, Simon, and me. At a certain point, she had no control anymore and descended into blackness, talking about God and the devil and redemption and the Catholic Church. We couldn't get her attention. She talked to the wall as if someone were there. We lay in the bedroom trying not to listen but unable to avoid hearing her rantings just outside our door.

"Do you think this is what they mean by a mental breakdown?" I whispered.

Monica kicked me softly and whispered back, "Yes, Leslie, that's exactly what this is." After a long silence, she said, "We have to call for help."

It was nearly daylight when we called the hospital, and a very short time later three men arrived in white coats with an ambulance and took Mom away. She was catatonic at that point, mumbling gibberish and completely compliant as they carried her out to the ambulance.

Nobody asked if other adults lived with us. Nobody asked if we would be fine. Nobody asked if we needed help. They just took Mom away, and in her place was a deafening silence.

It was the first time we had been around to see the escalation of her manic personality brought on by the drugs and alcohol. Her moods seemed to have a life of their own and I barely recognized her. Her blank eyes and vacant face confirmed that she had gone somewhere else. She didn't seem to be in her body anymore.

The sun came up, and we were all exhausted, but we made a pact that morning to continue to go to school, do our homework, and be good girls until Mom came back.

A small feeling of guilt began to grow inside. I needed to see Simon.

9

We went to school the morning after Mom was taken away as if everything was normal. We wondered why the hospital hadn't called to let us know about Mom. Maybe they had called during the day while we were at school? Maybe we should call them? Not knowing what to do, I called Simon and told him what had happened, including the part about her wanting to date him and threatening to tell everyone about us.

"Let's hope she doesn't do that." There was silence and then he added, "Let me go and check on her. I'll get back to you."

Giving in to the growing feeling of guilt, I asked Simon, "Do you think it's our fault?"

His voice boomed. "Absolutely not. How could this be our fault?"

Did I contribute to her cracking because Simon picked me? I wondered, but I didn't say this aloud to Simon.

Monica, Karen, and I lived alone in the apartment on Rooney Street for several weeks. We had family in Windsor—a grandma, two aunts, two uncles, and multiple cousins—but we didn't want anybody to know Mom had gone into the hospital. We especially didn't want Dad to know. We knew Dad would be pissed off at Mom and that they'd get into a big fight over what had happened. None of us were entirely sure the whole thing wasn't our fault after pouring out her alcohol and dumping her pills. And mine for dating Simon.

Dad would absolutely make it worse for Mom, so we made a pact not to tell him when he called. We secretly hoped that Mom would get out of the hospital in a few days, and nobody would be the wiser.

We went to school, did our homework, cleaned the apartment, cooked what little food was left, and tried to be good girls. I still saw Simon on the weekends, and he and Ron checked on Mom in the hospital and reported back that she was improving. Ron knew nothing about Simon's and my relationship, of course.

One day, leaving his house with my school backpack in my hands, I finally asked him what I had been wondering for days: "Should we go and see her?"

Afraid of how she would act and what she would say, I wasn't sure. Simon took my hand and held it, considering my question. I looked up at him and his eyes melted into caramels. "Yes, you should all three go and visit her. It's time."

We rode the city bus together from home. We brought her a homemade card with a heart on the front and a message from each of us about how sorry we were for the fighting.

A security guard in the lobby of the Hotel Dieu Hospital escorted us up the locked elevator to the eighth-floor psychiatric unit, where we asked at the nurse's station to see Paula Johansen. A nurse who looked to be only a few years older than Monica and me led us down a corridor and past several rooms where people lay in their beds. Yells and screams could be heard echoing down the hallway from around the corner. The three of us locked elbows together like we had a few years earlier in Nuku Hiva when we went to see our very sick dad in the rustic, rural health clinic, not wanting to see the elephantiasis or leprosy patients living there. This time we didn't want to see anybody freaking out.

We arrived at a corner room and stopped. There were two patients in the room. Mom was in the farthest bed from the door, lying flat without even a pillow under her head. When she raised her head and saw us, she yelled, "Come here, girls! Come here right now!" The other patient's eyes remained closed. Was she asleep? We inched our way closer, moving as a group, holding on to each other. Mom wore a thick white canvas-like hospital gown cinched at the waist by a thick strap that disappeared under the bed. Her ankles and wrists had the same straps. She lifted her head again and the chains rattled under the bed. Her black hair lay matted against her head; her dark eyes were large and desperate.

The floors, ceilings, walls, and bedding were white. The nurse in her crisp white uniform put a pillow under Mom's head so she could see us better. We congregated beside her, trying not to stare at the restraints attached to the now-visible chains on the underside of the bed.

"Come closer, girls."

Shock and horror settled over me. Mom began quietly crying and whimpering, her dark eyes pleading as they darted between the three of us. "Help me, girls. Help me get out of here." She kicked her legs and tried to raise her arms. The chains rattled.

A familiar feeling of helpless despair like a black cloud filled me up, pressing against my ribs and expanding like an approaching thunderstorm. There would be wind, rain, hail, and lightning, and there was nothing we could do about it. The dark side of life terrified me, and we were staring into its abyss. The young nurse came up behind us and asked us to step back a bit from the bed. My lips quivered. Sadness threatened to overflow from me as I pushed back the tears.

"How, Mom? How can we get you out?" Karen whimpered, taking her hand.

Her face looked familiar and yet not familiar. She had lost weight and her cheekbones stuck out a bit more than normal. "Call Grandma or Aunt Melanie."

"Okay, we can do that. We'll call them," I said, barely able to look into her glassy, bloodshot eyes. The black pupils were almost as big as the brown irises.

An older nurse who must have been watching from the doorway charged into the room. "Never mind, Paula. The girls can't help you. You must take your medication and then you will get better."

"Shut up, you nasty witch!" Mom spat at the woman. We all took a big step back but when the other patient began shouting incoherently behind us, we startled and took a small step toward Mom again, caught between both beds.

"Yeah, shut up, you bitch!" the other patient yelled as she thrashed her head back and forth and rattled the chains on the bed.

Stunned, I stared at the other patient. Her gray hair was matted against her head and her lips were cracked dry. My stomach clenched and my throat tightened. *Why did they have to tie Mom down?*

"Paula, if you keep spitting, I will cover your mouth so you can't speak."

The nurse looked at us. "This isn't a good day to visit. Your mother isn't doing well today. It's too bad you didn't come yesterday. She was much better yesterday."

I grabbed Karen's arm and started to back away. Monica took my arm, all of us watching Mom thrash like the rain and wind in a big black thunderstorm.

We sidestepped from between the beds and backed up. I said, "Mom, we'll come back tomorrow, okay?"

"Oh no, girls. You stop now. Listen to me. I have something to tell you." Her voice was commanding, and she sounded like her old self.

The nurse motioned us toward the door.

Mom continued in her commanding voice. "Monica, you're always asking if you're adopted. Your father and I made a promise never to speak about this ever. But I think you're old enough now to hear the truth. Don't you?"

Monica eyed her in suspicion, as we all seemed to be weighing whether she was telling the truth.

"Mom, stop. I'm scared," Karen said quietly, looking like she would fold in on herself and fall to a heap on the floor. Monica stood in stunned silence, waiting.

"You have a different father than Karen and Leslie. Your father was my high school sweetheart."

We stopped moving backward.

"What?" Monica was shaking her head like she hadn't just heard the truth she'd begged for since she was little.

Mom spoke in unbelievably lucid and clear words. Her eyes held Monica's, and her body was rigidly still. "His name is Bernie. Bjorn and I didn't marry until you were three months old. Go look at the marriage certificate and your birth certificate. When Bjorn came back from his year-long trip to explore the States, I was already pregnant, so we made a pact with Bernie to never tell you."

"But why did you make a pact to lie to me?" Monica asked.

"Because Bernie was getting married to somebody else and I wanted to marry Bjorn." All the tenseness left her body and she went limp, looking exhausted like a marathon runner.

"No more talking today," said the nurse in a tender voice, seemingly moved by the speech Mom just gave. "That's enough for now."

We left the hospital and took the bus home, each of us filled with our own thoughts and feelings we weren't willing to share out loud. In the apartment we found all the paperwork. Mom and Dad had been married three months after Monica was born.

Monica kept saying "I knew it" in a low, defeated voice. She threw herself on Mom's bed with her head buried in a pillow and screamed, "I knew it! I knew I was different from you two!"

I couldn't take any more sadness that day. It felt like my heart was melting in my chest, threatening to slide right out of me.

"Monica! It doesn't matter. We're sisters. Dad is your dad. He's been your dad your whole life. He loves you. He takes care of you. We're all a family. It doesn't matter," I said.

"Yeah, Monica, we'll always be sisters. Who cares what Mom says," Karen said.

Monica waited a long minute before raising her head off the pillow. "It matters, you guys. Dad is not my dad. He's your dad. I'm different and I've always felt like it. Now I have proof."

The heaviness around me felt as if it would pull me to the ground and devour me.

We continued to try to convince Monica that it didn't matter to us what Mom said, but a wave of anger built inside me at the deception. How dare they lie to us all these years. How dare they tell bold-faced lies to Monica repeatedly! It would never matter to Karen or me. We kept insisting she was still our sister and we loved her. And we did. But Monica took it very hard and withdrew over the following days and weeks. She was less boisterous and outgoing, more introverted and moody.

The phone rang every evening, but we were afraid it was Dad, so we never answered it. We weren't expecting to hear from him until after he'd made his way back to California. But none of us were sure where he was, and nobody had the guts to lie to him about Mom being in the hospital, or to tell him we knew about Bernie being Monica's dad. If we didn't answer the phone, then we didn't have to lie. We lived in our little world and never went to see Mom again. She was too scary. Eventually, we unplugged the phone so we didn't have to listen to it ring all the time. We went to school, did our homework, and hoped it would somehow work out.

We never called Grandma or Aunt Melanie. After that first night, we simply never discussed Mom being in the hospital or what she'd said.

Only when we ran out of food did we confront an emergency we needed to deal with. Staring at bare shelves and an empty fridge, I said, "I hope the rent and heating bill aren't due anytime soon." We all considered this for a moment as our stomachs grumbled for dinner. "Let's just tackle one problem at a time," Karen said. Monica kicked into normal mode and started to solve the problem of how to get groceries without any money.

10

I still spent intimate time with Simon on the weekends. I was able to get food there, but Monica and Karen were not. Simon never asked about our resources. He told us Mom was not getting better very fast, but we still held out hope.

We hatched a plan to ask the food bank downtown to help us. We made up a story and set off on the bus after school. We arrived in front of the welfare office right before dark. Inside we found a heavy-set older lady with a kind face sitting behind the counter.

"Can I help you girls?"

I stepped forward. "Our mother is home sick in bed. She's been that way for several weeks and we've run out of food. Do you think we can have some food until she gets better?"

The lady looked at us closely. When she smiled, it was as if warmth came right out of her eyes and filled my body. I liked her immediately. "Where do you live?"

"On Rooney Street," Monica said.

We had agreed earlier not to give any real information about ourselves, so when Monica said we lived on Rooney Street, Karen and I snapped around to look at her.

I tried a diversion tactic. "Yeah, our mom is fine. She's just got a bad flu and can't get to work across the river in Detroit where she's a nurse."

Monica gave me a little shove. The lady nodded and said, "Okay, let me see what I can do." She went through two swinging doors to the warehouse where we caught a glimpse of long shelves stacked with cans and bags.

We collectively held our breath as Karen said, "You said Rooney Street," looking at Monica, then she turned to me and said, "You told her our mom was a nurse in a Detroit hospital, Leslie!"

Neither of us said anything. She was right. We were terrible liars.

A few minutes later the doors swung open and the lady brought two full boxes of food to the counter. Two loaves of Wonder bread sat on top of one box. "Can one of you please put your names down on this list here, along with your address and phone number?"

I knew we couldn't say where we lived, so I filled in a bogus address on Rooney Street. I made up a phone number as well. As for the name, I put down Lisa Johnson.

"Thank you!" we all chimed as we took the boxes and left the office.

On the bus we laughed and giggled; we were so proud. It felt good to take care of ourselves, like we did when Dad was in the hospital in Nuku Hiva and we'd had to live on the boat all alone. But mostly we were happy to have food in the house again. We peeked through the boxes and found peanut butter and jelly, soup, chili, macaroni and cheese, honey, pancake mix and syrup, apples, and two jugs of milk.

"Let's make PB&Js for dinner with cold milk!" I said, licking my lips.

"I'm going to goop on the peanut butter so thick," Monica said.

Now we could make lunches for school and have something to eat before bed. We were surviving in the big bad city without Mom. We beamed with pride.

A freak winter snowstorm blew down big, thick snowflakes that filled the street and sidewalks fast. But as we got off the bus, nothing could get us down and we kicked the snow, yelling out loud to the weather gods, daring them to give us a snow day the following day.

It reminded me of being on the boat in a squall and talking to the weather gods, thanking them for the fresh water to wash our hair and clothes and reminding them not to send too much wind.

As we ran from the bus stop in the darkness to the apartment building, we saw a figure up ahead leaning against a car. The streetlight was just above, and I had to blink. It was a tall man with a shiny, bald head. I gasped and stopped running.

"Guys!" I yelled. Monica and Karen stopped too. We all stared, dumbstruck.

"Could it be?" I asked.

Under her breath Monica said, "Oh God, we're in trouble."

11

"Girls! Is that you?" Dad yelled. "Where have you been? I've been waiting here for over an hour, freezing my ass off." I knew Dad was mad just by how he stood leaning against the car with his arms crossed.

Running up to him, I said, "We went to get food."

He eyed the boxes we carried. "Where's your mother?"

We didn't respond until we got inside, where we answered all his questions, conveniently skipping over the Simon part. When we proudly told him where we'd gotten the food, he was raging mad. "How is it okay to take handouts?" He grabbed the groceries. "Get into the car. Now!" he yelled.

He drove fast, the car skidding on the snowy road as we turned down Wyandotte, the three of us sliding into each other in the back seat. He instructed us, "When we get to this place, you will tell them that Johansens don't take handouts. Got that?"

Monica, Karen, and I side-eyed each other, trying not to catch Dad's eye in the rearview mirror. He parked on the street and we carried the boxes inside, where he slammed the groceries down on the counter. The nice lady looked startled then perplexed and then a little scared. We knew how she felt.

He stared at Monica and me and nodded. "Go ahead."

In unison, we said, "The Johansens don't take handouts."

He ushered us out of the building before the lady could even speak and drove us to the grocery store, where we bought some food and went back to the apartment.

We felt like utter failures, as if we had done a horrible thing, taking care of ourselves and finding free food while Mom recovered. Nothing we ever did was good enough. I hated Dad. Never any praise, never any compassion.

A sadness descended after that. We made soup and crackers for dinner and ate in the thickening silence, waiting for Dad to upend our world. Anxiety swirled inside at the thought of him finding out about Simon. What would he do to me?

After quietly cleaning up, we went to our bedroom and closed the door, leaving Dad on the couch staring at the wall like he did when he was planning something. We could hear the wheels turning.

I knew Dad would find out about Simon the next day and I would be dead. In the bedroom, we were all too afraid to speak to one another, unsure if his razor-sharp hearing could listen to us through the walls. I forced myself to sleep to forget.

The next morning, we filed out of the bedroom and into the kitchen for breakfast. We found Dad in the same position as last night: lying on the couch, fully clothed, staring at the ceiling. Panic rose up in me. Nobody said anything. We were dressed and ready for school, so we sat at the kitchen table silently while Karen put out bowls and cereal. Usually, cartoons played on TV while we all rushed around gathering our things, but today, we sat in fear of what the day would bring.

Dad stood up. "You girls stay here today. No school. I'm going to see your mother. I will be back shortly."

After he left, we turned on the TV to distract ourselves as we waited for the hammer to come down on our heads.

Later that afternoon, when the key clicked in the lock and Dad returned to the apartment, we all sat up straighter and I involuntarily clenched my teeth. He went straight to Monica and took her in his arms. "I love you, Monica, and I don't want to hear anything about another dad. You are my daughter. We are a family." Then he kissed and hugged her again. Monica let herself be hugged, her arms hanging lifeless beside her, but didn't respond to him.

Then he turned to me with hardened, challenging eyes and said, "What's this I hear about the family therapist being your boyfriend?" His face was contorted a little, lips pursed together in anger. He was so mad.

I don't know why it struck me as funny, but my mouth felt like it would smile. I tried biting the inside of my cheek, refusing to speak, but the edges of my mouth went up. I turned my head down and looked at the floor.

"Well, is somebody going to talk to me?" he boomed.

He looked at Monica and Karen, who buckled under the pressure and spewed forth all the details of Mom, Alan, the fight, the Deep Purple concert, and Simon. I listened with a newfound hatred. They were such traitors. Why couldn't we just stick together?

But sisterly competition was always encouraged by Dad. When he treated me as the favorite, I blossomed in the sunshine of his attention, which made Monica and Karen mad. When he shone his light of love on them, they would say anything to disparage me. It was a divide-and-conquer mentality.

"I think it's time I meet this Simon," Dad said with something that sounded like glee in his voice. I shrank back at the scene he would make. He left the apartment again.

An hour later, he came back but didn't say a word about Simon. I was dying to know what had happened, but I couldn't do anything. I refused to beg.

I could imagine the big scene he had made with Simon's boss. How had I wished to be sailing in Fiji with him again? How could I have thought I loved him? In his usual fucked-up way, he stared at me as he cozied up to Monica and Karen on the couch, asking them about school, basketball, band, and life to coax information out of them. He took us out for a steak dinner, where they spilled all the information on our life in Windsor while I scowled at him.

He was jealous of Simon just like he was jealous of any male in my life who ever came near me. He loved to disguise his jealousy as the instincts of a protective father, but I knew better. I no longer needed him, wishing I could leave this family for good. I had Simon now, and maybe he would rescue me.

The next day, we flew out of Detroit on United Airlines, leaving Mom in that hateful hospital, leaving the apartment in shambles and abandoning our schools without saying goodbye. I wasn't able to speak to Simon before we left.

I loved Simon and felt torn away from the only man who'd ever loved me back. Staring out the airplane window, once again I wondered what my life would be like. We touched down in Los Angeles and I swore silently to myself that I would return to Simon as soon as possible.

12

I needed to find a way to balance on the shifting ground under my feet. Life changed so fast, whiplash became a state of survival. One day we were slushing through the brown snow, and the next we were walking barefoot on the sand in California again.

With *Aegir* at the bottom of the ocean, it seemed our sailing days were over. Dad bought a home-based business called A-1 Marine Surveys in Redondo Beach with the insurance money from the boat. We moved into a three-bedroom, one-bath house that even had a backyard with a barbecue! How normal.

The previous owners had started the business decades earlier and were ready to travel the United States by RV in retirement. We inherited everything. Dad got his king-size bed, and we girls shared the other two bedrooms. The house/business package also included a decades-old plaid couch, a 1950s-era fake wood dining room table, what looked like turn-of-the-century working appliances, sheets, bedding, and towels. We even found their gravy-stained tablecloths in the sideboard. They must have just packed their clothes and driven away like we did in Windsor. Dad had bargained well. We had everything we needed. We went from homeless sailors with a boat at the bottom of the ocean to furnished homeowners with a thriving business in a beachy Southern California community.

The business operated out of an enclosed patio in the backyard with tin walls and a roof, and even a few windows that opened to let in a breeze. Two desks filled up the space, one for the surveyor and one for the secretary. The file cabinets with years of historical marine surveys were kept in the garage.

The day we unpacked, Dad yelled from his bedroom across the hall, "You girls get settled and decide how you're going to divide up the two bedrooms." I could tell by the singsong tone of his voice that he was pleased with himself.

We owned very little, since everything had sunk to the bottom of the ocean with *Aegir*. We only had the winter clothes in our suitcases, having abandoned most of our things in the apartment in Windsor, including the bra I had purchased at the thrift store, knowing Dad would not allow me to wear a bra yet. His philosophy was that only pregnant women needed a bra and that all others should be European and be free and natural. So unpacking didn't take long, and we got right to bedroom negotiations. We settled on Karen staying in one of the twin beds all the time while Monica and I rotated into our own bedroom every other week.

"I go first, Lez. I'm going to love having my own room," Monica said as she disappeared around the corner and closed her bedroom door.

Dad called from across the hall, "Leslie, how fast are you typing these days?"

He was trying hard to get our relationship back to "normal"—whatever that was. I could just imagine him lying on his bed, fingers laced behind his head as he stared at the ceiling. "How about you type up the marine surveys for me?" Those damn wheels turned so loud they needed oiling. Here he was planning out my life.

I hated him deeply for not letting me say goodbye to Simon and for trying to worm his way back into my life trying to be all kind and considerate by *asking* me to work for him instead of *demanding*.

Aside from Simon, I'd hated my horrible, miserable life in

Windsor and would have done anything to get back to California, but now I had to deal with this—all his worming weirdness every single day. I didn't want to work for him but answered politely, "I haven't typed since eighth grade in Oceanside. I probably don't remember anything."

"It hasn't been that long, Leslie, just a little more than a year, so give it a try. The typewriter out in the office is just sitting there getting dusty. Practice. It'll come back to you."

He wasn't asking anymore; he was telling me. I rolled my eyes and continued to stuff the few things I owned in the dresser's bottom drawer. "Okay, I guess," I mumbled under my breath.

"I need a secretary, and I pick you." I could tell from his voice that he was smiling—actually enjoying himself. He would make me his typing slave just like he had made me his sailing slave on the boat. "Great," I murmured, throwing myself face down on the bed.

As we settled in, Dad began surveying boats, and I typed up the reports. He decided to pay me $1.50 per hour, since he couldn't justify paying a "novice," he said, the legal minimum wage of $2.30. I began to save for my great escape.

Monica, Karen, and I took turns cooking, submitting our menus to Dad on Sundays for approval, and taking trips to the grocery store with him. When my week came up, I enjoyed the planning and cooking process. I loved to bake, and after becoming an expert bread maker while sailing, I ventured out and added to my skills by baking pies, cookies, and more elaborate cakes. I also loved cooking stews and soups from the old cookbooks I found in the cabinet and experimenting with new recipes.

We didn't start school when we arrived in late April, because there were only about six weeks left in the school year, and Dad said that wasn't enough time to learn anything. He let us have the time to explore all the little beach towns nearby: Redondo Beach with the harbor, Hermosa Beach with its strand, pier, and hippies, and

Manhattan Beach with the surfers, volleyball nets, and its rich and monied everything. The two old bikes in the garage had us riding double on one and going to the beach often to get away from Dad. Money was tight so we shopped at the secondhand store for bikinis and summer clothes.

My thoughts drifted to Mom some nights as I fell asleep. Dread and guilt bubbled up about leaving her in that hospital, abandoning our apartment, and being swept away without a proper goodbye. If we ever talked about Mom when Dad was around, he would launch into diatribes about her, saying she was weak, a crazy alcoholic, an unfit mother and that it was best to stay away from her. "Let her go, girls," he'd say sometimes. But none of us could forget our mother. Keeping my armor up with Dad was a full-time job. We barely spoke and I considered it a great accomplishment to make it through a week without being yelled at or shamed.

One night in bed, Karen and I whispered together and decided to write Grandma and Aunt Joan to find out about Mom.

California was the A-side of life. The sun and sand of summer occupied most of my days. Windsor was the B-side. Getting an update on Mom, gaining my freedom, and my love of Simon occupied my thoughts.

13

"Leslie, want to come with me to deliver a boat from Honolulu to San Francisco?"

We were on the couch watching TV when he sprung the question on me, even though we weren't exactly living in the sunshine of our relationship yet. I hadn't attended school for the end of my freshman year, had the whole summer stretching out in front of me, and I was still mad at him, but the storm was passing over and clearing out.

He continued, "I need to go soon, and I need an experienced crew. Won't you come and help your dear ole dad? I'm planning for us to sail through the Hawaiian Islands for a few weeks before heading to San Francisco."

He was pandering to me. He knew just which words to choose. Calling me "experienced crew" was a compliment, and compliments were like water in the desert of our relationship. Telling me we were going to see the other islands too. He knew where my buttons were.

I missed the ocean, my dear and sweet friend. I missed the long days at sea and the sense of solitude and communion I felt while on watch. Even though Dad would be paid, I was expected to go as unpaid crew, just like everyone else he recruited, saying that the experience of the ocean crossing would be payment enough.

"I'll go if Raine goes with us," I said after thinking for a minute. My negotiating skills were improving.

Without hesitation, he said, "I'll call Myrna Loy tomorrow."

Myrna Loy was Raine's pot-smoking, drug-doing, sexy, hippy mom, who'd allowed all manner of surfers and skateboarders to hang out at her house while we were growing up in Oceanside. A smile spread across my face. I didn't say anything, because then he would have the upper hand again, and it was so rare that I had any power. *He needs me*, I thought.

Myrna Loy agreed to let Raine go. Dad also enlisted a sixteen-year-old surfer/diver/sailor named Ron that we knew from Oceanside Harbor. Ron was foxy with his long blond hair and buff body, but he had a serious cloud hanging over him and wasn't my type. Dad insisted he was a good sailor and wanted him aboard for deck work and watches. Being the stuck-up beach girls we were, Raine and I made a pact to ignore Ron in favor of meeting foxy Hawaiian surfer boys.

On June 5, 1976, Dad closed up the house and he and I headed out into the world for another adventure. Monica stayed on a ranch with family friends in Atascadero with horses, cows, goats, and chickens. Perfect for her. Dad arranged for Karen to stay with another family friend who just had a baby. Poor Karen babysitting again.

After our five-hour flight to Honolulu, Ron, Raine, Dad, and I made our way under cloudy skies via taxi the short seven miles to Kewalo Basin Harbor and boarded *Starship*, a 1950s-era, fifty-six-foot yawl. She was a sleek and slim Rhodes design with beautiful lines and a yellow stripe above the waterline. Dad opened the hatches, and we instantly plugged our noses. The stale and rancid odor confirmed *Starship* had been battened up for several weeks or months and never cleaned from the last party. Empty beer, wine, tequila, and rum bottles were strewn around the cabin. Marijuana roaches lay in an ashtray overflowing with cigarette butts. To top it all off, it smelled like the head was clogged.

Our crew grew by two when a quiet couple in their late twenties from Michigan, Beth and Phil, joined us in Honolulu. Dad had met them in San Diego a few months earlier when they were looking for crewing positions on boats headed for Tahiti. Everything about them looked conservative to me from their long shorts and glasses to their Bible—initially making me leery of them. We soon found out they were high school sweethearts and had grown up on Lake Michigan with dreams of opening their own boat business. It didn't take long before their stellar work ethics and hearts of gold won us all over. Beth felt like an older sister, and I welcomed an adult woman aboard. That way Raine and I could be teenagers and find boys.

Raine and I picked out our bunks in the crew quarters near the bow just as Dad yelled from the cockpit, "Girls, can you come up here so we can talk about chores?"

"Ugh," I groaned, "here we go. Dad's going to boss us around all summer. Just watch."

But after he assigned chores like cleaning the floors and heads once a day, sanding the teak railing, and hosing off the deck, he gave Raine and me unprecedented freedom to explore Ala Moana Beach and to walk a couple of miles to swim at the famous Waikiki Beach. We found matching puka shell necklaces from a street vendor and pledged to be best friends forever.

The plan was to spend two weeks sailing the islands after Dad took inventory of the boat and made sure everything was in working order for an ocean crossing. As the days progressed, we learned from the harbormaster and the employees at the marine store about the wild, naked drug parties the granddaughter Linda, more commonly called Elektra Flash, had thrown on the boat. *Cool name*, I thought. As we were sanding the teak railings one sticky, hot morning, several unfriendly large Hawaiian men checked us out as they walked past, eyeing the boat like they were taking stock. I nodded politely as we made eye contact but furrowed my brow with each new person who passed. I nudged Raine, who stopped sanding the railings for a sip of her lemonade. "Are you noticing all these dudes checking us out?"

Raine brushed the long brown hair from her shoulders. "Yeah. But I think it's the boat as much as it is us. I wonder if Elektra Flash ripped them off or something."

I moved my hand back and forth on the railing. "I'll tell my dad," I said, and then, after a moment, added, "I wish we could have met Elektra Flash, don't you?"

"Yeah, she was probably a lot of fun, but it's obvious she made people mad."

A short time later, a blond haole man and a woman with shaggy, sandy hair approached the boat. "Permission to come aboard?" the man said. They were both in their late twenties. He had glassy eyes, and the woman held the man's forearm to steady herself. They wore towels like they had just gotten out of a shower—his wrapped around his waist and hers around her chest.

"Dad? There's somebody here!" I yelled down to the engine room, smiling at the couple.

He came up on deck wiping the sweat from his forehead, and the man repeated his request to come aboard. "Permission granted," Dad said. When they sat down in the cockpit and let their towels fall to their sides, I saw that they were completely naked. I tried not to stare but grabbed Raine's arm and scooted closer to her. Ron looked over his shoulder only briefly to catch sight of the couple before swiping his long hair to the side and going back to work. His face was always so hard to read.

Dad didn't seem the least bit fazed by their nudity, which made it even weirder to me as they just carried on a normal conversation. Raine and I kept watch from midship, where we were supposed to be sanding the railings.

"Is Elektra around?" the man asked. His spiral-shaped koa wood necklace hung against his bare chest.

Raine and I stole glances at each other again.

"No, she's gone back to the mainland," Dad said, finally lifting his eyes off the woman's breasts to her eyes, her long turquoise dangly earrings swaying back and forth.

"Really? Well, let me tell you that we had some great times on this boat," the man said.

"We've heard stories." Dad nodded.

A few awkward moments passed when nobody spoke. The couple looked around at Ron varnishing and Raine and me on the deck in our bathing suits and suddenly realized we weren't loose and crazy or naked like the people they had partied with.

"Do you know how to contact Elektra? She owes me some money," the woman said.

"If you leave me your name and number, I can get it to her," Dad said.

After writing down their information, the couple put their towels back on and left. Once they were out of earshot, Raine and I burst out in a big laugh, but Dad snarled at me. "We don't know what we're dealing with or how much money Elektra owes people, so be quiet." I shrunk back and looked away. He continued, "We'll paint over the name tonight and move the boat to a different part of the harbor tomorrow."

A serious mood fell over the boat. I knew my dad well enough to know the fun was over and that after stocking the boat with food, we would be heading out on our tour of the islands.

14

We left Oahu a few days later on "a shakedown cruise" to Lanai, also known as the Pineapple Island, eighty miles away. A "shakedown cruise" always revealed problems that needed fixing, and the idea was to root out most of them before heading to San Francisco. Winds between the Hawaiian Islands can blow fierce and fast. That day was no exception. Our novice sailors, Raine, Phil, and Beth, were seasick, while Ron and Dad were unaffected. My sea legs were gone from living on land for so long, so I paid the price of queasiness for a few hours until my body adjusted. We were sailing up and down large mounds of water when a rogue wave crashed against the forward genoa sail, ripping it up the luff about eight feet. Dad and Ron made their way to the bow to take it down and put up a storm jib, which slowed us down and immediately straightened the heeling.

"Isn't that better?" I asked Raine. She was lying on the high side of the boat in her orange bikini, still wanting to work on her tan even though she was nauseous.

"Is all of this normal?" she asked, brows furrowed.

"The wind? The waves? The ripped sails? Or being seasick?" I asked, smiling and patting her shoulder in comfort.

"All of it," she said without opening her eyes.

"It's all a normal part of sailing. You'll feel better soon."

As we rounded the tip of Lanai, the sea became flat. The island looked barren and uninhabited as we approached Manele Bay. "Where are all the cute surfers, palm trees, and pineapples?" I asked Dad.

"The palm trees and pineapples are up a long, winding road that goes into the clouds and leads to Lanai City. As for the surfers, I have no idea." He explained that the Dole Plantation Company owned the island and that most of the people who lived here worked for them.

After anchoring and settling in, Beth made chicken and potatoes for dinner, which we ate ravenously. Having another woman aboard the boat who cooked like a professional and acted like my older sister was immensely pleasing. "Who's coming to Lanai City tomorrow morning so I can call Mrs. Olsen, the boat's owner, and order a new genoa sail?" Dad asked.

Raine, Ron, and I jumped at the chance. Beth and Phil agreed to stay on the boat.

The next morning, we caught a ride with a very nice Dole employee who let us sit in the back of his truck. Lanai City was set out in a square with cute little dirt roads crisscrossing back and forth. Dad found a phone booth outside the small library while Ron, Raine, and I looked for a store. "There's nothing happening in this town," Ron said after we found the grocery store.

"Everybody's in the fields picking pineapples," Raine said.

"Let's find my dad and go back to the beach and swim," I said.

On the ride back down to the coast, the nice Dole truck driver who dropped us off bestowed a case of pineapples on us. "Thanks," we all called as he pulled away in a cloud of dust.

That night Dad let Raine and me sleep on the beach alone. It would have been cool if some cute surfers had been around, but then he probably wouldn't have let us sleep ashore. Still, having some privacy and being alone with Raine for a whole night was a welcome change. We spread our sleeping bags out on the sand and dug a small pit for a fire. We could have pretended to be on a deserted island but for the three boats anchored in front of us. I rolled over on my back. Small stars began to light the heavens. The flames from our fire glowed more orange than blue.

"I'm so glad I got to come on this trip. Thanks for bringing me," Raine said.

Away from my dad, we fell into catching up about our love lives. She told me about the guy she was dating, Brett. "He's five years older than me," she shared.

I hadn't told her about Simon, but now I did—and let her know that he was sixteen years older than me. "Does your mom know about Brett?"

"No, he's a friend of hers. I've been seeing him on the sly for three months now."

The ankle-high waves crashed onshore. Down the beach, a group of seagulls huddled in a circle, cawing. The blue-and-purple sky hovered over us. Raine asked, "Did your mom or dad know about Simon?"

"They both found out. It was a bum rap," I said, and I told her the whole story.

After putting more driftwood on the fire, I asked, "Do you like Brett? I mean, is he the guy for you?"

"Nah, not really. I'm just having fun, I guess. What's Simon like?" she asked, propping herself up on her elbow to look at me.

I poured out my heart, telling her of my erotic experiences with Simon.

"Wow, that's incredible," she said when I was done. "Are you writing to him?"

"I snuck a letter to him and told him about this trip. But he can't write, because I live in a prison where everything I own is subject to search."

She laughed. "Your dad doesn't seem like a prison guard."

"You don't know him."

A long silence settled on us. I propped myself up on one elbow and looked at her. "Let's be best friends and sisters."

Nodding and smiling, she said, "I love you so much."

The fire died out and we climbed inside our sleeping bags, falling asleep late, staring at the stars.

15

The next morning, we sailed to Maui, only about twenty miles away, and anchored at Kaanapali Beach, which is not a protected bay but a beautiful stretch of sand. We anchored in front of the Royal Lahaina Hotel in forty feet of pristine water. At 2 p.m., the wind was blowing twenty-five plus knots, and by 3:30 p.m., our anchor chain had broken, and we drifted toward the beach.

Dad started the engine in a scramble, and we motored away from shore. Without another anchor aboard, we circled until Dad decided to send Phil ashore in the dinghy to buy another anchor.

Having a link in the chain break was highly unusual, and even though the chain was very rusty, Dad was suspicious of more shenanigans related to Elektra Flash. "I'll dive to the anchor in the morning and hopefully be able to see what happened."

Phil returned an hour later with news of a mooring we were invited to use. "It's by Black Rock Beach in front of the Sheraton." He pointed up the coast.

"Who offered that?" Dad asked. I could tell he was paranoid.

Phil took off his sunglasses and hat. "A man who works at the marine store. He said his friend is sailing in Tahiti and wouldn't mind."

"At least it's the perfect price—free," Dad mumbled.

Black Rock Beach was behind a point extending into the ocean, which provided shelter to moored boats. We motored over there, and by 6 p.m., we were securely tied to the mooring for the night.

We stood watch that night, keeping an eye on anybody who came close. In the morning, when Dad dove down to get our anchor, his suspicions were confirmed. One of the links had been cut cleanly about five feet from the anchor. He brought the anchor back to the boat just as a man from a neighboring ship approached us in a dinghy, claiming that Elektra Flash owed him $100 for repairs he had done to *Starship*. A dark-blue bandanna covered his head like a pirate. "I'll take that anchor you fished off the bottom as payment," he said.

Dad answered, "Oh no, you won't. It's the only anchor we have. If Elektra owes you money, that's your problem."

The man grumbled and headed back to his boat.

Raine and I conjured more stories about Elektra Flash and her parties and enemies. Dad played down the encounter with the other boater, but he couldn't hide his nervousness. He paced on deck, staring at the shore, squinting, or stood with his hands on his hips, his legs spread apart like the King of Siam. I could see him thinking and planning ways to keep us safe. It was a conundrum in our relationship that I felt unsafe while alone with my father and yet felt safest while with him in any kind of dangerous situation outside.

After fixing the chain, we reanchored in soft sand off Kaanapali and continued our nightly watches. Raine and I went ashore looking for some boy fun; we found a few cuties and lay near them while keeping an eye on the boat anchored just offshore, trying to act like we didn't know Ron, who was shirtless on the bow fixing something. When the boys next to us went out surfing, we followed them and bodysurfed until my bathing suit top came untied and I nearly lost it. Once Ron began waving at us, we knew we had to go back. We hadn't said a word to the cute boys by the time we had to pack up and return to the boat.

* *

While waiting for the replacement of the sail that had ripped on our trip from Oahu, Phil, Dad, and Ron examined *Starship*'s seaworthiness. The story wasn't good. They discovered a big crack in the engine, and, worst of all, the stuffing box was leaking badly around the prop. The mizzen staysail was jammed, and the spark plugs on the outboard dinghy engine needed to be replaced. Maybe worst of all, one of the two heads had backed up again and was now blocked entirely and couldn't be used. The engine crack was terrible, but the dry rot around the leaking stuffing box worried Dad the most. Wooden boats leaked, but almost everything aboard *Starship* was falling apart.

Raine and I stayed out of the way during the repairs, going to the beach and helping Beth shop for more food for our upcoming passage to San Francisco, which Dad optimistically explained would take between eleven and twenty days.

On a quiet, beautiful morning without the wind and high waves, Ron was wholly absorbed in studying a chart with Dad down below while I hung wet towels on the line, when a large crash startled us all. I turned around and saw that a Hobie Cat had rammed us. Dad flew up on deck and yelled, "What the hell was that?" When he saw the Hobie Cat, he yelled, "Watch it, will you?" in a fierce voice that scared me.

The man looked terrified. "I'm so sorry. I don't know how to operate this thing."

Nerves were raw, and Dad was suspicious that we were being targeted. Except for a minor scrape on the hull, there was no damage. We all nervously watched as the novice tried to steer the fast-moving boat back toward the hotel where he'd rented it.

After seven days of rocking and rolling in the Kaanapali anchorage, Dad was tired of waiting for the sail and being suspicious of everyone around us. We weighed anchor and sailed north around Maui to Honolua Bay, a much quieter anchorage. The big waves hit Honolua

Bay in the winter, but in late June, the bay was flat like a lake. There were no hotels, houses, or people anywhere. There were also no cute surfers.

The anchorage was pristine and quiet, and we barely moved on the water. Being more secluded from the public allowed Dad to relax and not be so suspicious of people approaching the boat, but it was also more boring for Raine and me. We kept busy embroidering, sewing, or getting French lessons from Beth. I knew a fair amount of French from our time in Tahiti, but Raine knew none. Beth had learned French in high school and college and was practically fluent, although she hadn't been to France yet. We practiced introducing ourselves and asking for directions to the closest bakery, but then Beth taught us how to say more fun stuff like "Où sont les garçons mignons?"—which means "Where are the cute boys?" We also asked her to teach us to ask where the nearest party was in case we met some nice people: "Où est la fête la plus proche?" We practiced those phrases ad nauseam.

Meanwhile, Dad worked on the boat's repairs with Phil and Ron. They tore the exhaust manifold apart and hauled it to town to find a welder. On each trip to Lahaina, they hauled five-gallon jerry cans filled with diesel from town. We needed to leave the islands with a full tank of diesel. Dad worried daily about how much money he was spending to get the boat ready and how long we'd have to wait for the new sail.

Delay after delay, first by the sailmaker in Newport Beach and then by Pan Am, who was flying the sail from California, made Dad a grumpy captain. In desperation, after eight more days of waiting, he flew to Honolulu to pick up our new genoa from Pan Am freight, but they had misplaced the sail, so he came back to Maui empty-handed, threatening a lawsuit. Pam Am agreed to send the sail to Maui if Dad paid $198 in freight charges.

After three more days, Pan Am had yet to locate the sail. *Starship* was turning into the bad-luck boat. Finally, after five more days of waiting, on June 30, 1976, the sail arrived at the Maui airport, and Dad hitchhiked there to pick it up. Once back on *Starship*, we packed up and prepared for our final stop, a visit to Moloka'i and the leper colony.

16

Unbeknown to any of us, Dad had been planning this visit to Moloka'i and the leper colony from the very beginning of our trip. Even though we were severely behind schedule due to the delayed sail, he was determined to bring supplies to the men and women living in the village of Kalaupapa, a generous and kind act by anyone's standards. This was completely in character for my father, and yet, another conundrum for me was how to reconcile an abusive, overbearing, and unfair father with this man who would go out of his way to bring supplies to people who had suffered their entire lives.

Our humanitarian and history lessons began the night before we left Maui. Dad took on a history teacher aura at dinner as we ate chili and cornbread on deck. "Starting in 1866, the Hawaiian government began sending thousands of men, women, and children afflicted with leprosy to Moloka'i to keep them away from the general population. This was back when they weren't sure how leprosy was spread." Sitting up straighter and expanding his chest ever so slightly, he said, "The disease is officially called 'Hansen's Disease' because, in 1874, a Norwegian doctor named Gerhard Hansen discovered the leprosy microorganism, and the journey to a cure began."

"Go Norway!" I said, hoping to earn some brownie points with Dad. He smiled at me, and I heard the points being added to my account: *cha-ching*.

"A cure was discovered in the 1960s, allowing the Hawaiian government to close the Kalaupapa leprosy colony. But many residents had to stay and live in isolation because they had nowhere to go."

"How sad," Raine said, and we all nodded.

"Yes, it is sad, but when we meet them in the village on Moloka'i, I assure you they do not want your sympathy," Dad said with force. We all nodded in unison.

He shared a handout with us, explaining some rules for visiting the village. We were not allowed to take pictures of the people but could talk to anybody on the street or in a public place. Bathrooms were only available at the public picnic grounds and the main office in town. We could visit the hospital only with prior permission. There were no restaurants in town, and eating should only be done at the public picnic tables. Reading the document made our visit very solemn. Respect and compassion felt like the order of the day.

We left Maui midmorning for the fast half-day sail. Our new genoa performed beautifully, and we arrived on our final island under cloudy skies, anchoring in Kalaupapa Bay directly in front of the town. That night, it rained and the wind blew. The cabin leaked in various places. We rocked and rolled in the high surf, but by morning, everything had calmed.

We loaded the dinghy with clothing and our supplies and carried them in bags onto the island, looking for a church elder. The town seemed deserted, and I didn't want to look too closely or peer into any screen doors. I knew what leprosy looked like from my time in French Polynesia. I had described the deformed hands and feet, the lesions, and the discolored skin to Raine before our visit.

The dirt road through town was lined with large estate houses painted in various pastel colors, giving the town a warm and welcoming feel. Everything was well taken care of and freshly painted, although no people were visible anywhere, not even in the one grocery store or at the post office. Were they hiding from us?

Nineteen

Arm in arm, Raine and I walked together in the eerie silence of the town. Ron followed Dad, while Beth and Phil walked slightly behind us. Nobody spoke. All we heard was the wind blowing. We saw a cross high up on the church spire at the other end of town and headed for it. As we walked, sadness came over me. My imagination took hold, and my mind's eye saw hundreds of people hiding just out of sight, watching us through windows and slits in wood, peering around corners. The isolation they felt living outside society for their entire lives must have been immense. Having been granted their freedom only seven years earlier, in 1969, some had no place to go that wouldn't treat them as outcasts, so they had to stay. My heart swelled for these people I couldn't see. I clutched Raine's arm more tightly.

Finally, we reached the church and spoke with a priest about donating our goods. He thanked us and promised to distribute the items to the villagers. "Since the leprosy colony is technically closed, only a few hundred people live on the island now."

We returned to the boat in silence. As we sat on deck eating another delicious meal, Beth said to Dad, "Thank you for taking us to this island and showing us this village. Even though we didn't see anybody, they are in our thoughts and prayers, and we're grateful for the experience." Dad smiled and nodded. We all chimed in with our agreement with Beth. It was confusing to be proud of my dad. Usually, I hated him and didn't want to be anywhere near him, but now, I wanted to hug him. But I didn't.

Later that evening on deck, I witnessed the first stars hanging over the gorgeous volcanic view of the plateaus. The Hawaiian ancestors had shared the same view more than one hundred years before when King Kamehameha V established the leper colony in 1866. Seeing history alive in front of me filled me with awe and respect. I prayed for Moloka'i's people, sending them love, kindness, and peace.

* *

On our final day before crossing to the mainland, the repairs to the stuffing box and steering components continued. Ron, Raine, and I fished with the poles off the boat, and, to our amazement, Ron caught a ten-pound papio, which we identified as edible in a book below deck. We barbecued it that evening and discovered it tasted buttery and went very well with rice and the rest of our pineapple.

Our first official crew meeting took place that night before we left for San Francisco as we sat around the cockpit with our plates of fish, rice, and pineapple. "With luck and some decent wind, we'll sail two hundred miles a day," Dad said.

I did the math in my head: 2,300 miles to San Francisco meant we might only be at sea for twelve or thirteen days. Easy deal. Twelve days at sea was a nice thought. It gave me enough time to commune with my beloved ocean while not being so long that it would be boring. I wished to be back on the mainland as soon as possible to call Simon, even if I had to call collect. I needed confirmation that he still loved me.

Dad continued, "The rhumb line from Moloka'i to San Francisco is a northern trajectory, meaning we will most likely have to tack back and forth a few times."

Beth said softly, "I hope we can make it in less than twenty days because our food stores are down from all the delays."

Dad considered this. "Do you think we have enough food for twenty days?"

Beth thought for a moment, then said, "If we catch some fish, it'll help. If nobody is too picky, we have lots of rice and a fifteen-pound can of cashews." She laughed nervously. I thought about the realities of rationing rice and cashews the last few days at sea. No fun.

Leaving with less than the desired amount of food wasn't ideal. Dad had spent so much money on repairs and the new sail that he said, "It'll be fine. Leslie and I need to go on a diet anyway. You all will have plenty of food for the trip."

Beth looked at Phil and then at Dad. I shrunk into myself. The air was heavy, and my face was beet red. Everyone's eyes darted away. Ron cleared his throat, picked up the nearest line, and began coiling it. Beth stood up and started collecting the empty plates. Phil helped her. I was grateful for the distraction and ran to my bunk to hide.

Dad had been trying to put me on a diet since I was little, but I never had any stamina when it came to fasting. I always cheated on his imposed diets, and he called me names like "stupid little weakling" or "Fatso," trying to motivate me, but it never did. Not much had changed when it came to Dad scrutinizing my body.

I wished I could call him out. If I could have, I'd have taken a deep breath, stood up, and said "Shut up, old man, with the belly hanging over your shorts. How dare you criticize my teenage body. You're a creep and a horrible dad for making me embarrassed like that in front of everybody. I hate you." But I would never have called him out like that. He probably would have pushed me overboard, laughed, or berated me for speaking up.

While I was huddled in my bunk reading, Raine took my hand. "Come up on deck with me. There are flying fish all around. It's crazy."

"Where's my dad?"

"At the navigation station. Everybody else is out of sight. Beth and Phil are in the galley, and Ron is reading in his bunk. Come on, it's incredible."

I followed her to the bow, getting as far away from everybody else as possible. The night air was cool, and a few early stars peeked out from the heavens. We dangled our legs over the edge of the boat and watched the sky come to life. Flying fish skimmed the surface of the still water, speeding through the air and then diving back down again. Was something chasing them, or were they celebrating the coming night where they could hide from predators in the dark?

Raine leaned into me and whispered, "Forget your dad. You're not fat and don't need to lose weight."

I laid my head on her shoulder for a second and whispered, "Thank you."

17

We sailed away from the Hawaiian Islands under cloudy, wind-driven skies on July 3, 1976.

"I'm sort of scared," Raine said quietly.

"Don't be scared. Some parts will be hard; other parts will be so amazing you'll forget how hard it was."

This would be my third ocean crossing in less than two years. The number of days we spent at sea sailing to San Francisco would be added to the seventy-two days I had already earned: twenty-three from San Diego to Nuku Hiva, a few more sailing between the Marquesas, Tuamotu, and Society Islands, and forty-two from Tahiti to San Diego. That thought made me proud. Still mad at Dad for the diet comment, I tried to make it through as many days as I could without talking to him.

The first afternoon at sea blew a hard and steady twenty-five knots. *Starship* climbed the building eight-foot waves like a professional, sliding down the other side elegantly. Raine, Beth, and Phil were seasick again, so Dad, Ron, and I took all the watches. We were sailing almost due north and the chill in the air bit at my skin. I played my guitar and sang James Taylor, Carole King, and Bob Dylan songs to keep myself company the first few days alone on deck, reminiscing about the Deep Purple concert in Detroit. My life had changed so completely since then, it was unrecognizable even to me.

But being at sea felt like communing with a dear friend. I loved the ocean and had missed her terribly while living in the snow of Windsor. Looking around at the wind, the waves, and the boat plowing through the water in that familiar up-and-down motion made it hard to believe that the drama around Simon, my mom being hospitalized, and Dad spiriting us away from Windsor had happened just four months earlier.

On the third morning, Beth showed up in the galley and made coffee and muffins for breakfast. A welcome change from oatmeal every morning.

In the cockpit together, Dad took a big bite of his muffin and, looking at Phil, Beth, and Raine, said, "At some point, you must start moving around. The seasickness will fade." He looked directly at Raine and said, "Keep taking the Dramamine."

"It won't stay down," Raine whimpered, and Beth nodded her agreement. Raine's mouth turned up a bit, and I thought she'd smile, but then she ran to the side of the boat to dry-heave again.

"Starting today everyone will take their own watches and we'll see how it goes," Dad said, sweeping his eyes around the cockpit.

Raine and I did our two-hour watches together. That way we could go to the galley for hot tea and food, not that she was eating much. The boat had an autopilot so manual steering wasn't necessary, but paying attention to freighters and other sailboats was crucial. On watch, our job included keeping the logbook up-to-date by writing down the heading, wind speed and direction, and boat speed every hour.

Dad impressed upon us the importance of staying alert, since we would be sailing in some of the most heavily trafficked waters in the world as hundreds of freighters a day entered San Francisco Harbor from Japan. Of course, a trip with the salty Sea Captain Bjorn Johansen wouldn't be complete without a few man-overboard drills and official navigation classes with sextants and declination tables. It was good to be back to the exercises of life aboard.

As the days progressed, the logbook filled up with everyone's stories about the number of freighters they saw on watch, along with whales and dolphin sightings. Beth and Phil had grown up sailing on Lake Michigan and were especially wowed by the ocean and all her bounty. We caught a mahi-mahi soon after leaving Moloka'i, and after eating it, Phil and Beth were never seasick again.

One morning while on watch alone, I was in my own world reminiscing about Simon when Dad, Phil, and Ron appeared on deck, ready to reef the main sail. I smiled big, knowing Dad would vehemently object to my thoughts of Simon in bed beside me.

"What are you smiling at?" he barked.

"Nothing," I said, feeling dangerous at my many forbidden thoughts.

He thought he controlled me, but I knew he didn't. I could think whatever I wanted to, whenever I wanted to, even when he was standing right next to me. He would never control me or my thoughts.

Ever since I was six years old, Dad had photographed me naked in the name of art or something. My first memory was of being made to stand naked on the beach with Monica and Karen, all of us holding on to each other and crying from the cold while the waves lapped at our knees. He yelled at us to stop crying and smile, but we couldn't. Nothing stopped him from snapping away with his camera. I dreaded it every time it happened over the years. Of course now, on our first warm and sunny day, there he was as Raine and I sat on the teak deck trying to bathe. She had a nice lather on her head while washing her hair as I stood over her naked, ready to dump a bucket of water, when I looked up—*click, click, click* went his camera.

"Dad! Stop!" I yelled. He ignored me and kept looking through the viewfinder, snapping away.

He hadn't changed a bit. What a lecherous old man. I hated him. I promised myself that someday I wouldn't ever talk to him again.

About a week into our journey, we were struck with days and days of no wind. "I guess this is what they call the 'Aloha High,'" Dad said without fanfare. True to his word, he fired up the engine, but soon after, the engine's shaking caused a leak around the prop, which filled up the bilge. We began pumping shifts to keep the water below the floorboards. Dad and I regaled the crew with stories of *Patricia* and our around-the-clock pumping shifts on our forty-two-day sail from Tahiti to San Diego.

We flopped around in the quietness for six days, running the engine off and on while Dad and Phil tried again to fix the rotting wood around the prop. Ron took on the navigation, practicing taking shots of the sun with the sextant every day and plotting our course for Dad. He wore his blue bandanna tied around his forehead to keep his long blond hair out of his face.

We still had to do our watches even though we just sat motionless on top of the water. Raine and I sang with the guitar, traded books, practiced our French, did macramé, swam a few times, and tanned ourselves. "You girls should put zinc oxide on your noses and cheeks. They're always peeling," Beth said, acting like an older sister. We begged her to let us bake cookies or cook dinner one evening, but she was reluctant with such small amounts of food left on the boat. She had the meals planned out to the very ingredients, doing an excellent job rationing the supplies and yet providing us with delicious meals.

Finally, we got away from the Aloha High and found some wind.

After twenty days of sailing, on July 23, 1976, we arrived at the entrance of San Francisco Harbor in the thick, soupy, and chilly wet fog. With no radar aboard, there was no way to navigate the harbor's entrance. "We'll have to wait outside the harbor until morning with all the other freighters who can't enter," Dad announced.

"I wish we could see the Golden Gate Bridge," Raine said quietly.

"Let's hope the fog lifts in the morning," Ron said, staring ahead into the fog bank.

Dad imposed an overnight all-crew watch. Beth and Phil were given the stern, Dad was at the wheel, Ron and Raine were on either side of the cabin, and I was on the bow. All night we listened for the freighters getting close in the thick fog while our eyes and ears played tricks on us. We could never be sure which direction a sound came from.

Dad came to the bow to check on me. "Staying up all night burns calories, Leslie."

I shivered and ignored him, but he continued, "You know we could both lose a few pounds tonight."

"Why do you say I'm fat, that I need to diet?"

"I don't say you're fat. I say we need to lose a few pounds. We come from hardy stock." He patted my thigh for emphasis. "We've been sitting still at sea for twenty days. I think we're both a little heavier."

I stared into the fog, refusing to speak to him. After a few minutes of silence, he squeezed my knee and returned to the helm. I hated him.

All night my eyes played tricks on me as I munched on the last of the cashews to stay awake and piss off Dad. If I stared long enough at the fog, I could make myself see a cement wall or a colossal tanker bearing down on us. The smell of fish, seaweed, and seals filled my nose. The low rumble of engines idling and the intermittent blast of the foghorn in the distance was a rhythm that wore on my brain. I struggled to keep my eyes open and stay alert.

The fog finally dissipated with the sunrise. To celebrate, I did a little dance on the bow. Raine and Ron joined me.

As far as the eye could see, massive freighters hovered and loomed over us. We entered San Francisco Harbor exhausted, motoring under the famous bridge filled with cars and people living entirely different lives than us. We docked in Sausalito only to fall straight into bed for a long morning nap.

The goodbyes were teary as we hugged and promised to stay in touch. Beth and Phil headed to Seattle to visit friends. Raine and Ron flew back to San Diego.

Dad and I stayed in the Bay Area for a few days after Elektra Flash's grandmother, Mrs. Olsen, refused to reimburse him for all the repairs needed to make the crossing, including the new sail. Four days later, without any luck in securing his fee, we officially handed over *Starship*, leaving Dad no choice but to sue for his money.

18

Back home in Redondo Beach, I called Simon collect from the pay phone at the gas station across the street as soon as we arrived. Nothing could stop me from continuing my love affair with him. It was a Sunday, and I knew he'd be home cleaning and reading the newspaper.

When he answered, his voice wasn't as cheerful as I thought it would be. He seemed genuinely surprised to hear from me. After awkward hellos, I didn't know how to bridge the gap and mend the damage, so I asked him if he had received my letter. "Yes, it was very nice. Thank you."

"Is everything okay?"

"Yes, I'm just surprised to hear from you, and taken a bit off guard."

I knew Dad had confronted him, but I didn't know the story, so I asked what had happened. Apparently, he'd caused quite a scene in the office with the administrative staff, yelling and demanding to speak to Simon and his boss, threatening a lawsuit if he ever contacted me again.

"Wow. And what did you say?"

"I didn't say anything. I just waited for him to leave."

A long silence hung over us. I asked if he had a new girlfriend.

He let out a long breath. "Yes, I'm seeing somebody."

"I knew it. I could feel it." After a few seconds, I added, "So it's over between us? You don't love me anymore?" The cloudless cobalt-blue sky outside the phone booth hovered over me.

"Leslie, you're gone now. I'm not sure if I'll ever see you again."

"You will! I'm coming back. I'm saving my money and I'm coming back. Didn't you read my letter? But I'm not coming if you have another girlfriend."

His voice was stern. "When you return, we will put ourselves together again, but in the meantime, I'm casually dating."

"What's her name?"

"Why does that matter?"

I stared at the cars in the gas station, taking a deep breath. "I'm going to date too."

He didn't answer, but said, "Keep calling me, okay? I care about you."

"But you don't love me?"

"I want us to be together when I use those words."

"Yeah, okay, sure," I said, dejected, and hung up.

How could he be dating? Didn't we love each other? Apparently not. But we had shared real love! When I left the gas station, the hurt turned into anger. How dare he.

I made a resolution not to call him again and dragged myself around feeling betrayed and sad for weeks. I ignored the nagging feeling inside that I should move on.

In tortured agony at having to work in the same office as Dad, I typed up the stupid marine survey reports in the mornings and went to the beach in the afternoons whenever I could. A sick feeling grew in my belly at the thought of school starting and maybe having to repeat ninth grade because my three months of school in Windsor probably wasn't enough to count as a "school year." When Dad registered us, the schools insisted on placement tests, since we hadn't been in a Californian school for over a year and a half, and Dad had not brought our school records from Windsor.

We each took our tests one afternoon a few weeks before school started. The questions were easy, which made me doubt myself. Had I misunderstood them? I wrote an essay about some facts they gave me and was confident I'd nailed that part. I didn't want to think about the math problems I'd skipped over.

A few days later, Dad brought three envelopes to dinner and placed them next to his wine glass.

"What are those?" I strained to see the return address.

The hint of a devilish smile came across his face, but he said nothing. He took a bite of roast pork, boiled potato, and green beans, using his knife to cut and place the food on the back of his fork in the Scandinavian way. We had been raised to eat this way, but our mother said we should cut our food, put the knife down, transfer the fork into our right hand, and put the food in our mouths that way—the civilized way. They fought about it at times. Dad called that absurd, insisting we eat like Norwegians. They fought about other stupid things, too, like how to put tinsel on a Christmas tree. Dad threw it; Mom placed it strand by strand.

We ate in silence, waiting for the King to reveal the contents of those damn envelopes. He loved the drama of it all. Eventually, he put his utensils down and wiped his mouth. "You've all passed with flying colors."

"Yes!" I cheered, arms lifted, hands waving. Karen and Monica hooted and hollered. I would enter school as a sophomore, Monica as a junior, and Karen as an eighth grader.

Dad beamed at us, proud we weren't dummies and thereby vindicating himself as Master Teacher in the School of Life and Sailing. "It's like you girls are a grade ahead," he said as he took a gulp of his wine, continuing to pontificate and gloat. "It doesn't say much for a school system when a student can miss more than a year and still pass a placement test."

"Yeah, it sure doesn't," I said, taking my dishes to the kitchen. "Maybe we don't need to attend school at all. Maybe we can learn in life like we did—"

Before I could finish, Monica objected, "I *want* to go to school and make friends."

Dad spewed raspberries, ignoring Monica's comment. "You're not that smart, Leslie. In fact, you're downright slow most of the time, so shut up, will you?"

I rolled my eyes as I placed the dishes in the sink, mumbling under my breath, "I hate you."

"I'm with Leslie; I don't want to go to school if we don't have to," Karen said, bringing plates from the table. I smiled, grateful for the support.

Dad, as always, had the final exasperated word. "Well, you have to! None of you are smart enough to skip out of school."

19

The fall semester began the following week, with Dad insisting we all learn to play a school instrument. Playing the guitar didn't count in high school, so Monica quickly claimed the flute, which left me the only other cool instrument: the saxophone. But because we walked to and from school and I'd have to carry whatever I chose, I picked the third-coolest instrument, the clarinet. After Dad said no to Karen playing the drums, she chose the trumpet.

On campus, I still felt like an alien, but one from a closer galaxy than Windsor. Redondo Beach was at least a beach community, but I still languished alone between classes and at lunchtime, feeling wholly inadequate, like a drifter in the desert of my life. I reluctantly daydreamed about two-timing Simon and how I would get him back once I had my freedom. I dreamed about being old enough to get in my car and drive away, or about sailing with Raine and John de la Cruz. Some ruts in my brain would not go away.

Marching band was my only fun. I counted steps while playing the songs, turning and marching in my line. I wasn't the first chair, but I wasn't the last chair either.

Hoping to find something in common with my classmates, I hung around the fringes of the lunch tables, longing for one of the girls in my classes to say hi, but they never did. I wondered what was wrong with me, but never figured it out.

Sailing, snorkeling, and discovering new worlds occupied my thoughts. From afar, I admired the most popular girl in the school and wondered what it was like to be loved by all. Some days, I met Monica for lunch, and we commiserated until she joined the basketball team and, just like in Windsor, suddenly had a team full of friends and no time for me.

Escaping reality became my focus and I occupied my thoughts dreaming about the future and being done with school. I broke down and called Simon from the gas station pay phone, crying to him about wanting to return to Windsor. Part of me could not believe I was dreaming of Windsor. My life was so strange. No matter where I was, I wanted to be someplace else. The grass really was greener on the other side. I could see it with my own eyes. Would I ever be free and happy?

Simon told me, "If you come to Windsor now, I could get in trouble and lose my career. You can't come back until you're older."

"You mean I have to wait until I'm eighteen?"

"I think so. Otherwise, I could lose everything."

On the metal shelf below the phone, "C+B" was scratched with a heart around it. I had been tracing the heart while Simon spoke, tears falling as the sadness and isolation filled me up. "So, I'm stuck here for two-and-a-half more years. Great!"

"It's not that long. We can talk all the time."

"I have to go. I have homework." I hung up.

Life became humdrum compared to all the life-and-death excitement we experienced while sailing, or with Mom in Windsor. School was boring. At home, I practiced my clarinet, cooked during my week, and typed the stupid survey reports for Dad in the afternoons and evenings after I finished my homework.

Dad had stopped insisting we sleep naked, and since we didn't have to share a bed with him anymore like we did in Oceanside before we left for Tahiti, he couldn't make his move on me in the middle of the night. We all wore pajamas to bed for the first time in our lives. When it was my turn to have the bedroom alone, I'd slide a chair in front of the door so Dad couldn't get in and crawl into bed with me. He hadn't made any moves on me since I screamed at him at sea on our way to Tahiti, but he continued to creep me out, leering and watching me from afar.

One Saturday, while cooking breakfast, I heard Dad's voice. "Coffee ready?"

I turned around, and there he stood, butt naked. "Dad! You're naked!"

His face filled with a proud smile. I turned away, rolling my eyes.

"We shouldn't be ashamed of our bodies."

"Whatever, just leave me alone."

His equipment down low was so gross. How could anyone be attracted to that?

He loved making me feel uncomfortable and awkward.

Another day, after showering, I saw him walking naked around the house, mumbling, "Where are my keys?"

Does anyone need their keys when they're dripping wet naked? Geez. What a creep.

Once, he told us, "Don't be shy about being naked, girls; it's the most natural thing in the world. Feel free to go without clothes whenever you wish."

Yeah, right. You're a tripping old man.

One day, from the back seat of Dad's Cadillac, the Paul McCartney and Wings song "Silly Love Songs" came on, and I started singing quietly. On the chorus "I love you," I looked at the sky, my thoughts on Simon. The light changed to red, and we stopped. Dad turned down the radio and twisted around to face us in the back seat. "If there's anything you want to know about sex, just ask me. I want there to be an open door of communication between us."

My face flushed, and he winked at me. I snapped my head away to look out the window, wanting to die.

Avoiding Dad was my biggest priority. I developed radar for where he was in the house in relation to me, and if he came close, I moved. The only exception was our massive orange-and-brown plaid couch in the living room. The sectional sofa was as big as two king-size beds when all the square pieces were pushed together. More than a dozen pillows and multiple blankets promised protection. Crawling up and finding a corner far away from him meant I could surround myself with the pillows and blankets like a wall. Dad watched his shows—*60 Minutes*, *Kojak*, *Baretta*, *M*A*S*H*, and *All in the Family*. Sometimes, I watched quietly from the corner of the couch covered in pillows, but mostly I stayed the hell away in my bedroom. Some nights I'd be reading in the bedroom, and he'd yell with his sweetest voice from the couch during a show, "Leslie, can you make me some toast and jam?"

I'd haul myself out of the bedroom and make him two pieces of sourdough toast with lots of butter and strawberry jam, putting everything away and wiping the counters so he wouldn't yell at me. I'd bring the toast to him on the couch. He never said thank you. "A glass of milk, too?" he'd croon. I'd get him the milk and make it back to the bedroom and my book, and he'd yell again, "Leslie, can I have two more pieces of toast, pleeease?"

I wanted to scream, cry, or run; I don't know which.

Sometimes when he asked me for multiple favors, I'd yell back, "Can't Monica or Karen make it this time? I'm reading."

"No! I asked you. I want you to make it."

Monica, who was also reading in her bed, would say, "I did it last night, so stop complaining."

"And I did it the night before that. So there!" Karen added.

They snickered at me as I hauled myself out to the kitchen again to make him another round of toast and jam. I willed myself not to throw it at him.

He'd go out some nights and work late in the office other nights and I'd curl up on the ginormous couch to watch *One Day at a Time*, *The Six Million Dollar Man*, or *The Bionic Woman*. In the fall of 1976, the debut of *Charlie's Angels* changed my life. Now I knew what I wanted to be in life: a detective.

Finally, we had strong women to watch, and I dreamed about being a combination of Lindsay Wagner and Farrah Fawcett. Lindsay was smart and confident with a strong personality, and Farrah was beautiful, sexy, and capable. I wore my hair like Farrah's and tried to dress like Lindsay and Farrah, daydreaming about my adult life.

20

Finally we received a response from Grandma. I quietly gathered my sisters by waving the small envelope with the loopy grandma writing around their faces. We gathered around the bed, squeezing together, bumping heads to read the news.

Monica read: "Dear Monica, Leslie, and Karen, The weather here is warm. How is the weather there?"

Grandma always started her letters with the weather and it was so annoying. "Why can't she just cut to the news?" Karen said, falling back on the bed and staring at the ceiling.

Monica continued, "Your mother is out of the hospital and is doing well. She plans to move to California soon to be near you girls."

"She survived that place," Karen said, sitting up on the bed with more glee than I had heard in a while.

"Is there more?" I prodded Monica.

"Yes, just be patient. I'm getting to it." She cleared her throat and held the letter like the court jester reading a decree. I rolled my eyes but didn't say anything. "She will write soon. She'll need an apartment and a job, and I hope you girls can help her get settled."

"I wonder when she's coming," Karen said.

"Do you think she's going to be mad at us for not trying to get her out of the hospital?" I asked.

We all just stared at one another. Monica tossed the letter down on the dresser. Was Mom still mad at me for dating Simon? Did she regret telling Monica about her biological father? When was she coming? So many unanswered questions. Our prison-guard father opened the bedroom door with force, like he was trying to catch us all hiding money or smoking cigarettes. It startled all of us. "What are you girls hiding in here?" His eyes searched us and then he looked around the room, landing on the letter on the dresser.

"That's not yours," I said as he reached to pick it up.

"Everything in this house is mine. You are mine. All your clothing, your schoolwork, everything is mine. You live under my roof."

Monica backed up and sat on the bed beside Karen and me and said, "Yeah, but that letter is addressed to us, and there are laws about stealing mail."

Damn! Monica hit that nail on the head and found her voice. I was impressed, even if Dad wasn't. He laughed big and left the room with our letter. I called after him, "Mom's moving to California. Did you know?"

Dad called back, "Yes, I knew."

"Then give us our letter back!" I called again from the bedroom. But there was no answer.

With a whisper, Karen said, "He didn't know. Mom would never write him after he stole us from Windsor."

Monica and Karen looked as defeated as I felt, like we had just dropped our ice cream on the sidewalk. There wasn't anything to do but wait for Mom to arrive.

Being a satellite in school and sitting far away from the other students at lunch confirmed my alien status. Most days, I ate alone and read my book with one eye on the student population in case anybody approached. That's how I met Pat, the twenty-something school gardener and surfer with sandy blond hair. It started with a wave and a hello, which happened multiple days in a row until Pat took out his sandwich and sat in the shade on the garden wall a distance from the picnic table where I ate.

"Where are all your friends?" he asked, his brown eyes shining.

"We just moved here. I don't know anybody yet," I said, pushing my hair away from my shoulders like Farrah did.

"You know me." He sipped his Coke.

"Doesn't count. You work here," I said, half smiling at him.

"I can assure you that I count. I used to go here."

I nodded, smiled, and kept reading.

Our relationship grew slowly and naturally over the following weeks.

One afternoon, after listening to me complain about how much I hated high school, Pat told me how I could get out early. "Go ask your counselor about the California High School Proficiency Test."

I learned they gave the test twice a year and I could take it if I was sixteen and enrolled in school. I would be sixteen in January and if I passed it in April, they would give me a high school diploma. An opening to my potential freedom had appeared.

On my long walk home that day, I stopped at the liquor store to buy a cold Coke and couldn't wait to drink it. Cracking open the red can in front of the store, I leaned back and guzzled it in front of a car resembling a silver rocket. A man, maybe in his early thirties, with dark hair, warm eyes, and a big smile, came out of the store. "It's hot today, isn't it?" he said. I stepped back and let him pass, nodding my agreement. "Is that your car?" I asked.

"Yes, it is. You like it?" He stopped at the car door.

I nodded again. "What is it?"

"A 240Z."

"It looks like a rocket." After a few minutes of chitchatting about the weather, he asked where I was headed.

"Home, and I've got to run. If I'm late, I get in trouble," I said, feeling more alert to his advances as I backed away.

"Can I offer you a ride?" he asked quietly. He stood behind the open door. His warm brown eyes welcomed me.

"No thanks. I'm happy to walk. Bye. It was nice meeting you." I turned my back and walked away.

The next day, when I stopped for a Coke, there he was again, and after talking more about movies and books, I accepted the ride. Dad had flown to a business meeting and wouldn't be home until late.

His name was Jason, and he wore a dress shirt tucked into his jeans instead of a T-shirt. He seemed important and he told me he was an inventor.

"Like Thomas Edison?" I questioned as we drove down Hermosa Avenue.

He shook his head. "No. I'm nothing like Thomas Edison, but my inventions are unique, and I sell them to all kinds of people, some well-known."

"Like what? What have you invented that a famous person bought?" I almost demanded, anxious to see who he knew. *Does he know Farrah Fawcett?*

"I invented the first locking gas cap so people can't siphon gas anymore." I knew there were long lines at gas stations. He continued, "I also make clocks. The poet, Rod McKuen, bought a golf ball clock that I installed at his house."

"My mother loves Rod McKuen. I grew up listening to his poetry."

I liked Jason. He was different, like me. After a short time, he dropped me off near the house and gave me his phone number.

Jason and Pat were angels sent by God. Pat kept me going to high school because I looked forward to laughing and spending time with him at lunch, and Jason entertained me with his fancy, moneyed ways. They were older men, yes, and maybe they initially had designs on me, but neither of them ever made a move once we got to know each other. I told them my secrets of sailing and adventure. They listened and were thoughtful and kind. That's how I made it through my first semester at Redondo High.

21

Dad was waiting when I arrived at the breakfast table on the morning of my sixteenth birthday. "I have a surprise for you. Get dressed, and we'll go."

I bowed my head. Dammit, I had plans to drive to Venice Beach with Jason if I could get away. I finished my breakfast and got dressed.

"You will always be the favorite," Monica said, lying on the bed.

I rolled my eyes and continued dressing. "I didn't ask for this. I don't want to go," I whispered.

She closed the bedroom door so we could talk. "Dad didn't do anything for Karen's or my birthday, but of course, precious Leslie has a birthday, and Dad takes her out alone for something special."

"How is this my fault?" I opened the door and walked out.

Dad waited in front of his great big gold Cadillac Coupe de Ville. "Where are we going?" I asked, sliding into the front seat.

"I told you, it's a surprise."

Twenty minutes later we pulled into Torrance Airport and parked on the tarmac near a small airplane with an orange-and-brown stripe.

"Whose plane is this?"

Dad smiled at me in his all-knowing way. "Mine, now get in. We're going for a ride."

"You have a plane?" I said, trying not to be impressed, because I didn't want him to think I admired him. He didn't answer.

Standing nearby, I watched him prepare the plane, referring to a three-ring binder of information and several checklists. "You know how to fly this?"

"Yes, I do," he said, laughing. "You don't know much about me, do you?"

I cringed because I made a great effort to avoid him. I knew he used to work for United Airlines as an instrument technician at San Francisco Airport when we lived in Redwood City, and that he flew small planes with his friend Rudy when we were little, but that's it. I can't say it surprised me that he owned a plane, because very little Dad did surprised me anymore.

Our shoulders touched as we strapped into the tiny cockpit and put on our headphones. I scrunched in but then relaxed and let our shoulders touch again. "It's small in here," he said. His reflective wraparound sunglasses hid his blue eyes, but the corner of his mouth lifted slightly as he flipped switches and started the engine. Avoiding my own reflection in his glasses, I looked out my side window. The takeoff made the plane rattle and shake, but everything smoothed out as we gained altitude. The day was clear, bright, and sunny, and I could see the Pacific Ocean in the distance. Dad squeezed my knee, and I involuntarily squirmed and smiled. His voice crackled in my ear. "King Harbor," he said, dipping the wings. He had worked there surveying boats. He pointed out the sights as we flew over Palos Verdes Peninsula with its rolling green hills and houses clinging to the cliffs. He also pointed out the dozens of freighters in San Pedro Harbor.

"Take the yoke," he said, removing his hands from the steering wheel.

My head whipped around in disbelief. "What?" I said, but only saw my reflection in those damn glasses.

"Go on, take the control in front of you. I'll walk you through flying the plane."

We were headed to Catalina Island across the twenty-three miles of open ocean. I didn't want to touch the steering wheel that looked like upside-down female reproductive organs, but I did. Gently, I put my hands on the fallopian tubes.

"You can pull, push, and turn the yoke."

"No thank you. I'll just hold it," I crackled back at him through the headset.

He laughed a big Kojak laugh and insisted I hold the yoke for a few more minutes. "Okay, I'm done," I said, returning my hands to my lap.

He took the controls, shaking his head and smiling. "Consider that your first lesson."

"I don't remember asking to learn how to fly a plane."

He smiled at me. We flew the rest of the way in silence until we arrived at a very short runway. Dad said, "Brace yourself."

I grabbed the edges of my seat with both hands and pushed myself back.

The wheels touched down, and the brakes brought us to a stop right before the cliff drop.

"Not much room for error," I said, ogling the blue sky before us.

"Nope. Not much. Happy Sweet Sixteen, Sweetheart."

I finally took a breath and released myself from bracing. "Thanks, Dad," I mumbled.

On Catalina, we made our way to the "Airport in the Sky" restaurant, the sun beating down on us. Dad carried a small, unwrapped cardboard box in one hand. A distant herd of buffalo gathered on the brown hill under a group of oak trees. Inside, a customer service desk greeted us. We took our seats at an empty table. After ordering our burgers and fries, he slid the box across the table to me. I pulled apart the flaps and found a 35mm Minolta camera and four rolls of film.

"Dad! Wow! I love it!" I brought the viewfinder up to my eye and focused on Dad's beaming face across the table.

"I thought you could take up photography."

"Sure. That's sounds fun." I lowered the camera to the table and ate my hamburger. Sirens went off in my head. Every gift had strings—I'd learned that early in life. He could be generous with many people, but never with me. What game was he playing?

He smiled genuinely at me with warm eyes, and I felt guilty for feeling suspicious. I tried to accept the gift as innocent, hoping I wouldn't regret it later. Yes, I was interested in photographing the ocean and nature but hated him directing my path in life. I endured the rest of the afternoon with him being super pleased with himself, constantly looking for reassurance that I liked my gift. Once home, I brought the box with the camera and film to the bedroom and flopped down on the bed.

"Get off. You're in the other room this week," Monica sneered.

I got up and went into the other bedroom. Karen was lying in her bed, and Monica appeared at the door.

"What did you get?" she scoffed.

"A camera and some film." I rolled over and eyed them. Monica was angry with lips pursed and eyes on fire. Karen looked on quietly, but I could read her face. She was hurt.

Somehow all this was my fault.

22

The second semester of my sophomore year began with making a much-needed girlfriend, Cyndi. She was new and sat right next to me in English. Her blonde hair was styled in a flip around her face like Stevie Nicks. We had lunch together, and I introduced her to Pat. She lived with her mother and younger sister in an apartment near school. It didn't take us long to start cutting classes and hanging out at her apartment a few days a week, drinking beer, dancing in her living room, and watching TV. Cyndi introduced me to her mother's Virginia Slim cigarettes, and I took to them like a natural. Both of our moms smoked all the time, so it wasn't anything novel. Each time I took another drag of the Virginia Slim, I coughed and felt nauseous, but I stuck with it, and before long I could smoke an entire cigarette without throwing up.

Cigarettes and beer filled up the cavernous hole growing inside me. They made me forget the anxiety and pain and let me relax. I would do anything to escape the emptiness of that hole.

My plan to take the High School Proficiency Test started with convincing Monica to take it with me as moral support. Walking home from school, I pleaded with her. "Come on, Monica, please take it with me."

"Did you tell Dad both of us would take it?" she asked.

"No. Because you haven't agreed yet, but I'll talk to him."

Her long strides had me running to catch up to her. She was only two inches taller than me but could walk so fast. "I don't want to get out of high school early. I like school and all my friends."

I couldn't imagine feeling that way. "I know. Just say you'll take it with me, pleeease?"

"Okay, fine," she said, giving in and flicking my shoulder with her finger.

I skipped around her, singing, "Thank you, Monica. You're my favorite sister and always will be."

She smiled at me. "But I'm not leaving school if I pass."

I nodded quickly, blowing her kisses and still skipping. That same afternoon, as I typed up a marine survey report for him, I asked Dad if Monica and I could take the test. He pondered and said, "You think you're smart enough?"

"Yes, I know I can pass it."

"I'll think about it," he said, leaving the office.

I squirmed and wondered and hated waiting for the answer.

That night at dinner, he asked about our plans if we passed.

"We won't even find out until August," I said. "Can we think about it?"

"No. You need a plan now."

Looking at Monica chomping at her pork chop, hoping she would play along and give Dad a reasonable answer, I said, "I'll get a full-time job and start college," because that's what he wanted me to say. Actually, I would be going to Windsor to live with Simon and start my adult life.

His blue eyes were lasers. "Do you honestly think you're smart enough to pass this test and then go to college?"

I picked up a bite of salad and held the fork. "I passed the placement test and learned to navigate with a sextant. Or did you forget I was pretty good at it?"

His fork came up in warning. "Be careful, Leslie. Nobody likes a braggart."

I lowered my head, shame filling me with that familiar sour feeling. *Why can't he acknowledge my hard work and encourage me to continue? Why does he always have to pick at me?*

Dad turned to Monica, who spoke without delay. "I'll get a full-time job and start community college."

I smiled in thanks and knew I owed her big.

After a few moments of silence, he said, "All right, you girls can take the test and see if you're smart enough."

"Thank you, Dad!" I blurted out. "You won't regret this."

That night in our bedroom, Monica made sure I knew how much I owed her. "You can pay me back by cooking for me when it's my week, cleaning the bathroom when it's my turn, and paying me ten dollars."

"Monica! Come on."

She flipped her long blonde hair behind her shoulders. "It's up to you. I'll take the test if you do those things."

Of course I agreed but felt beaten and used.

In early spring, Mom arrived and moved into a two-bedroom apartment in nearby Hermosa Beach. On the appointed day, we all walked to her place after school. "I hope she's not weird," Karen said from behind us.

"I hope she doesn't bring up what happened in Windsor," I said.

"Yeah, let's not relive the whole Simon thing, okay?" Karen said.

"Shut up!" I called to her.

"I hope she doesn't talk about her Bible," Monica said. We all nodded at that thought.

Her apartment was at the top of a steep hill, behind a garage in a two-story house. It was dark inside and didn't feel welcoming. Mom looked fragile and tender, air hugging us as usual and brushing our cheeks with a kiss. It had been a year since we had seen her. We sat in her bedroom around her bed on the floor. She leaned back against the wall, her face filled up with a smile. She told us she'd found a job as a licensed vocational nurse at South Bay Hospital. "That's great," I said.

"How are you girls doing in school? It's so good to see you," she said.

The air was thick with anticipation of her weirdness. "We're doing fine. We play instruments, and I'm on the basketball team," Monica offered.

My eyes scanned the nightstand. No drinks or pill bottles, thank God. "Monica and I are in the marching band. We play at halftime during the football games. I play the clarinet, Monica the flute, and Karen plays the trumpet," I said, then added, "Karen's not in the marching band."

"She knows I'm not in high school, Leslie," Karen remarked, her words dripping in sarcasm.

I flashed her a quizzical look, hoping not to have an out-and-out argument on our first visit. "I know," I said quietly.

"There's a nice red bougainvillea in the back," Mom said randomly. "Can you see it?"

I nodded as I turned my head to look out the back window of her room. "It's gorgeous," I said nervously, adjusting my shirt.

Mom sat back against the wall on her bed hugging her knees, studying us with a slight smile. We filled the emptiness with idle chatter, telling her tidbits about our lives with Dad, but nothing that might anger or alienate her. It was like walking a tightrope, which we were good at. We had played this game with her our whole lives. We'd learned to gloss over all the bad stuff, to smooth it out—consciously denying anything bad ever happened. Our job as her children was to act like everything was okay no matter what. We chatted about our classes, grades, tests, or whatever came to mind that didn't stir any pots. I hoped she didn't ask about Dad.

Itching to leave at the first opportunity, Karen tested the waters. "It's my night to cook, so we'd better head out soon."

I wondered if we'd stayed long enough or made her feel good enough. She would surely start ranting at us if not, but she answered. "Your father has you girls cooking now?"

"Now? We all cooked on the boat when we sailed," I said, hoping that wasn't too confrontational.

"We take weeks. This week is my week, and I'm making pot pies," Karen said.

I grabbed my backpack. Monica and Karen did the same, and Mom walked us to the door. "I talked to your father about setting up a schedule for each of you to come one at a time and stay the night."

"Okay," we all said together, just outside her door.

"Bye, Mom. See you soon," Monica said.

When we got far enough away, I said, "I don't want to sleep there."

"Me neither," Monica said.

"I wonder if Alan is still alive," Karen said.

We walked the rest of the way home in silence.

On my first overnight visit a couple weeks later, the dread threatened to consume me. Was she going to yell at me about Simon? About how we didn't call Grandma or Aunt Melanie? Was she going to pump me for information about Monica's reaction to hearing the truth about her biological dad?

I entered the apartment ready for battle, but her energy was low, and her kisses and hugs were tentative as usual. We ate ham-and-cheese sandwiches on her bed, side by side, staring at the wall of black curtains keeping all the light out. I tried to fill up the silence. "I'm taking the High School Proficiency Test in a few weeks." I took a big bite of my sandwich. She didn't ask any questions, so I moved on. "Band practice can be so hard when they change the routine. We're supposed to march in the formation of our mascot, the seahawk."

Still, nothing. This was hard work. The oppressive silence threatened to swallow us alive. "How's your job? Do you like South Bay Hospital?"

"It's fine. It's a job." She set her plate on the bedside table with three-quarters of her sandwich uneaten.

She turned on *All in the Family,* and Archie and Edith Bunker filled the room with barbs and sarcasm. She laughed under her breath when Edith yelled at Archie. I tried to laugh, too, but it came out strained. I excused myself to do homework and go to sleep. When I got to my little bedroom with the mattress on the floor, I closed the door and shook the weirdness off.

Had something broken inside Mom from staying in the mental health hospital? She was wholly disconnected. She was here, but the right pieces were not in the right places.

23

As time progressed, we all found a new normal. When Dad was away on business, Mom came to the house in the evening to have dinner with us and watch TV. She drove a cute white 1971 Datsun 1200 Coupe. Sometimes, she'd take us out for pizza and let Monica and me practice driving in the Alpha Beta parking lot. She didn't yell at us anymore or drink uncontrollably. She seemed more stable in some fragile way, even though something was not quite right with her. I just didn't understand what it was.

Sometimes, I told Dad I was at Mom's but would sneak off for a long car ride with Jason up to Malibu and Santa Monica. I was getting better at keeping secrets and telling lies.

In April, Monica and I walked to the high school to take the High School Proficiency Test. I struggled through the entire three-and-a-half-hour test, not having studied much. When it was over, I felt dismal. Monica glowed as she recounted the questions and answers.

Arriving home, Dad called, "Leslie! Come here now!" from the enclosed patio that functioned as a backyard office. His mood lately had turned solemn, with more criticism and anger for everyone. None of us knew why. It could be a bank loan denied, a business offer that fell through, a request from our mother for money, or maybe a refusal from some new girl he was dating.

I went to the backyard office and stood in the doorway. "What do you want?"

"Don't talk to me like that. I want you to do your job. You are so stupid and make so many mistakes, I'm surprised we get any work done in this office."

I looked at him for a long time, waiting for more, my face dead of expression.

He picked up some papers. "Look at this report. You're not capitalizing the first letter of a new sentence. Why not?"

"I don't know. I think it looks cool that all the letters are the same size. It's a new thing I invented."

He bellowed, "Unbelievable! You have shit for brains, so don't use your brain while you're in this office. Just type the reports using all the right punctuation."

"Okay," I muttered.

"Retype this report and cover letter now. I'm not paying for this either." He threw the papers at me and left the office.

I redid the work while daydreaming about my next cigarette and beer. I had almost perfected the skill of thinking about a different thing while typing a document. The words went into my eyes, through my brain, and out my fingers. Once I was in the flow, I could think about something else. It took some time to get the hang of, but now I could think about where to apply for a new job as a waitress while typing about boat keels, depths, mast height, and dry rot.

With the money Dad was paying me, I had only managed to save about $75 because I kept buying new clothes. I looked cute, but my wallet was thin, and I needed to stop spending. Otherwise, my escape from this hellhole would never happen.

24

I studied the back of the Honey Pops cereal box, which had a maze that went through the forest to find the treasure. But mainly, I was using it to shield myself from Dad, who invariably sat across from me at the breakfast table.

"Monica and Leslie, I have decided you girls will attend a wilderness survival course in Colorado for the month of August."

I peered over the cereal box at Dad.

"You two leave in nine days, so you'd better start training today." He looked at Karen. "You can't go because you aren't sixteen yet, but you'll do something similar when you're old enough."

Karen shrank, scooching down, clearly disappointed. Being two years younger meant she couldn't always do the same things as Monica and I could. I felt bad for her and wished she could join us because leaving her behind felt wrong.

"What's a wilderness survival course?" Monica asked.

"What it sounds like! Don't be stupid," Dad said. "Fair warning that I paid six hundred and twenty-five dollars for each of you to go, so you better get in shape fast. It's an all-girls program through Outward Bound." That familiar puffed-up chest and grin meant he was proud of himself and we were supposed to be happy.

My surprised look at the price quickly turned into a sour face. "All girls? Why?"

"Yes, all girls, so you can focus on the survival skills. I'm not sending you there to find a boyfriend."

This was obviously not the time to ask questions. I gathered my bowl and cereal box and headed to the kitchen. Dad continued, "I'm going to Asia and Australia to find a stolen boat for an insurance company."

He explained his new business venture to us, saying that sailboats were disappearing worldwide, and insurance companies were on the hook to pay out. Not all the boats were sinking, so there was fraud. "They need something called a nautical bounty hunter to find these supposedly sunken boats."

"You're going to become a bounty hunter?" I said, smiling, imagining Dad with a gun strapped to his waist and a big cowboy hat.

"Yes, I think so. There's money to be made finding these missing boats."

I was impressed, despite myself. Now he wasn't just delivering boats but finding stolen ones. Cool!

"What will I do while you're all gone?" Karen asked.

"You'll stay here with Beth and Phil and watch the business."

He held up the Outward Bound flyer and looked and Monica and me. "You two should start getting in shape immediately. I doubt either of you can run very far."

I stared at the flyer, and must have been looking at it with a giant blank face because he bellowed, "Are you stupid? The Colorado Rockies are fourteen thousand feet up. We live at sea level." Monica and I blankly looked at each other, not making the connection when he added, dripping in sarcasm, "Sea level is lower. So, get going."

With that, the King left, taking the flyer with him.

I hated running. I never did it voluntarily, ever! Running without a bra was painful. I still wasn't allowed to wear one, which was a constant source of shame and humiliation at school. Dad was oblivious, and I didn't dare mention needing a bra to exercise. In lieu of one, I wore my bikini top to train in. It wasn't much support, but it was something.

We invited Karen to come running with us, but she declined. Built like a smaller version of me, she hated running as much as I did. Monica was the only runner in our family, built long and lean with her skinny legs and torso and noodle arms. At least with our swimsuits under our clothes, we could jump in the ocean at the end of our run as a reward. We turned right as we left our driveway and faced the enormous 190th Street hill. We only made it halfway up before stopping to walk. "We're pathetic," I panted.

"We're going to suck when we get to Colorado. I bet everyone else will be in better shape."

"Ughhhh," I groaned.

After ten minutes, we started running again. This time, we made it to the strand, where we tore off our clothes and ran into the surf. The ocean cooled us off and we bodysurfed a few waves before turning around and running the two miles back.

Later that week, Dad took us to purchase hiking boots and insisted we wear them every minute we were awake until the day we left. We even ran in them. They were heavy, slowed us down considerably, and gave us blisters, but we didn't complain. I wanted to go to Colorado and be away from Dad for almost a month—yes, please! We put bandages on our blisters and soaked our feet in cold water at night to toughen up the sores. We worked out twice a day, adding miles to our run, hoping it would help with the drastic elevation change.

A few nights before our flight to Colorado, I plucked up enough courage to ask Dad what the survival course would be like. In a good mood, he said, "The brochure is on my nightstand. Go and get it for me, will you?"

I ran down the hall, grabbed the little booklet, and brought it to him. He read to us about carrying a thirty-pound pack, learning which plants to eat, how to find ourselves on a topographical map with the compass, and how to plot a course.

"Can I bring my camera?" I asked, having recently purchased a wide-angle lens.

"It'll add weight to your pack."

"I don't care," I said. "I want to take it."

"Let me think about it."

I wondered how much thirty pounds was, so I went to the bathroom and stood on the scale. I weighed 136 pounds. After getting a suitcase from the garage, I stood on the scale again: 148 pounds.

"What are you doing down there?" Dad yelled from the living room.

"Seeing how much thirty pounds weighs!" I called back.

I added books to the suitcase and stood on the scale again—170 pounds. It was just dawning on me how heavy thirty pounds was. Maybe I'd reconsider the camera after all.

25

The next day, Monica and I stumbled onto the front porch and fell down panting after a three-mile run. My period was heavy that day. I had cramps and felt like throwing up. I rolled on my side and clutched my stomach, moaning. We were running in our hiking boots and wearing daypacks filled with books to simulate the weight we would carry. Dad came out to the porch and threw a letter at me. It drifted down to the ground as he said, "I knew you couldn't pass it. You didn't try hard enough, Leslie. You hardly studied, and this proves you're stupid."

The California High School Proficiency Test results had arrived. I grabbed the letter, trying to see what it said.

"Monica passed!" he said with a happy, sarcastic attitude, throwing her letter at her.

I peeled myself off the porch and went to the kitchen for water. Dad followed closely behind me, practically pushing me as he spoke. I could feel his breath on my neck. "You will return to Redondo Beach High next month as a junior. Got that little girl?"

"Yes," I said quietly.

"You are just not smart enough, Leslie. In fact, you're downright stupid." The door slammed behind him as he went to the backyard office. Monica arrived in the kitchen, grinning. She shrugged her shoulders as I stood at the sink, guzzling water. She held my gaze as she gulped a glass of lemonade from the fridge. There was nothing to say. *Why'd she have to pass?* Life wasn't fair. I hated Dad for reveling in my failure. I wished he would die so I could live my life in peace.

The day before we left for Colorado, Dad agreed to let me take the camera and bestowed two rolls of film on me. He refused to drive us to the airport, saying we needed to figure it out for ourselves. "I'm not going to baby you any longer."

Any longer? Since when has he babied us? With airline tickets in hand, he gave us both a crisp new $20 bill for the taxi ride and then left for his own trip, barely saying goodbye.

Beth and Phil had arrived to take care of the business for Dad and stay with Karen, who moped around. There was nothing we could do to cheer her up.

The following morning, we decided Monica would pay for the taxi going to the airport, and I would pay for the cab coming home. We made lunches for the plane ride and snacks for the bus ride into the Rocky Mountains. I hid my $20 bill under the pullout pad in the sole of my boot.

"I hope we're in good enough shape," Monica said on the way to the airport.

"Me too," I said, staring at the bumper-to-bumper traffic on the 405 freeway. My stomach churned in anticipation of the next few weeks. *Will it be fun? Will I be smart enough and in good enough shape?*

At baggage claim at Denver Airport, we introduced ourselves to a man holding an OUTWARD BOUND sign. He checked our names off the list, and we loaded onto the bus with several other girls who had flown in that day. After a silent two-hour bus ride, we unloaded into a pristine meadow in the Collegiate Peaks mountain range. In the distance, I could see a long row of orange-colored nylon backpacks lying flat on the grass.

"Welcome, girls. Gather around," a woman with long red hair said with authority.

We dragged our suitcases and duffel bags across the meadow surrounded by thick trees and stood behind the backpacks. The bus drove away, leaving us stranded in the wilderness. I sized up some of the other girls: a dainty-looking girl, a tomboy, a timid-looking girl avoiding eye contact with everybody, and a girl dressed in a fringe vest and cowboy boots. *Is everybody as afraid as Monica and I are?*

The red-haired woman continued, "I'm Donna, and this is Carly and Nancy, the other leaders for this section." Carly smiled and gave us a peace sign while Nancy, in her tie-dye tank top, just nodded.

All the equipment we would need for twenty-two days in the wilderness lay in front of us—a tent, a sleeping bag, a green Styrofoam bedroll, a climbing helmet, gaiters, a tin plate, bowl, cup, knife, fork, and spoon. Without warning or fanfare, Carly, Nancy, and Donna began undressing. "There's no better way to connect with nature and wash off the cities, the buses, and the airplanes than to strip down and swim together," said Nancy.

The girl with braids next to me tentatively began unbuttoning her blouse. Monica and I locked gazes, looking around for proof we had to do this. Panic and fear rose up from my chest. A blonde girl wearing a patchwork skirt and platform shoes backed away from the circle. I moved to the back of the group with Monica, and we pretended to be unbuttoning our shorts. The fear of being naked in public made my throat close, and memories of all those times Dad had photographed us nude on the boat threatened to paralyze me. *Why is everybody always trying to get me naked? This part wasn't in the brochure!*

Within a few minutes, the leaders were butt naked, wearing goofy smiles, hooting, hollering, then running down to the nearby stream. One by one, we all undressed and, before long, were laughing, screaming, splashing each other, and getting clean in the freezing melted snow water, except for the girl in the skirt. She stayed with our stuff in the meadow, writing in a journal.

Sun spears shot through the canopy of trees and lit the stream like a ballroom. Light danced on the water. My inhibitions and fears disappeared as all the girls looked exhilarated and happy. "Hi! I'm Fel," an older girl said to me.

"I'm Leslie, and this is my sister Monica."

I was filled with an enormous feeling—love or something so pure it caught my breath as we played together in the water.

After our swim, we dressed and were sorted into three groups of eight girls each. As sisters, Monica and I were not allowed to be in the same group. Monica went to stand with her group, and we stared longingly at each other from across the meadow.

We divided the food we would all carry so the weight would be evenly distributed. We carried whole wheat flour, baking powder, cornmeal, spices, raisins, dried apricots and dates, vegetable oil, brown sugar, honey, tea, peanuts, salt and pepper, a cheese block, peanut butter, carrots, and potatoes.

When that was done, Nancy gathered us together again and showed us how to make homemade biscuits for our dinner with peanut butter and honey or cheese if we preferred. We were each given a map of the mountains and a compass if we didn't have one.

As we sat around the campfire that night, we learned each other's names. I felt close to these strangers already. Being naked in nature took me to a deep place quickly. Maneuvering through the groups of sleeping bags and girls, Monica and I found a place to sleep next to each other, her lying on her back and me on my side facing her.

"What do you think?" I whispered.

"I think it's going to be fun. I like the girls in my group."

"I hope we're in good enough shape," I said, for the umpteenth time.

"I think we'll be fine. I don't think some girls even trained before they got here."

I fell onto my back, and we were silent for a few minutes before

I realized Monica was sleeping. The stars and the depth of space mesmerized me like I would be devoured by it. The meadow was a circle, and the trees provided a frame around the night sky with their branches and leaves. The view rivaled the ones I'd experienced at sea. Nature, whether in the vast ocean or the wooded mountains, was a presence that filled me up inside. The empty, lost feeling that had permanently occupied my body since we arrived in Redondo Beach was gone. I said thank you to the universe and felt grateful to be there.

Before falling asleep under the sky, I wrote a poem.

Simplicity

Everything about nature
Is real and alive . . .
Peaceful and truthful.

Nature never lies.

Every branch and leaf is
So honest yet so naive.
They've been through it all—
The storms, the sun, the people,
And the tragedy.

They would tell you anything—
If you asked.

In the morning, we munched on raisins and made tortillas with melted cheese on top for breakfast. We were all given journals to document our time in the wilderness. Nobody had to tell me twice to keep a diary. I was thrilled to have approved and sanctioned paper and pencil and began to write immediately. Dad wasn't anywhere around, and I could write my truths. Hiding the diaries when we got home would be something I could figure out later.

After breakfast, my group left the meadow, walking down a wide dirt road. I walked next to Fel, the girl I'd met in the stream, and discovered she was a PE teacher from Long Beach. Our group leader, Donna, the redhead, had big blue eyes and fair white skin. I flashed to the novels where I'd read about women with "alabaster skin" and knew instantly this was what they meant.

Donna said, "Check your compasses, girls. You'll see we're headed west. Try to follow along on the map as we hike today."

I took out my map and compass, found the road we were on, and verified we were headed west-southwest. So many thoughts and feelings welled up, it overwhelmed me, including that I was probably the youngest in the group. I had never been in a group of older women like this before.

Donna was a warrior and a goddess who oozed kindness when she smiled. Every time we came to a lake, she encouraged us to run through the woods nude, sometimes in slow-motion single file, imitating the person in front of us, and sometimes as fast as we could. The flesh and muscles on my thighs, stomach, and breasts bounced and moved in a way I had never felt before. Being naked in nature with these women and feeling safe was foreign but welcome. I released a big breath I'd been holding, maybe my whole life.

I was by far the most well-traveled person in our troop, which gave me a sense of maturity and confidence even though I was the youngest. We made camp after hiking nearly fifteen miles. Donna gave us lessons on map and compass reading and answered all our questions at dinner, like "How do we pick a leader each day?" (group consensus), "What if we run out of food?" (she'd order more for the next resupply), and "When can we see the other groups?" (at the end of the term). I was exhausted after the hike and wanted to sleep.

Before bed, I wrote in my diary about my love of the trees. They spoke to me in a language I had first experienced when we lived on Midgaard, our ranch in Paradise, California, years earlier. At nine years old, I had my special place under a canopy of craggy old oak trees between two large boulders. I wrote poems and sang to nature there, communing with the trees. Lodgepole pines and cottonwoods, Douglas firs, Colorado blue spruces, ponderosa pines, and aspens were all around us. I loved them all. They sounded like a poem. The connectedness of everything seemed to flow through them and into me. Was I right that they were lovingly watching over us? It sure felt like it.

The following day over breakfast, Donna said, "See this X here?" She pointed to her map, and we all found the spot on our own maps. "Meet me here tonight before sunset." And without any more fanfare, she left.

"What? You're just leaving us?" a girl we called Chicago Sue said. She was from the Windy City and everyone seemed to be getting names based on where they were from. At twenty-one, Chicago Sue was almost the oldest on the trip. She reminded me of Raine, not only because she was full-figured but also because we hit it off immediately.

Donna didn't answer.

"Who wants to be the leader today?" Carla asked. She was sixteen, like me, from Los Angeles, and had already begun to get on my nerves. She talked with her mouth full and interrupted when others were speaking.

"I'll do it," Fel offered. At twenty-three, she was the oldest. I learned her real name was Felicity.

Nobody objected, so we had our leader for the day. There was no time to waste, since we had another fifteen miles to cover that day. Fel was a great leader, encouraging us and finding the best route to our destination. She was athletic and rugged. I struggled slightly on the second day with carrying my heavy pack and keeping to the front of the group, but I was grateful for a big cup of tea with honey at lunch with my tortillas and peanut butter before hiking the second part.

Several of the girls lagged, walking very slowly. Nineteen-year-old Tennessee Sue spoke with a drawl and twang and was in a world of her own and we all felt sorry for her. Her parents had tricked her into coming to Outward Bound. She had had a complete meltdown when she arrived at Denver Airport and discovered she was going on a wilderness survival course for twenty-two days instead of to the resort she had been promised.

26

Our days piled up as Donna taught us about the plants and animals around us. At night we heard coyotes howling, bats flying, and owls hooting. We wondered about bears, but Donna assured us they would never confront a group as large as ours.

We summited two mountains and walked along the highest ridges. The first was Hagerman's Pass at 14,000 feet. We stood on the Continental Divide staring out over the horizon and trees below. The wind nearly blew us off the top as our hiking boots struggled to find solid ground among the shale, loose rocks, and dirt. "Hold on to me, or we'll blow over," I called to Chicago Sue. She grabbed my hand. "Let's not die up here, okay?" Donna stood with elegance and ease as the other girls lined up so we could all enjoy the view, some crouching to minimize the wind and others sitting down. Like the ocean's immensity, here, too, was a vastness that made me feel small and humbled. The clear blue sky and horizon in the distant expanse before us begged attention. Below us the Colorado Rocky Mountains, green and lush at the tree line, promised protection and warmth.

Donna explained the view. "Look around, girls, all the rivers on this side of the mountains," she indicated the east side, "flow to the Atlantic Ocean, and on the other side, the rivers flow to the Pacific Ocean."

Awe and wonder filled me up.

The second mountain range, which we summited with Donna a few days later, was Mount Grizzley at 13,988 feet. This time the wind was quiet, almost like the world was holding its breath. The cloudless view felt royal. Pride and gratitude filled my heart for being able to stand in such a majestic place. We each found a safe spot to sit and made tea and honey while eating our morning snack of nuts and dried fruit. A solemn spiritual consciousness hung over all of us as Donna read a quote by Sir Francis Younghusband, a British army officer, explorer, and spiritual writer. I wrote it in my diary later that night.

> *To those who have struggled with the mountains, they reveal beauties they will not disclose to those who make no effort. That is the reward the mountains give to effort. And it is because they have so much to give and give it so lavishly to those who will wrestle with them that [wo]men love the mountains and go back to them again and again . . . The mountains reserve their choice gifts for those who stand upon their summit.*

As part of the requirement to pass the survival course, each of us had to be leader for the day twice. I had avoided it as long as I could, feeling unsure about whether I could wrangle a group like this, with so many difficult personalities. Fel and Caroline with the Curls had both led twice and tried to rule the group like the president and vice president picking the next leader each morning. But after the first morning, the rest of us revolted. We didn't want to be dictated to by them and so I volunteered.

Studying the map and the X where we were due to meet Donna for dinner, I decided on our route. We had thirteen miles of hiking over a mountain and into the next valley. Self-doubt filled me up. I could hear Dad in my head saying, "You can't lead. You're too stupid."

But I had read charts and maps on the boat when we sailed—even navigated with a sextant and calculated our position using declination tables. A small voice inside whispered, "You can do this now in the mountains. There are actual landmarks here, unlike the middle of the ocean."

We set out on a very dense and wooded trail, going up the mountain in single file. I couldn't shake the doubts screaming inside my head. The elevation quickly became so steep that Carla whined, "Are you sure we're going the right way?" She was a pain in my ass!

I didn't answer but decided at that moment I would forever call her Complaining Carla. She might be a California sister from LA, but she bugged the crap out of me.

"Did you measure the elevation change on the map? This is very steep," Becky from Kentucky called from the back of the line.

I stopped hiking and said, "Let's take a ten-minute break," and pulled out my map. The elevation lines were getting closer together, meaning it would be steeper ahead. That morning, with my nerves and Dad's voice screaming at me, I had not seen that.

I broke the bad news to the group. "We have to backtrack to this trail here," I said, pointing to my map. Groans filled the air. We began hiking back down the way we came and I shrunk inside as a heavy, dark feeling enveloped me like a thick blanket, and the negative voices inside continued to berate me until Becky from Kentucky said, "At home in Lexington, I hardly walk to the store. None of my friends would believe I'm doing this."

"Me too," Caroline with the Curls chirped. "I don't think I'd ever walked more than a mile before I came here."

Grateful for the distraction from my negative thinking, I listened to the girls talk. I had a hard time thinking of something positive to say—of being diplomatic—so I stayed quiet. I felt their disappointment. It weighed heavy on my heart and I scolded myself. An additional three miles added to our hike was not welcomed by anyone. "You're a failure," Dad's voice bellowed inside.

That other voice inside whispered again, "Just keep walking." The tears hovered just below the surface and my lip quivered. Catching up to me, Fel put her arm around my shoulder. "You're doing fine. Dig in. We'll get there soon."

I smiled at her and put one foot in front of the other. When we got close to the X on the map, the sun was ready to set, and all our stomachs were grumbling for dinner. With my head hung low, thinking, *Dad's right. I'm not a good leader. I don't know how to do anything*, I heard Chicago Sue say with a bright face, "There's Donna."

I looked ahead and saw her sitting on a boulder like a Roman goddess reading a book, her hair piled high on her head in a bun. We threw our packs down, and the floodgate of grievances poured out with Complaining Carla leading the charge in ridiculing me. I sat away from the group. Disappointment and loathing filled me up. "I'm sorry, guys, I really am."

I wanted so much to make Donna proud, be a good leader, and maybe even be a star student. *What a crock. I'm the worst!*

Whenever I spiraled into self-hate like this, I couldn't stop myself from piling all the mistakes I'd ever made on top of this one. Stopping it was like trying to grab something slippery headed down the drain. The burden grew heavier inside.

Donna quietly listened from afar to all the complaints and talked about map-reading and leadership skills as she began preparing for dinner. "Let's move on and start cooking dinner. I'm starving!" she said.

Grateful not to be lambasted in front of everyone, I slunk away and began gathering firewood so we could cook—anything to be away from the group. I couldn't bear the thought of facing Donna alone. Chicago Sue and Fel followed me into the woods, showering me with words of comfort and kindness. Fel said, "Ultimately, you were successful so take heart. It was your first time leading and you're one of the youngest." Chicago Sue added, "Don't beat yourself up. You'll do better next time."

She was right and wrong, because the next time I led the group I didn't make the same mistake with the elevation but had bad luck. Halfway up the mountain, we reached a gigantic boulder blocking the trail. In the first few seconds I fell into my old behavior and silently berated myself but then decided there would be no backtracking today. We just needed to get around that damn boulder.

Setting our packs down, Fel and I climbed up the skinny path on a steep cliff to get around the boulder. I called for everyone to take off their packs and hand them around the boulder to us before climbing around themselves. It was time-consuming and treacherous, but everyone made it around and we continued on the trail. Ragged and sore, we found Donna a few hours later at the appointed place. Several girls complained about my leadership skills again. I stayed quiet knowing it was just bad luck that the boulder had rolled onto the trail.

Our survival skills in this wilderness course wouldn't be complete without a day of rock climbing on the tallest granite wall we had seen in the mountains. The challenge of finding crevices and cracks for my hands and feet going up gave me abrasions and blisters. Donna worked the ropes from above while rock climbing expert teacher, Lisa, who met us for the day, coached us from the bottom. Rappelling took a little more courage, as we had to jump away from the wall and descend a few feet each time. I got the hang of it quickly and enjoyed the ride down. Thank God I kept up with the other girls and wasn't a dweeb at rock climbing.

One of the most challenging days happened shortly after our rock climbing experience. Soft-spoken and somewhat fragile, Liz was leading us through a thick wooden section of the mountains into a barren valley with green hills on either side and a creek at the bottom. The valley was half in the shade, half in the sun, and it reminded me of a photograph in *National Geographic*. We found Donna by the river and ran up to her like little cubs who had found their mother after a long separation. "Well done, girls! Welcome to the most beautiful valley I know." She beamed at us.

We all stripped naked except for our hiking boots and ran a loop along the edge of the valley leaping and jumping from large boulder to large boulder, then we sat down and took off our boots so we could wade in and out of the water splashing each other until we laughed and nearly cried from the cold. Last in the line, I watched as the women ran, bounced, flopped, and swung their bodies. I let go of my inhibitions that day and felt freer than I'd ever felt. We sang from the tops of our lungs—the chorus to John Denver's "Rocky Mountain High." The feeling was euphoric.

Collapsing around our packs, digging for food like starving cubs, we ate greedily from the jar of berry jam Donna had brought us, slathering it on our homemade flour tortillas. Life felt rich and good and full. We were at almost 11,000 feet; the temperature was falling fast, so we gathered around the fire closely. Donna encouraged us to tuck in together for warmth instead of sleeping alone.

Ten days earlier, Fel had asked if I wanted to buddy up on cold nights, and I'd said yes. I admired her leadership and strength. We shared a sleeping bag on several cold nights, and it all seemed fine. That night, it was my and Fel's turn to fetch water when she confided that she "liked" me. Stunned, I stood up from bending down to the water and stared at her, hoping I had heard her wrong.

"Oh, sorry, I've shocked you. I thought maybe you knew."

"How was I supposed to know? I thought we were friends."

"We are friends. I want to be more." Her mouth was tight but her eyes glowed.

I smiled my friendly sixteen-year-old-girl smile and reminded her I had a boyfriend I loved very much while my insides did backflips and somersaults of embarrassment.

I sort of knew about lesbians. In elementary school, the kids called me Lez and Lezzie as they snickered. I didn't know what they meant until one of the older kids explained it to me.

On our walk back to camp with the filled water bottles, I realized there was no way to get out of sleeping with her, since everyone had buddied up already. My fears of being assaulted in the night reared up. Memories of Dad forcing me to sleep naked in the same bed as him and then mounting me while I slept came rushing back. I tried to act normal, but my insides flip-flopped, and I couldn't eat dinner. That night we lay in our double-zipped sleeping bag, both of us wearing almost all the clothes we owned because it was so cold. I huddled to one side as far as possible, thinking, *Why me? Why did she have to pick me?*

I didn't sleep much. Fear and flashbacks filled my head with images of waiting for Dad. My trauma was still so fresh and even though Dad hadn't tried anything on me for a few years, my radar was up. I never thought I had to put my radar up for women. At least I wasn't naked in my sleeping bag with Fel.

Sometime in the middle of the night, all hell broke loose when the water-laden clouds rolled into the valley and it began to blow and pour rain. Rushing to put our tents up, we climbed inside hoping the thin fabric was enough of a barrier. It wasn't. Fel and I hunkered down together in the same tent, inside our double sleeping bag trying to stay warm, hoping the rain would stop. But the creek turned into a river and the water underneath the tent grew. We couldn't ignore it any longer. We both sat up in the dark. "I'm soaking wet," I said. "We're practically floating," she said.

By 4 a.m., all the girls were outside their tents. We sat in rows on the slope, up from the pooling water, holding a tarp over our heads as torrents of water assaulted us. Shaking from cold, we huddled as close as we could, trying to doze off as we leaned against each other, teeth chattering, shivering, and utterly miserable.

The storm passed and pale-blue light filled the morning sky. I tried to be grateful but was destitute in my thinking. It would take another few hours before the sun peeked over the ridgeline and hit our bodies so we could feel the direct rays on our skin. Everything we owned was soaking wet. In her cheery voice, Donna rallied us, "Come on, girls, wring out your clothes and sleeping bags and hang them on the bushes to dry."

Our attempts to make a fire with the wet wood finally succeeded. We had hot tea with honey, which had never tasted so good, and hot oatmeal and more honey. Our moods improved immensely. A short time later, the sun finally peeked over the ridge, and we stood in wet clothes facing it with puckered skin and hair tied up, jogging in place and doing jumping jacks for warmth, worshipping the weak heat it brought.

This was the second time in my life I'd been so cold and wet my body shook involuntarily, quaking on its own while I silently prayed to Helios to warm me. The first time was our near-death experience sailing on *Patricia* when we almost sank in a huge storm.

At 10 a.m., Donna said, "Pack it up, girls. Let's go find that heat." We followed her out of the waterlogged valley into a low meadow, where we stayed for the day, soaking up the sun, drying out, and napping.

The beauty and suffering juxtaposed against each other the previous twenty-four hours felt like the Colorado mountains were in cahoots with the Pacific Ocean. I didn't know they were friends and wouldn't soon forget it.

Life was slightly awkward with Fel for the next several days, but she gave me my space and respected my wishes. A few days later, we shared a laugh about something silly, and all was smoothed over and forgotten. We never shared another sleeping bag.

27

Nearing the end of the course, we had three hurdles to clear before our time in the Rocky Mountains ended. The first was the three-day solo, the second was the final examination hike, and the last was the mini marathon we had to run.

I had never spent three days and nights alone without food, and most of us in our group had significant fear going into the experience. Donna explained that everyone would have plenty of water and must stay at the spot where she placed us. In other words, no day hiking. "Commune with nature, meditate, write in your diaries, sleep, rest, sing, draw, anything. I'll check on each of you girls every day although you probably won't see or hear me do it."

She explained that if we had a problem, we should tie our bandanna to one of the branches near our tent and she would see it. "Don't panic and don't worry. You are not in any danger. I will be close by. Maybe that will give you comfort. Try to push yourselves to finish this solo. You'll be a new person once you do."

That sounded good to me. I wanted to be a new person without my father's voice in my head telling me I was a piece of shit all the time. Donna placed me in a gorgeous little spot beside a stream under aspen trees. The rushing water was so loud it drowned out all the other forest noises. Filtered light came through the canopy and I could see up and down the river a good distance. It was cold in the shade all day and I had to seek out patches of sun in my small area for warmth. The first day was new and exciting. I wrote, slept, drew, and sang, but as I got hungrier, loneliness and depression descended on me. I started my period and knew why I had been so irritable the previous days. I had period supplies, but the cramps made me want to lie on my sleeping bag inside the tent and moan. What stopped me was my fear of sleeping too much during the day, which would leave me awake at night. I did not want to be alone in the dark. So I stayed busy talking to the trees, writing, singing, and washing laundry in the stream.

On the second day, my body felt ready to get moving. Hiking fifteen miles a day every day for the past two weeks was routine. But I had nowhere to go. The hunger pains disappeared but the familiar cavernous, hollow feeling inside came back with a vengeance. It filled up with all my self-doubts and hates. I relived my mistakes as a leader. Why did I feel this canyon of emptiness when I wasn't busy? When we were sailing, Annie had taught me about meditation, so I tried to meditate, sitting on my sleeping bag crisscross applesauce with my fingers in a circle resting on my knees. After a few minutes of sitting quietly, trying hard to focus on doing everything right, I let out a scream, fell over—clutching my empty, aching stomach—and went to sleep.

A dream about Mom woke me up. The guilt of having been so mean to her flooded over me, drowning me in regret. There was no place to hide—no distraction from it. I cried and cried, apologizing to Mom, wondering if I could ever make it up to her, asking for forgiveness from the god of nature. I threw in a prayer of forgiveness for leading the girls the wrong way up the mountains. I blew my nose into my bandanna and washed it in the creek so many times it never had a chance to dry. I used almost all my toilet paper blowing my nose the second day. All I heard was Dad's voice calling me a baby, telling me how stupid I was, that I would never amount to anything, and to buck up.

On the third day, I felt lightheaded and dizzy. I wasn't hungry anymore but wondered what we would eat first when the solo ended. I spent hours taking pictures of the trees, telling them I loved them, and the stream, and the light at different times of the day. Then I wrote a poem about each photo, trying to describe it. I looked for Donna in the forest, hoping to glimpse her, but I never saw her. My poetry about nature and the trees went in my journal, but I mainly wrote about my love for and admiration of Donna, hoping I would turn out like her in my twenties.

For Donna

Long red hair—
Big blue eyes.
That's what Donna
Looks like.
She's gentle with feelings
And hard on lies.
She loves the wilderness
And if you look close enough
You can really see
The wild in her.
Pink, pink cheeks
And a grin as
Big as the sky . . .
That's what Donna looks like.

At daybreak on the fourth day, I felt lightheaded when I saw Donna smiling from across the stream. "You did it. Solo is over. Follow me."

Other girls were already in a meadow not far away. I felt a rush of love and kindness for all of them. Rhonda and Liz rubbed dirt marks off each other's faces, giggling and getting their fingers wet with spit. Chicago Sue ran up to hug me. Complaining Carla and Tennessee Sue sat next to each other, watching the reunion. "We're starving," Complaining Carla said. The prescribed method of ending a fast began with hot tea and honey, then yogurt and berries. The sweetness of the berries exploded in my mouth. Next we could have a cup of oatmeal. Everything tasted so good.

Proud that I had finished the three-day solo, I wondered when I would start feeling like a new person.

28

After sixteen days, our time neared an end. On the final day of the regular group experience, Donna led us into the valley to reunite with the two other groups, including Monica. I searched for her in the crowd and found her watching as we entered the meadow, straining to see if it was me. My heart exploded; she never looked so good. I dropped my pack and ran to her, and we hugged and laughed. Her long blonde hair was tied up in a ponytail and she was thinner. We huddled together, sharing our joy and agreeing that all our traveling with Dad to Tahiti and Windsor had helped us endure this challenging experience.

The final examination was our next hurdle in the program and after meeting up with the entire group, we were all sorted into three new groups according to ability and strength. Monica and I were strong hikers and placed in the same final group. "You both show signs of great stamina and good map-reading skills," one of the other leaders, Nancy, said. I tried not to dwell on my failures in leadership, quietly accepting the perceived honor of being in Monica's final group, who was a force with her speed and agility, and I intended to give her a run for her money. Nancy continued, "We're making an exception this time, putting sisters together. Are you both okay with it?"

Monica nodded and said, "Yes, I'm great with it." She grabbed my hand and squeezed it.

I nodded with a big grin, thinking we worked well together—*when we aren't with Dad, otherwise we'll tear each other apart.*

Rhonda was the only girl from my group who joined us. I felt ambivalent about her, as she was the only girl I hadn't gotten to know very well. She had skinned knees from a fall but never complained about it. Ohio Kelly, with a big cross around her neck, came from Monica's group, and Lisa, with the southern accent, was brand new to Monica and me.

The five of us left the meadow the following morning, all working together with no clear leader. It felt right to hike by consensus, and I hoped it worked. We were headed to our first checkpoint eighteen miles away in search of a mound of rocks stacked in a pyramid shape. It held written directions to our next checkpoint and the time we had to get there.

After hiking up switchbacks for almost five hours, we found ourselves on a ridge by Mount Harvard. Giant black thunderheads built all around us. The terrain was barren, like the desert. The path at the top was narrow, loose rock and very steep on either side. We walked in a row along the ridgeline holding our arms out for balance, focusing each minute on our next step. If we slipped, we could tumble down several hundreds of feet. The wind gusted and the clouds hung low over our heads. Rain began to fall. "Let's jam it off this ridgeline and get some shelter," Lisa called. I nodded and looked for a way down. Monica pointed and we followed her.

We hiked a few more hours, avoiding the heavy downpour of rain behind us, finding checkpoint 1 easily. Making camp nearby, we read our instructions for the next day. Checkpoint 2 was over twenty-three miles away. We all groaned. None of us was excited about the heavy challenge ahead.

We studied our maps during dinner, discussed which course we would take the next day, and worked together like I wished we had in my original group. We agreed to an early start so we could hustle over two mountains and make it to checkpoint 2 before dark.

Rhonda said, "Hey, look at this: U.S. 24 is below us. We won't need to hike all that way if we hitchhike up the highway and then head back into the mountains to find our checkpoint."

I liked the idea. Monica waggled her eyebrows at me with a grin. Looking closely at my map, I said, "We might not have to hike more than eight miles."

"We could sleep in," Monica said wistfully, staring at her sleeping bag.

Everyone agreed it sounded like a good plan. None of the leaders would know.

We got a late start the following day. After tea, tortillas, and peanut butter, we left at 10 a.m., hiking down the highway near Vicksburg, an abandoned mining town. The weather was all sunshiny and we were hopeful for an easy day.

Exiting the forest, we met a lovely couple from Texas in an RV who offered us a watermelon. We split the entire thing open on the side of the road and ate like starving people, scooping out handfuls and shoving it in our mouths and laughing. Dripping in watermelon juice, we must have looked very uncivilized.

We said goodbye to the nice people and headed out to the highway. Stuffed with watermelon, I just wanted to lie in the warm sun and nap. But we walked on, putting our thumbs out, hoping we could catch a ride to the trailhead. An older man in a red pickup truck stopped, and we all jumped in the back and settled in, very pleased with ourselves. We passed a sign for the town of Buena Vista, three miles away.

"I bet they have pizza in that town," Lisa twanged. She was turning out to be quite fun. I liked her and her southern drawl.

"Pepperoni pizza," Monica drooled.

The thought of pizza ruined us. None of us wanted to return to eating tortillas, dried fruit, and oatmeal. We were sick to death of it.

Nineteen

The older man dropped us off, and we began hiking up the trail over the first mountain. My legs felt heavy, and my body felt sluggish. The watermelon slowed me down, and the truck ride stiffened my muscles.

"We've miscalculated. The checkpoint is at least sixteen miles from here," Ohio Kelly said with a dark look.

"We're not going to make it," Monica said. We all took out our maps to confirm.

"If we don't make it to checkpoint 2, they will send out the cavalry. We're supposed to be the best hikers in all the groups," Rhonda said.

"We're screwed. They'll kick us out and our father will kill us," I said, looking at Monica.

"That watermelon is like a rock in my stomach," Lisa mused, staring off into the sky.

We stopped hiking and stood in a circle. "What should we do? At this pace, we won't arrive at the checkpoint until after midnight," I said.

"Let's admit defeat," Ohio Kelly said.

"What does that mean?" Rhonda asked.

"Two of us will go into that town, Buena Vista, call Base Camp, and check in, telling them we got lost. Maybe we'll say one of us sprained our ankle."

"Now we're making shit up and lying," Lisa said.

The stress in the group was palpable. "We can't do that," Monica shouted.

"Our only other choice is to keep hiking all night," I said.

"If we can even find that stupid rock pyramid in the dark," Rhonda said.

The longer we debated, the more time we lost. We finally decided that Rhonda and Ohio Kelly should go to town and call. The rest of us made camp in a small meadow under a nearby canopy of trees. The sick feeling in my stomach nearly made me throw up. Monica and I eyed each other, and I could see she was also scared of the consequences we were facing in failing to make it to checkpoint 2.

"Damn that we slept in and ate all that watermelon," I said as we sat around the fire eating tortillas and cheese again for dinner.

Ohio Kelly and Rhonda were gone a long time. We gathered wood for the night, and then I paced at the edge of our camp, searching the distance for them.

"Do you see them yet?" Lisa called, throwing another log on the fire.

"No," I called back.

An hour later, they returned happy and laughing. Rhonda said, "We ate pizza and drank Cokes. It was heavenly."

"What about Base Camp? What did they say?" I said, anxious to hear our punishment.

"Carol at Base Camp was pretty mad," Ohio Kelly said, "but she gave us directions to checkpoint 3, saying we should finish the course and make our next resupply by tomorrow evening."

"God, we're such losers," Lisa groaned, and I agreed.

"Losers with candy bars," Rhonda teased, holding a handful of Snickers bars in the air.

"What? No pizza for us?" Monica said.

"Nope. We ate it all. Do you want your chocolate bar or not?" Rhonda sang out.

We grabbed ours, Monica and I shoving half the candy bar in our mouths in unison.

We were quiet for a minute. The birds chirped high up in the trees, and the sound of rustling nearby made me turn. I stood up but didn't see anything.

Rhonda added, "So that you know, we didn't say anything about a sprained ankle."

Thank God, I thought. At least we hadn't lied in addition to cheating.

The maps showed that checkpoint 3 was Cottonwood Pass, more than twenty miles away. A heavy day of hiking lay ahead of us again, but the sun was still up, and the town was so close . . .

"There's no reason to be glum. We're already in trouble, but if we make checkpoint 3, I'm sure everything will be fine," I said with a big smile.

A feeling of letting it all go came over us. We were already in trouble. What was the difference, anyway? We listened with envy to Ohio Kelly and Rhonda's stories of town. After all, we had a plan, and Base Camp knew where we were, so why not see the town of Buena Vista? Why not enjoy ourselves before we faced the firing squad?

For all her encouragement and seeming wildness, Lisa didn't want to go to town, and Rhonda and Ohio Kelly had already been, so Monica and I took off by ourselves, making it to the highway and sticking out our thumbs. I felt light as a feather without my thirty-pound pack. A girl in a green Gremlin on her way to work at the motel picked us up. She dropped us at the liquor store in town. Using Monica's remaining change from the $20 taxi ride to the airport, we bought gum, candy bars, and a Coke, then stopped for an ice cream. Cars cruised back and forth as we walked down the main road licking our ice creams, honking like it was the 1950s. This town was filled with mountain men and wannabe John Denvers. They honked at us, and we waved back.

We saw a flashing red neon Pizza sign and went inside. The jukebox blared a country song I didn't recognize, couples danced, and crowds of men played pool and shot darts. A cute cowboy with a square jaw and a mustache invited us to play pool. "Sure," I said, and took a pool cue. He offered us a slice of his pizza; we ordered Cokes and swayed to the music. My eyes drank in the scene of people. The music had my head buzzing. It felt like going from solitary confinement to the middle of a raging party in two steps. Dozens of men in boots and cowboy hats drank beer and did whiskey shots. Women in tight jeans and button-up cowgirl blouses huddled around the men, swaying to Waylon Jennings's "Good Hearted Woman."

I felt wonky and far away, yet I stood there observing the commotion. "I'm going to the bathroom. Are you okay?" I asked Monica. She, too, looked like she was having trouble assimilating to our environment. "Yeah, I'm good."

I left her with the cute cowboy, leaning over the table to make a pool shot.

The bathroom was a revelation. There were porcelain toilets and for the first time in more than eighteen days, I sat properly instead of digging a hole and squatting in the woods.

Washing my hands, I glanced in the mirror and cried out. My face was long and drawn, and I had lost weight. My cheek had a big smudge of dirt, and three big red mosquito bites demanded too much attention on my forehead. *I'm a wild mountain woman.* My unbrushed hair hung around my face in a ratty mess. Running out to the pool hall, I grabbed Monica and dragged her into the bathroom. "Look! Look at yourself."

We stood side by side and studied ourselves in the mirror. She squinted. "My God, I'm filthy and very skinny."

"I know. Look at this dirt smudge you didn't tell me I had on my cheek."

"I guess I didn't notice it. It's been there for days."

"Oh fine. Thanks a lot. My hair looks like I stuck my finger in a socket."

"Mine too. Look at my teeth," Monica said, "I'm disgusting."

We spent the next twenty minutes fixing ourselves up as best we could, practically bathing in the sink with soap and water. When we left, it was late. Some guys from the pool hall gave us a ride up Highway 306, and we hiked back to camp in the dark to find the other girls already asleep.

We left at first light, with Lisa waking us up and offering hot tea and honey. "The town was so much fun. I wish we lived nearby. I could hang out at that pizza bar every night," Monica said as she packed away her sleeping bag. "Yeah, it was crazy looking in the mirror," I said, sipping my tea and lacing up my hiking boots.

The elevation gain for that day's hike was more than 4,000 feet. We needed to forget about the boys and the pizza and remember how to hike so we could get to Cottonwood Pass. I struggled to find the energy that had been so easy to tap into earlier in the trip. My body was working against me, maybe because of all the junk I had put in it the previous night.

"This sucks," Rhonda called from the back of our group. And we all agreed.

When we arrived at checkpoint 3, we were greeted by all the other groups. We laid our packs down, and the three group leaders circled us. "Come with us," Carly said. She looked clean with bouncy hair like she'd had a shower. We followed the three leaders around the bend away from the other girls.

"You have all failed us greatly, and we're very disappointed in you," Nancy said, eyes twitching.

Donna brushed her long hair back and nodded. "We have never had a group cheat and stray so far from the intended course."

We all looked at our feet. I kicked the dirt, not looking any of them in the eye, especially Donna. My stomach roiled. Donna shook her head at Rhonda and me, visibly disappointed.

The next day was our last. We were going home, but before we received our certificates of achievement, we had to run eight miles at Cottonwood Pass Summit, which was 12,000 feet in elevation.

Monica came in first out of all twenty-four women, and I came in second to last, walking most of the way. I seemed to have no control over the guilt and shame that grew inside. After the run, I wasn't hungry or thirsty and went off by myself around the bend from everybody else, wondering if people could die from shame and guilt.

"Hey, Leslie, I found you," came Donna's soothing voice. I could barely look her in the eye. She slid in beside me, and we quietly stared at the vast mountains before us for a few minutes. Her voice was calm and quiet as she studied me and the view alternately. "It looks like you're pretty upset. Can I suggest you work on forgiving yourself?"

"I hate myself. I know I could have completed the course. I didn't need to cheat." My voice quivered, and I looked away, afraid of bursting out crying. The lump in my throat hardened.

"Hating yourself won't help. Try accepting your mistakes. None of us are perfect, and learning to accept our mistakes is key to growing up."

"Accept my mistakes? How do I do that?" I walked a few steps away from her, shaking my head.

I knew how to stuff my embarrassments and mistakes down. I had learned to berate myself, say terrible things, and bury it all in the pains and hurts I never acknowledged or dealt with. I was good at that. But acceptance? How?

Donna patted my shoulder gently, and I saw her smile from the corner of my eye. She leaned over and kissed me on the cheek before returning to the group.

I tried to stop hating myself and to accept my failings and lack of stamina, knowing they were just thoughts in my head.

On the flight home, I read the handwritten letter on Outward Bound stationery, signed by Donna.

> *Leslie has had an Outward Bound experience full of thought-provoking experiences. It is my hope that she will continue her exploration of leadership skills, developing her awareness tools for other individuals. Throughout the course Leslie continually set her expectations for herself so high that she often found herself struggling to meet her anticipated goals. I know that Leslie is very*

aware of this and hope she will continue to look realistically not only at what it is she would like to do, but at those things that she can do.

Leslie is a very capable individual and I wish her lots of luck.

29

Dad was still gone on his big trip when we got home from Outward Bound at the end of August, which allowed Monica and me to settle in and catch our breath. Beth and Phil welcomed us warmly. Karen had a thousand questions. I hoped Dad would be gone for weeks.

Mom took us out for pizza the first night home. She looked good with her black hair coiffed high again and her mouth painted red. "You're both so skinny," she said, picking at her food. She brushed Monica's long hair back from her shoulder. "Was it tough?"

I straightened up, proud to be skinny, but prouder Mom noticed. "Yes, it was hard," I said, gazing at Monica, who nodded with big eyes and a piece of pepperoni pizza in her hand.

"I've been starving for a month," she said, shoving a huge bite of pizza in her mouth.

"I missed you guys," Karen said with a sweet, longing look. "You still have a hollow leg, don't you, Monica?"

Looking at Karen, I said, "You looking forward to being a freshman this year?"

"Yes, finally, a high schooler like my big sisters."

School was due to start in only a week. The dread weighed heavy on me.

* *

Nineteen

After three days of telling myself not to, I called Simon from the pay phone across the street. I told him a little bit about where I'd been for the past three plus weeks. "Are you still seeing somebody?" I asked.

"No. It didn't last."

"So can I come to Windsor now?" He waited too long to answer, so I rushed in and said, "I get it. The answer is still no."

"I don't want to lose my career, but please believe me, I miss you terribly and wish you were in my bed right now."

"Me too. I wish I were there as well."

I hung up and ran to Cyndi's apartment, where we smoked Virginia Slims and drank a few beers.

I got home a little buzzed and found Dad in the kitchen with Beth and Phil, wrapping up a conversation. Suitcases sat near the front door. I got a glass of water from the sink and waved hi to Dad, not wanting to interrupt. My stomach clutched at the sight of him. He was skinnier, too, and tanned, and his face was relaxed and happy. There was an unusual aura of calm around him.

Phil and Beth left, and with the screen door slamming, all politeness, kindness, and peace left with them. "Monica and Leslie!" Dad called out. "In the living room, now!"

Arriving in the living room with a handful of used film canisters, I tried to crawl up onto the couch and claim a corner, but he stopped me with his hand, indicating I should stand. Monica and I stood shoulder to shoulder like good little soldiers being summoned by our father/king. "Tell me about your time in Colorado."

"I got first in the mini marathon," Monica announced.

"Congratulations!" the King said, and turned to me with raised eyebrows.

I took a step backward. "I'm not a runner like Monica. Look at her. She's a cheetah for God's sake."

He rolled his eyes and twirled his finger in the air like "Get on with it." I decided blurting it out was the best way. "I finished second to last." I hung my head.

"You're too heavy. You have always been too thick." He stared at the lower half of my body.

I shrunk inside, my chest caving in just a little, but I stood my ground. I wanted to yell and scream at him that I'd lost weight on the wilderness course and was skinnier than ever, weighing only 126 pounds. But I said nothing.

"Dad," Karen chirped from the dining room, where she was setting the dinner dishes. "They're both so skinny."

The King scowled at Karen and raised a finger in warning. He addressed us. "I had interesting mail—a report of your time in the wilderness. So please continue to fill me in on your lessons and don't leave anything out."

Monica and I exchanged a glance and crumbled right then and there. We confessed most of our mistakes, leaving out the more damning details the counselors didn't even know. We blamed the other girls as bad influences and said we knew we'd made a mistake.

"A mistake? No. You cheated," he snarled at us.

Neither of us spoke. The shame and guilt grew inside but I refused to look the part. *Fuck him.*

He ranted on about how much money he had spent on us, how embarrassed and disappointed he was, and, of course, how stupid and worthless we were. The barrage of bullets landed in their usual places, but I refused to show him a wound. I closed my eyes, looked up at the ceiling, and shook my head slightly.

He looked directly at me. "Are you smoking?"

I squinted. "What?"

"You heard me. Are you smoking cigarettes?"

"No."

He looked at Monica and waved his hand in dismissal. "You can go." She slunk into the kitchen with Karen.

"You're a liar. You're a fat liar. You smelled like smoke when you came home. The entire kitchen smelled like smoke when you walked in."

"So what? I don't care."

He scooched off the couch and towered over me with a menacing look. "Correct me if I'm wrong. You failed the proficiency test, you cheated on your wilderness final, you came in last in the marathon, and now you're lying about smoking. What else are you up to?"

"I came in second to last. Not last," I whispered under my breath.

"Oh excuse me, second to last." He grimaced at me. "I'll ask you again: What are you up to?"

Why can't he die? Why can't I be eighteen already and get out of this stupid family? "Nothing! I'm not up to anything." I turned and ran to the bedroom. "I hate you and can't wait to leave this family."

His maniacal laugh followed me down the hall. "Don't let the door hit you in the ass on the way out."

Monica and I were grounded for two weeks. On the night we were supposed to go to Mom's, Monica was allowed and I wasn't. When I asked why, he said, "Because I don't trust you, Leslie. Monica can stay with your mother though. I trust her."

Fuck you! We both cheated on that final. Not just me!

Our sentence included weeding the entire property, front and back, cutting the lawn, planting new rose bushes, cleaning out and organizing the garage, and washing his precious Cadillac. I avoided eye contact or even being in the same room together. All I thought about was running away. As if he could read my mind, I'd be pulling weeds in the backyard, and he'd repeat his new favorite expression, "And if you're planning to run away, don't let the door hit you in the ass on the way out."

I had run away before when I was thirteen and we were getting ready to leave on our around-the-world sailing trip. It was a time when he insisted my sisters and I sleep naked, like the Europeans. Monica, Karen, and I had to rotate sleeping in his king-size bed, since we only had two twins in the other bedroom. We all dreaded our nights with Dad. On a night when it was my turn to share his bed, he came home drunk and climbed on top of me. I screamed, jumped out of bed, and locked myself in the bathroom. The next day, I tried to run away—but it only lasted one night. He found me the next morning on the other side of the harbor, sitting on a bench.

"Don't let the door hit you in the ass on the way out" was his new mantra. It was his way of telling me he didn't care if I ran away, but I knew he did. I pulled weeds to the rhythm of it, making my resolution to leave firmer. I couldn't go to Simon until I was eighteen, so where could I go? I scoured my mind for somewhere else to live as I scrubbed the kitchen floor and cleaned the bathroom toilets. I considered asking Mom if I could live with her but immediately changed my mind. The freedom would be tremendous, but I'd always have to put up with her moods and weirdness.

Then I remembered Annie, my dear, sweet sailing friend from our trip to Tahiti. Maybe I could live with her and her parents in Pacific Beach. If not, I would run away to Windsor early and Simon would have to deal with it.

The next time Dad left the house, I called Annie, desperate, asking if I could live with her. She agreed to talk to my dad. I dared to hope for a change—that Annie could save me from my life.

Unbelievably, Dad agreed to let me move to Pacific Beach with Annie. When she picked me up, I kissed and hugged her wildly. She became my de facto guardian and enrolled me in Mission Bay High and I moved in with her on her twenty-six-foot sailboat.

I rejoiced in my freedom and being out from under the King's thumb, watchful eye, and unreasonable rules. I bought a pack of Virginia Slims and smoked *at* him every time I took a drag. *Fuck him. I will be somebody in this life. I am smart enough. I can do anything I want. Fuck him!*

30

At Mission Bay High as a junior, my alien and dork status continued. Not fitting into my third high school was excruciating. *Is it me?* I promised myself I'd stay in school and study for my second attempt at the State Proficiency Exam, which was being given in October.

But I also needed money. I needed to get back to Simon and stop spending the money I earned on frivolous things. I needed to get serious about leaving home.

I borrowed Annie's ten-speed bike and found two jobs, one at the Sea World chicken restaurant, where I worked the lunch shift, and the other at Jack in the Box by the sports arena, where I worked the evening shift. At Jack in the Box, the manager put me on the drive-through window, and I worked until 2 a.m. most nights, when we'd get slammed after the concert or sports events let out. I loved the fast pace of the drive-through and was good at juggling all the orders. Finally, I was good at something. How depressing that it was fast food.

Annie attended classes at San Diego State, getting her physical education degree while working. Even though we went days without seeing each other, Annie decided that fall to rent another boat in the harbor, leaving me on her first boat. She was dating, and she wanted her space. I never asked about what it cost her or if I should contribute to the rent. I loved the autonomy. I was living on my own and loving it!

Monica wrote to me that Mom was drinking again and not going to work. She asked me to come home, but I just couldn't. I wrote back saying that I was staying in San Diego and never heard anything more.

I lied to Annie about attending classes at Mission Bay High and she passed the lie on to Dad. Everything was working out beautifully. On the day of the second proficiency test, I couldn't calm down, so I drank a few beers in the cockpit of my sailboat home. Slightly buzzed, I took the bus to the high school and sat for the three-and-a-half-hour test. When it was done, Annie was waiting in front of the school in her sunshine-yellow Karmann Ghia. What a sight! I was parched with a pounding headache and starving.

"Congratulations, Nearly Normal. I know you passed." Her smile was infectious, and I felt better just seeing her. We celebrated by grabbing some tacos at the beach.

I called Simon and gushed my love at him, not telling him about the nightmares I'd been having recently about him not loving me anymore. He reassured me that he loved me, but it felt hollow. The more months that passed, the more it occurred to me that maybe I'd never get back to Windsor.

The months ticked on. Thanksgiving and Christmas came and went. I worked every moment I could. Jason came to see me in San Diego and took me out. He was so good to me all the time. Life was beautiful living on the boat by myself—wonderfully peaceful.

When the proficiency test results arrived, they went to Annie's parents' house. I had to ride my bike to their house after work, nervous and anxious and feeling like I could throw up. The results would change my life either way. When I got there, Annie was waiting at the house, her gauzy white dress rippling as she stepped aside to let me enter. "Here's the envelope," she said, handing it to me. "Good luck!"

I tore it open and to my utter despair, I saw that I'd failed for the second time. I screamed, crumbled the letter into a ball, and threw it across the room.

"It's okay. You can retake it," Annie comforted me.

"But not for months. I'm such a loser," I cried. "I'm never going to get out of high school."

"Stop that ugly thinking," she said, wrapping an arm around me.

"But I'll have to move home now. I'm sure Dad won't let me stay."

"I'll talk to your dad. Don't worry. Everything will be fine."

The failure funnel claimed me and my entire life. It sucked me down and I was spiraling out, unable to stop the momentum.

Working the drive-through window the next day, a familiar Norwegian-accented voice bellowed out the speaker near my head, "I'll have a hamburger, french fries, and a Coke." My heart sped up. I stared at the speaker, cleared my throat, and repeated the order. I was getting better at thinking on my feet. He was not going to trip me up. I would not let him. When he reached the window, I took his $10 bill and made change.

"It's time to come home, Leslie. This little experiment has failed spectacularly," Dad said.

"Yeah, okay," I mumbled, handing him his food. "I get off at eight."

He waited for me in the parking lot, and I drove home with him that night, a complete failure at life except for the $240 I had saved since moving to Pacific Beach. It was my only win.

31

Spring semester 1978 began, and I fell back into a familiar rhythm with Pat, Jason, and Cyndi. I was more careful about smoking and learned to avoid detection by carrying mints, switching to a clean shirt, and always using Cyndi's mom's perfume before leaving her house.

Instead of the marching band, I enrolled in photography and oceanography. Maybe I could combine my love of photography with my love of the ocean and learn to be a scientist. School-sanctioned field trips to the tide pools excited me and I clung to those classes for dear life.

So much had changed at home while I was living in San Diego. Karen was halfway through her freshman year and was typing for Dad now, doing all his marine surveys and letters. She was his indentured servant. I decided to study all the time so I could pass that damn test when it was given again in April.

Monica was a senior in high school and worked at Alpha Beta, the neighborhood grocery store. Dad gave her permission to drive one of his precious Cadillacs, but that only lasted until a drunk driver totaled hers and three others parked on our busy street. What was the deal with Dad collecting all those cars? Nobody knew. Monica was dating a cute boy, and they planned to go to the prom together. Mom and Monica had joined a born-again Christian church called

Faith of Our Fathers. Walking home together from our first day at school, I asked about the church.

"I like the people," Monica said. "They're trying to help Mom."

"How?" I asked, giving Karen a skeptical glance as she shook her head.

"They're trying to cure her of drinking," Karen interjected like they'd had this discussion already. Monica shot her a sour look.

I asked Karen, "So you're not attending this church?"

"Not a chance. It's so weird," she said.

"Weird, how?" I asked.

"The pastor chants funny sounds, and his eyes roll back into his head, his arms wave frantically at heaven as he blesses the congregation, and all the people echo him. I went one time and it gave me the creeps."

I furrowed my brows at Monica. "The church is trying to cure Mom of her drinking? How does that work?"

"We pray, chant, and give witness to people at the beach with her, trying to get her involved."

"That's weird, Monica. How long have you been going?"

"A few months and it's not weird. You should come and see. I love it," she said with pride. She quickly walked ahead of us using her long strides, ending the conversation.

More quietly, I said to Karen, "If it helps Mom not drink, I'm all for it."

"It won't," she said resolutely. "She's not happy at all, even with the church. She hasn't gone the last few weeks, but Monica didn't tell you that."

"Great," I said, "I'm supposed to go over there Saturday night and stay."

"Just bring your schoolbooks and stay in the bedroom," Karen advised.

* *

That Saturday, I walked up to Mom's house with my backpack full of books and clothes. She wasn't home, so I settled into my room, unpacking my bag, cleaning the bathroom, vacuuming, and pulling the sheets off both beds and washing them. I pulled open the curtains to see the bougainvillea bush and a large acacia tree. Patches of blue sky were visible through the branches. Usually, the window was covered with a dark-blue sheet. A little TV sat on the dresser with a Bible on top. Another Bible on the nightstand invariably held a plate with leftovers from the night before. All of it crowded around a single lamp. I cleaned it all up, dusting and wiping everything off. The overhead light switch was taped over as a reminder not to turn it on. "It's like a spotlight, and I feel guilty with it on," she consistently said, so we had to sit in near darkness on her bed to talk to her.

She clung to her Bibles like a life preserver, swimming in blackness. Even our visits didn't give her much joy. We'd arrive, and she'd use that fake smile for five minutes, then close her door and tell us to do our homework. On good days, she'd ask about Dad, who he was dating, and what the woman was like. Sometimes, when Dad would pick us up, she'd come to the door dressed overtly sexily with full makeup, trying to lure him back.

I promised myself I would never be like her. I'd never do the things she did.

After finishing cleaning, I was hungry and in the kitchen foraging for food to cook dinner when the lock clicked and Mom opened the door.

"Hi, Mom!" I beamed at her from the kitchen doorway.

"Leslie! I forgot you were coming," she said.

My heart sank a little, since I had been dreading the visit. She was wearing her white nurse's uniform with faded red lipstick and white bouncy shoes with big rubbery soles. "I have the worst headache," she mumbled as she disappeared into her bedroom.

The fridge contained a chicken breast, cucumbers, and a jar of black olives. Whipping up a basic dinner, I knocked on Mom's door with a plate. "Come in," she said.

I found her in bed in her pajamas, reading her Bible in a dark room with a glass of amber liquid on her nightstand. "I have dinner here for you. Can't I open the curtains a little?" I said, whisking into the room.

"Please don't. The glare from outside makes my head hurt."

I handed her the plate of food. "Is there any bread?" she asked, taking the plate from me.

"Yes, I can make some toast for you." I left the room.

"No. I just want a piece of bread and butter," she called after me.

I brought her the bread and sat on the edge of her bed. The plate of food sat untouched on her bedspread. She ignored me and continued reading her Bible. After a few more minutes of watching her read, I went to my bedroom. I didn't see her again that evening and left the following day. Why was I even going over there?

Dad had been in a good mood since my return from San Diego, but I still avoided him in all cases. According to Karen and Monica, he'd begun doing his paperwork at the greasy spoon coffee shop down the street called Norm's. He liked a waitress there, which I witnessed firsthand on Saturday morning when we arrived for breakfast.

Sitting in our booth, I watched Dad search the restaurant with his piercing blue eyes, and I could tell he had found her when his face went smooth and calm. She was young, maybe twenty-five, of medium build, with brown hair in a high ponytail and pink ribbon. She stayed away, even though I saw them make eye contact.

Our food came and Dad scarfed down his bacon and eggs in three bites. "I can't get Veronica's attention," he said.

"She's not our waitress," I said, looking at her working the counter.

Karen squinted at me in a warning.

Dad kept staring at her, nodding when Veronica looked near us, but she didn't make eye contact with him again. I took a bite of pancake. "Maybe she's mad at you," I said, trying to joke about it. "What did you do to her?"

He scowled at me, and Monica kicked me under the table. "Ouch," I said, glaring at her.

Dad licked the egg off his fork and visually lined it up with Veronica, swinging it back and forth with a grand gesture, eyeing her and the trajectory of the fork. Then he threw the fork across the restaurant, almost hitting her leg. The fork made a clang as it landed and slid past Veronica's foot. She looked up and squinted at Dad.

People at multiple tables turned to look. "Dad! What are you doing?" I said.

"Shut up," he muttered under tense breath, his eyes never leaving Veronica. She slowly walked to our table, ponytail swinging from side to side. Her round cheeks and button nose were cute. People went back to eating their meals. She stood in front of our table, fierce eyes locked on Dad. I liked her. She wasn't backing down. Yay!

"Yes, can I help you?" Veronica said with angry eyes and a tight mouth.

"Can I have more coffee?" Dad said.

She turned and walked away, saying, "I'll tell your waitress."

I shoved a bit more pancake in my mouth and noticed that Monica and Karen were prepared to exit quickly. I grabbed my purse.

"You girls walk home," Dad said.

We slid out of the booth and headed down 190th Street to our house. "Jesus, what's wrong with him?" I said.

"Stop it, Leslie. Just stop it. You come home and act all cavalier around us, talking to Dad like you're equals or something. Just stop," Monica said as she fast-walked right past me.

"You've been gone a long time. Things have changed." Karen sped up to catch Monica.

"Clearly," I mumbled, walking behind my two sisters. "I'm not afraid of him. Fuck him!" I shouted.

They walked faster.

32

Valentine's Day arrived clear and bright, with a blue sky and calm winds. My sisters and I walked home from school, dragging our feet. None of us were anxious to get there. Monica walked ahead, her long blonde hair swaying back and forth against the pockets of her jeans. "Did you get any valentines today?" I asked Karen.

She looked up at me with her freckled face. "No, but I like a cute guy in my PE class."

"Cool," I said as we headed down the hill to the house.

"Did you?" she asked.

"No. I'm counting the days until I can retake the High School Proficiency Exam and get the hell out of here."

Monica turned around. "You're retaking it again?"

"Yes, and shut up. I have to pass that stupid test."

"I already did pass," she said, gloating.

Entering the driveway to the house, we saw Dad on the porch waiting for us. *He's mad; oh God what did I do?* But he had on a sly smile as we approached the front porch. "Happy Valentine's Day, girls! Can you all sit at the dining room table for a minute?"

Shit! What now? We dropped our backpacks inside the door and headed for the dining room table. Three places were set with blank paper and a pen. He lorded over us with the same sly smile. "Sit down," he said. I couldn't remember seeing this smile before.

He stood at the head of the table. "Okay, you have sixty seconds to write down one thing you want. Go!"

"What? What did he say?" Karen said, searching Monica's and my face. My eyes were wide.

"Are you kidding?" I said.

Our eyes darted back and forth around the table. I shrugged my shoulders. Dad looked at his watch.

"We can write down anything—anything at all?" I said.

He nodded. "You have thirty seconds left."

I stared at the mocking, blank white paper. *Think!*

Karen finished first and flipped her paper over, grinning. While Monica stared at her page, I quickly wrote down my wish and turned my paper over. Monica scribbled something right before Dad said, "Time!"

His smile unnerved me, but his words were unexpectedly kind. "Happy Valentine's Day, girls. Let me see your three wishes. Karen, you go first."

Karen flipped over the paper, proud of herself, and said, "New clothes."

Monica revealed her wish: a bicycle. When Dad looked at me, I smiled knowingly because he had just given me the ticket to start the adventure of my life. I held up my paper, which showed the amount of $200. He reached into his pocket, pulled out a wad of cash, and peeled off ten $20 bills.

Monica and Karen stared wide-eyed at him, then at me.

"No fair," Monica said. "I want cash, too."

"Then you should have written it down," I said, feeling like I had picked the golden door.

"But I didn't think we could write anything," she said, searching the room for a sympathetic face, and then added, "or that he'd give it to us."

I grabbed the wad of twenties and left the room, my body vibrating happily. In my bedroom, I lay face down on my pillow and screamed into it.

With the money I'd saved in San Diego and this $200, I had enough to get the hell away from here.

If I could live through the next three months with Dad, and pass that damn proficiency test, my life would be my own. I could see my freedom. I could almost touch it.

33

The day after Valentine's Day, Dad called me into his office. "Take a seat, please," he said in a voice kinder than I had heard in a long time.

Please? Oh God, what does he want? I sat at my old desk, radar way up. He was only ever nice to me when he needed something.

He sat at his desk across the small room and told me about his new business, A-1 International Marine Recovery. He talked to me like an adult, explaining his latest venture point by point. "I've been hired to recover a fifty-foot sloop missing from Miami."

"Okay, that sounds pretty groovy," I said tentatively. I didn't ask why he was telling me this because I didn't want to piss him off. His fuse was so short that he could take back the money he had just given me the day before. I had no rights. No power. Plus, I didn't hate his guts as much as usual, so I kept my mouth shut.

"I can see the puzzled look on your face. Just listen," he commanded. "The owner financed the boat with the bank, the bank insured the loan, and then he sailed away four months later. Nobody's seen the boat in months, and no payments have been made since the first one."

Dad was playing the role of Bosley, explaining the next job to Charlie's Angels. *Charlie's Angels* was still my favorite weekly show, although Farrah Fawcett was gone. I searched my mind for which character I would be now.

Dad continued, saying that the finance company was looking to recover their money from the insurance company. "I'm working for the insurance company trying to find the boat in the Bahamas."

"How do you do that from here?" I said, channeling Farrah even in her absence from the show. There was no one else I wanted to be.

"It's not easy. I'm making calls, looking at charts, and researching possible ports."

I couldn't stand it any longer, finally blurting out, "Why are you telling me all this?"

"I was wondering if you wanted to help me sail the boat back to Miami once I find her." He said it nonchalantly, and I almost mistakenly assumed he respected or liked me.

"I want to help with the recovery," I ventured.

"No. It's too dangerous. You can cocaptain the boat back to Miami. You're ready to get your captain's license next."

"So officially, I'll be first mate, and everyone will know I'm first mate, and I'll be treated like one?" I needed to insist on the title being public. He was a slippery fish when it came to giving me credit for work done. We'd made three ocean crossings together, and during each one, I was only "acting" first mate, but he would never say it out loud. Whenever male crew came aboard the boat, they automatically ascended to that position just because they were male—even if they didn't know how to sail. It was maddening. I deserved the acknowledgment. And I almost had enough sea time to apply for my captain's license.

He nodded, and a proud smile came over his face. "Official first mate," he repeated.

"You're going to be the other cocaptain?"

His sudden burst of laughter startled me. "That won't work. You and I are too similar. I've hired a guy who trains captains to deliver the boat back to Miami." The doorbell rang, and Dad leaned over to look through the window at the front door. We heard Karen talking to somebody who asked for Dad. He went to the door and all I could think was: *We're too similar? Are you kidding? No way! I am nothing like you.*

He left with the man, giving me time to think. His offer was pretty exciting. *Damn him! Always throwing me a curveball.*

As Monica stirred the spaghetti, garlic wafted through the house. Climbing up onto the couch, I snuggled in the corner, stared out the front window, and watched the cars speed by outside. I needed to think.

Karen climbed up onto the couch with me. "What's Dad up to now?"

I ignored her, but she repeated her annoying question, so I answered. "He has another delivery," I said absent-mindedly.

"I want to go. Why doesn't he ever ask me?" she said.

"I don't know. Ask him yourself." I turned away from her and tried to think of a way to convince him to let me go on the recovery. I wanted to be Farrah Fawcett.

The next day at school, the recovery was all I could think about. After school, I raced home as fast as possible, hoping to catch Dad in a good mood. I peeked into his office. *Yachting World* magazine held his complete attention. "Dad?" I said hesitantly.

"Come on in," he said, waving his hand like he was expecting me.

Sitting in our same spots, we picked up our conversation from the day before. He explained that he wouldn't go to the courts to get the boat back. "It takes too long to go the official route," he said, "because once the guy knows we've found him, he'll just sail off in the middle of the night again."

I nodded my head, following the thought he was laying out for me.

"Instead," he said, "I'm planning to steal the boat back under the noses of the island police and government."

"Wow!" I said. "Really?"

"It's dangerous," he said. "We must take the boat while the entire crew is gone."

"Who will help you sail her away from the island?" I asked, unclenching my jaw, realizing I had been grinding my teeth.

"A newly hired crew that I'll bring to the island," he answered matter-of-factly.

I sat up straight in my chair. "It's not too dangerous, Dad. I can handle it."

"This isn't *Charlie's Angels*."

"No, it'll be Bjorn's Angels," I quipped.

Jesus, I was pandering to him, making myself sick. But now that I had said it, I was too afraid to look at him. I was playing with fire. Did I want him back in my life in this way, working with him toward a common goal, talking daily, strategizing, and planning? I summoned all my strength, looked him in the eye, and in a business voice repeated, "I want to help you recover the boat. Please?"

He shook his head slightly but didn't say anything, then picked up a paper on his desk and began reading it. That was my cue to leave, and I did. *My God, I'm begging!*

On Saturday morning, Dad joined Monica and me around the breakfast table. Karen was at band practice. "I found a boat on the Dutch side of St. Maarten that matches the description of the stolen boat."

"How cool. When will you find out if it's the right boat?"

"Tomorrow. I have somebody down there now taking pictures of it, and once I verify that it's the right boat, I'm headed out."

"Please let me come," I asked meekly, afraid I had asked one too many times and he would yell at me.

"Leslie's going with you to St. Maarten?" Monica said, perking up now.

"Shut up, Monica. We're discussing something important here," I screeched at her.

Dad studied me with seriousness. "How can you help?"

"I don't know. Can't you think of something?"

"No. I can't think of anything. It's going to be too dangerous."

"Dad, please? I want to go. I could get aboard the boat as a cook if they needed it."

He stared off into the distance, thinking. He squinted, considering the idea. "No. It's too dangerous."

"Come on! I can do it. You know I can do it."

Karen arrived home and joined us around the breakfast table, listening intently.

Staring out the window again, Dad was quiet for what felt like an eternity. "Since you're so interested, how about coming today to check out a ski boat that went missing."

"Okay," I said without even thinking. This was Dad's fourth or fifth ski boat recovery.

"Can I come?" Karen said.

Dad shook his head. "Maybe next time."

I ran from the table to the bedroom and put on shorts, a tank top, and running shoes, ready for my first lesson in undercover work. Farrah would be so proud.

34

We left immediately for a neighborhood outside Los Angeles in the valley. Part of me couldn't believe I was working with Dad again—actually collaborating with the enemy.

After driving an hour, we arrived in a newly built neighborhood where the houses all looked the same with sapling trees and tiny green front lawns. Most cars were in garages, making the street look even more barren. For a Saturday, it was tranquil. No kids outside playing, nobody mowing their lawn or gardening. Only one person was in their driveway: a man with a baseball hat, washing his ski boat.

"There it is," Dad said as he pointed to the boat and the man about fifteen houses away.

He parked around the corner because there was no way to blend in or hide on such a barren street, especially with a striking bald man driving an orange Cadillac de Ville. Later we would laugh that Dad looked like a pimp cruising Hollywood Boulevard in the show *Baretta*. If the neighborhood was vanilla, Dad was orange sherbet.

"Just walk down the street and pretend you're looking for your girlfriend and you don't know which house she lives in. When you pass the boat, get the CF numbers and return here."

"That's it? I can do that." I got out of the car.

As I walked down the street toward the ski boat, I saw the man polishing the boat as I approached. He eyed me up and down. I was probably going slower than I should have been. The sun felt like a spotlight on me, making me aware of every muscle jiggle in my body. My heart kicked and pounded in my head, and my feet were lead. The man stared at me suspiciously, or was it just my nerves? Every sense was heightened. I dug deep inside and remembered how often my father had photographed me, watched me do things, or leered at me. I had learned to ignore him and focus elsewhere, denying reality. I swallowed hard, and found the confidence to walk with purpose, smiling at the man. "Hi. I'm looking for Shelly Jones. Do you know which house she lives in?" I said it in as casual a voice as I could manage.

I glanced at the CF numbers on the front of the boat, but too many sensory explosions were happening inside, and my eyes blurred a little as my mind raced. I tried to control my sweaty palms, racing heart, and muscle twitches as I stood before him. He had curly brown hair, big black armor-piercing eyes, and thin lips, which he licked. He studied me suspiciously, scanning the area around us. I hoped he couldn't see the explosion of nerves happening inside me. I casually glanced at the CF numbers again and got "3651." I stood my ground, also glancing up and down the street.

"No, I don't know anybody with that name on this street."

"Okay, thanks." I walked on.

He came out to the sidewalk and watched me walk away. I could feel his eyes on my butt as each cheek moved up and down. *Don't trip*, I thought. Peeking back to look at the CF numbers again, I saw him scowling at me, so I turned around and walked past a few more houses before I crossed the street and headed back toward Dad on the other side. The man kept polishing his boat and studying me. I nodded at him while scanning the numbers one last time. I got the last two letters: "AE." The radio call letters returned to me from my sailing days, so I silently repeated "3651 *Alpha Echo*."

I decided to knock on another door to keep my cover. A woman with a baby on her hip answered and I asked for Shelly. She had kind eyes and looked genuinely disappointed that she didn't know a Shelly. I thanked her and returned to the sidewalk. I peeked down the street at the guy who was still polishing his boat, still watching me.

Returning to the car, I collapsed onto my seat and blurted out, "CF 3651 *Alpha Echo*." My breathing was heavy. You'd have thought I had run a marathon or robbed a bank. Adrenaline coursed through me, and I wiped my wet hands on the car seat.

"Calm down, Leslie," Dad said.

"That guy was menacing. He's suspicious. He knows something's up."

"Okay, let's get out of here." He started the car, and we made our getaway.

"I'll have my guy pick up the boat tonight in the early morning hours. What a stupid guy, not changing the CF numbers," he said.

On the freeway home, I thought of everything I'd do differently. That man had psyched me out, and I got too nervous. I could do better. I *would* do better.

Breaking the silence, I said, "Admit I did a good job."

After the longest pause, he finally relented and said, "You were fine. You got the CF numbers."

"So I can go to Staint Martin and help recover that sailboat?"

He took a deep breath and eyed me with those blue lasers of his. "Yes, but you must follow my instructions to the letter. Understand?"

"Yes, I understand. Thank you! I won't let you down." My heart raced inside my chest, and I was glad I didn't have to hug him.

35

After we landed in Miami, Dad met with the insurance company while I hung out at the hotel pool. The insurance company funded the venture and sent a "bag man" with the cash Dad would need to pay for information about our target, Joe Cohen, and his crew, possibly bribe officials, and pay a crew to be "ready at a moment's notice."

The next day, we flew to St. Maarten. Again I summoned Farrah Fawcett. I just wished like heck I looked more like her.

Just like the plan with the ski boat, Dad would hide out of sight. He didn't want to blow his cover. We worked on my "story" and decided I would tell the truth about my age but lie about where I was from and the fact that I could sail, saying I was a runaway from Minnesota who needed to earn some money and a place to stay.

Another part of my cover would be that I was a runner. After coming in second to last at Outward Bound, I hoped I could pull it off. But the story would account for my leaving the boat each morning to meet Dad and tell him everything I had learned the day before.

The bag man turned out to be a gorgeous hunk of a man named Richard with warm, inviting brown eyes. He arrived with a briefcase full of cash for Dad that he doled out as needed. It was *Charlie's Angels* to the max.

Joe had a fifty-one-foot Morgan named *Princess* docked in the capital city, Philipsburg, in Great Bay Marina on the Dutch side of St. Maarten, near other charter and dive boats. He and his crew were chartering every day with boatloads of tourists. Dad and I settled into a hotel nearby. He gave me two $100 bills, which I put under the pullout sole of my tennis shoes. "You must always wear these shoes," he told me, explaining the money was for getting off the island whenever I needed to.

"I will. I promise," I said, biting my nails, trying not to overthink it.

Next, he gave me two small white pills, which I kept in the bottom of my bathroom bag. "I got these pills in Tijuana. They dissolve instantly in a drink, knocking the person out for six hours." My job would be to put one pill in Joe's drink when the opportunity arose, at some party or dinner.

On the second morning we were there, it was time for me to make contact with Joe and his crew. I walked down the cobblestone streets to the smallish harbor where three docks lined up against the rock jetty at the end of Great Bay Beach. Carrying my backpack and wearing my bikini top, a sarong tied around my waist, and the all-important tennis shoes, I wandered down the first dock and asked several people on sailboats for a position as a cook. Joe's boat, *Princess*, was docked only a few slips from the gate on the second dock. A man sat in the cockpit. He had blond curls visible under his hat and watched me approach different sailboats as I watched him. After receiving a few noes, I approached *Princess*.

"Good morning. I'm looking for a job and a place to stay. Any chance you need a cook?" I said, calmer than I had felt in days. My nerves were still. I felt comfortable on a dock, near a sailboat, and, most importantly, talking with sailors.

"Captain's away but will be back shortly," he said. "We do need a cook, so come back in an hour."

It was almost too easy.

I approached a few more boats, then went to the beach for a few hours, swam, and lay down, using my sarong as a towel. A waiter from a beach hotel took my order of rum and Coke without question. The legal drinking age was eighteen, and I surely looked it at seventeen. It was so nice to be considered an adult, and I hoped Dad wasn't watching me from afar.

In the late afternoon, I returned to *Princess* and met Joe, who was dark-haired and dressed in white linen pants and a blue-and-white tropical shirt. He must have been close to Dad's age and was barefoot with intense smallish blue eyes, similar to Dad's. The rum and Coke helped relax me. I set my backpack on the dock and pulled my hair into a ponytail. "I'm looking for a cook's job and a place to stay," I said as nonchalantly as possible.

"Come aboard, and let's chat," he said, indicating I should sit across from him in the cockpit. "Where are you from, and how did you end up on this island?"

The man I had met earlier was down below at the table in the main salon. He watched me, as did a few other people in the cabin.

"I'm from St. Paul, Minnesota. I've always dreamed of escaping the snow and living on an island."

He nodded and offered me a glass of wine. I accepted and took a sip.

"It's a good time of the year to come to the warmth of the islands," Joe agreed and then asked, "Do you sail?"

"No, but I'm a quick learner."

"It's okay. We have three crew for the sailing," he said, nodding toward the cabin. "Any chance we can get you to cook dinner tonight?"

"If you like what I cook, will you give me the job and a place to sleep?" I asked, feeling bold.

"You've got the job, young lady. I'm just hungry and want dinner."

"Thank you. You won't regret this." I went below to the galley, introduced myself, and said, "Let me look at what you guys have."

The other crew were handsome-faced Allen, a hunk in his late twenties and Joe's first mate, who I'd met earlier, along with an older couple with weathered faces, Seth and Jade, who were deckhands and entertainment for the guests. They seemed to be near Dad's age, too.

I whipped up a simple spinach marinara spaghetti, with lettuce and tomato for a salad. That, with some leftover French bread, had everyone impressed enough that my spot was secured.

Over dinner, the others asked questions about the Minnesota snow and my family. I told them I had two sisters named Julie and Jenny, which were actually my cousins' names. I described the Windsor winter and didn't get too specific. Feeling loose and happy, I asked them as many questions as they asked me.

Allen seemed disaffected by everything, was aloof, quiet, and uninterested in anything, including me, thank God. Seth and Jade were gracious and kind, gushing about the dinner while they told me they were starting their own charter business on another island soon. Joe was quiet except for the gleam of lust in his eyes. He watched me with a wily grin and kept offering me more wine as soon as I took the last sip.

After cleaning up, I moved into my bunk in the forward cabin across from the head. With the first hurdle cleared, satisfaction settled on me—I had gotten aboard as a cook. I closed the curtain on my gently swaying bunk and fell into a light sleep, tipsier than I had ever been.

The unfamiliar surroundings startled me awake a few times in the night. Adrenaline mixed with alcohol prevented any sound sleep. Little did I know, it would be weeks before I'd have a good night's sleep again.

Up early with a pounding head, the last thing I wanted to do was go for a run. Guzzling a large glass of water, I put on my shoes and headed upstairs. The morning was clear and calm. Joe was in the cockpit drinking coffee. "Where are you heading, young lady?"

"For a run. I won't be long. I'll make breakfast when I return."

"We sail today at 11 a.m., and we need to get to the store for supplies."

"Okay, I'll be back in thirty minutes."

It was 7 a.m. I ran up the beach as fast as possible, looking around for Dad. My stomach roiled. A hangover combined with nerves and anxiety left me struggling to breathe. I alternated walking and running until I heard Dad call my name from a beach café. Around the side of the building, I rushed to tell him everything that had happened in the last twelve hours.

"That's such good news." He studied my face, brushing my cheek with the back of his fingers. "Do you feel safe there?" he asked, looking down at my tennis shoes.

"Yes, they're buying my story. It's no problem."

"Excellent. If you ever feel unsafe, leave, go to the airport, take the next plane off the island—no matter where it's going—just get off the island. Okay?"

"Yes, Dad, you already told me that. I have to get back. We have a charter this morning."

Dad's warm smile spread across his face. He winked at me, and I took off running.

I had cleared the next hurdle. Dad and I were working together as Bosley and Jill Munroe did on *Charlie's Angels*, meaning Joe's days were numbered on St. Maarten.

36

Our first charter went off without a hitch. The half-day routine included taking tourists sailing around the island to snorkel and swim. When they came back aboard, I served lunch. Then we sailed back to the harbor—easy peasy.

We did that a few days in a row and gelled as a crew, meshing and laughing as we prepared the boat for the charter, cleaned up when we returned, and I cooked. I hid the constant thrum of nerves that lay just below the surface. They accepted me as a runaway from Minnesota who could cook. Everyone did their job beautifully, and I fit in with these people. I made sandwiches, served drinks, and stayed below deck like someone who knew nothing about sailing.

Seth and Jade sailed the boat and snorkeled with the guests. They were kind and generous, taking me under their wing like a little sister. In the evening, Seth played the guitar, and Jade sang songs.

Foxy Allen wore aviator sunglasses and board shorts, and was usually bare-chested while he steered the boat, anchoring and docking like a pro. He liked sweets, so I made a batch of chocolate chip cookies and got a rare smile when I offered him one.

Joe wore reflective sunglasses and a straw hat, always scanning the horizon like a peregrine falcon. In the evenings after a few drinks, Joe stared at me, licking his lips. He was lustily closing in on me. He rarely left the boat. If he did leave to go to the bank or some other errand, Allen kept watch from the cockpit as if expecting somebody. Joe was suspicious of everything and everyone, including where I went on my run each day. He didn't like me leaving in the morning, but I insisted I needed the exercise and he never tried to stop me.

My nerves were raw, and my stomach was a chaos of fireworks. I could barely eat and only wanted more alcohol or cigarettes. The trick was to look busy and relaxed but not too relaxed. To be alert, but not too alert. If I relaxed too much with the alcohol, I might do something to blow my cover, like reaching to coil a line or adjust a sheet to stop a luffing sail. I had to be on guard. I was undercover. It was draining. A reprieve didn't even come with the light sleep I got.

I ran to see Dad every morning to report the day's activities. He had taken up residence at a local beach motel but was at different cafés on the beach every morning. I never knew when I'd hear "Leslie!"

I always felt rushed and nervous about getting caught, so I'd talk a mile a minute while Dad studied me with a worried look on his face. The lines around his eyes and the creases in his forehead seemed to be getting deeper. No matter how much mundane information I gave him, he drank it in like a desert survivor. "Tell me everything so I can get a sense of the dynamics on the boat." My biggest intuitive hit was that Joe was hiding something. It was no big surprise. I came back to this theme again and again in sharing the day's events with Dad.

"Can you ask Jade about it without setting off any alarms?"

"Maybe," I said nervously. "We shower at the same time sometimes, and she goes with me to the grocery store. I'll try to bring it up."

"Be careful. Always be careful," he reiterated for the hundredth time.

"I know, Dad. I am careful."

Being undercover wasn't as fun as it looked on TV.

* *

That evening, after my shower, I ran into Jade in the bathroom. After some small talk about the day's charter, I asked, "Why do you think Joe and Allen watch everybody so closely?"

"I don't know. We've only been aboard a month or so. Seth and I wondered if maybe he has lots of cash aboard, or maybe some diamonds."

The following day I found Dad at the same breakfast café. I told him what Jade had told me.

"Okay, good job. That's valuable information. I've found two local guys to help us when the time comes," Dad said. "Keep your ears open." He handed me a slip of paper. "This is the hotel we will meet at on St. Thomas. Put it in your shoe with the money."

"Okay." I tucked it underneath my sole before I headed back toward the docks.

Later that day we took five guests out: a mother and her two daughters and an older German couple. On the way out of the harbor, Joe yelled, "Get that damn sail up, Seth!"

I was up on deck, helping the guests with cushions and offering drinks. Jade gave me a wary side glance that said, *Buckle in. Joe's on edge again.*

Without wind, we motor-sailed for an hour. The German couple made themselves at home on the bow, staring over the edge at the water lapping against the hull. The mother and her daughters sunned themselves near the cockpit. We anchored in pristine waters near a coral reef. Just as the guests were coming back aboard after snorkeling, a black Dory boat, maybe twenty-five feet long, approached us at high speed, cut the engine, and floated to within thirty feet. There were scuba tanks visible, but no people. We faintly heard someone yelling, "Help," from inside the cabin of the dive boat.

Joe opened a cockpit locker and pulled out a shotgun. He pointed it at the boat. "Take everyone below!" he yelled.

I went into autopilot mode—ushering everyone below with great efficiency and steady nerves.

"This is crazy," Jade whispered, eyeing me with panic. I nodded.

Joe yelled to the boat, "Come out now!"

A tanned, scruffy-haired man came out from the Dory boat, eyes frantic, hands in the air. "My wife is sick," he said. "We need help."

Joe didn't answer.

Jade came forward with me to look out the porthole and whispered, "Allen just got another gun out." Our gazes held for a minute.

"Please help!" the man said again, disappearing into the cabin.

Another younger man wearing a mesh tank top came out with his hands up. "Whoa, whoa, whoa! What's up with the guns?"

The Dory boat had floated to the other side of our ship now, so we raced back to the main cabin to get a better look.

"Who are you?" Joe demanded.

"I'm the captain. Who the hell are you?"

Joe didn't answer. The captain continued, "I lost my engine. A customer just had a heart attack. I've called for help, but nobody's answering on the radio."

Joe and Allen didn't put their guns down. "We'll call the harbor patrol for you," Joe said. Allen went to the helm, turned on the radio, and reported the medical emergency. The harbor boat answered immediately, saying they were on their way.

"Man, what's wrong with you? We need help, not guns," the dive boat captain said.

Joe finally lowered his weapon. "Seth, go and help them."

"I don't have any medical training," Seth said.

After a moment of whispered talking between Joe and Seth, we heard the splash when Allen dove in, then watched as he swam to the boat, hoisted himself onto the dive platform, then disappeared below deck.

The German mother asked, "Has this ever happened before?"

Jade and I both shook our heads.

Jade said to all of them, "Don't worry. Everything will be fine."

I hoped she was right.

I made rum and Cokes and poured wine. Jade and I didn't hesitate to partake.

I peeked my head out of the cabin hatch to check on things. It had been twenty minutes since Allen had called for help and swum over to the dive boat. Joe was oblivious to our guests, who were fixing a death glare at him on the dive boat. Finally, they carried a woman out of the cabin and laid her on the boat deck. The captain performed CPR on her.

Seth stood on the bow of our boat, scanning the horizon with binoculars. "There's the harbor boat."

Joe returned the gun to the locker just as the harbor patrol arrived at the Dory boat. The rescue commenced, and Allen swam back. The rescue boat left with the patient, saying they would send a tow boat for the Dory.

Our afternoon was over, so we raised the anchor and began motoring back to the harbor.

"Come on up, folks. The excitement is over. I'm sorry about that," Joe said, leaning through the companionway, trying to act normal about the whole affair.

Our guests went topside one by one, looking around, grateful for the fresh air. "What was that?" the German man said, scanning the area.

"Just a misunderstanding, that's all. I'm sorry for the scare. Everything is fine now," Joe said, standing behind Allen at the helm. One of the daughters, wearing a purple sarong, looked ready to heave over the side. Her sister, in a matching pink sarong, seemed fine.

After everyone had taken a seat, Joe explained about pirates in the sea around us, trying to convince them they were safe now. But when we arrived back at the dock, everyone left quickly without a thank you or a smile.

Seth and Jade put away the snorkel equipment and cleaned the boat as Joe and Allen whispered together on the dock. Below, cleaning the galley, I watched the men through the porthole. Nobody had eaten the food, so I wrapped it up and put it in the refrigerator.

After Seth and Jade were done with their chores, I offered up a round of drinks.

"Yes, drinks for everyone," Joe said. "What a day, right?"

Seth, Jade, and I took our drinks down below in the cabin while Joe had his in the cockpit, taking up his habit of scanning the horizon. Allen left the boat for a few hours, going who knew where.

My nerves were wrecked. I wanted to go find Dad, but there was no way to make excuses under such scrutiny and paranoia. So I drank and smoked instead.

"Can I have another?" Joe called to me down below in the cabin.

"Coming now," I said, and brought him another rum, looking for an opportunity to say something without having him explode at me. He was relaxing, evidenced by his slight smile when I handed him the drink. "Hey, Joe," I managed, "I'm not sure what happened today, but it scared me a lot. I didn't realize sailboats had guns aboard, or is it just this boat?"

Seth and Jade gathered around me at the entryway hatch. Jade touched my leg. "Hey, Leslie, let us up," she said.

I moved aside, and they climbed out of the cabin, sitting in the cockpit close together. "We're with Leslie. It was too much today. Guns are too much."

"Hey, guys, I'm sorry about today. I freaked out a little. I'm sorry," Joe said. "It won't happen again."

"The guns go, or we go," Seth said, grabbing Jade's hand.

I felt the same way. I knew Dad wouldn't want me to stay after finding out what had happened.

"I'll get rid of them tomorrow. I'm sorry about what happened today. Please don't quit. We have charters booked for the next week." He tried to act like it was nothing, but it was a big deal, and I was glad Seth and Jade felt the same way.

37

I ran down the beach to meet Dad the next morning. I decided I'd tell him about the Dory and the medical emergency, but not the guns, knowing he wouldn't let me keep staying with the crew.

The bag man, Richard, was with Dad at the hotel when I arrived. He was beautiful and dressed like a local. Tiny sparks flew between us when our eyes met. His black hair and smoldering dark eyes were not his best quality. It was the ripples of muscles struggling to get out of his long board shorts and T-shirt.

"We need to get everybody off the boat," Dad said. "How can we do that?"

"I don't know. Allen and Joe only leave one at a time."

"Keep your ears open. It's been eight days now. We need to take the boat soon."

That day, we took seven people out on a charter. Joe was semi-normal again, nervous and worried, but that was typical. Everything went smoothly, and once we were back at the dock, Joe left while Allen kept watch. He called us together in the cockpit and said that it was Joe's birthday on Saturday and that he wanted to do something special for him.

"I can bake him a cake," I offered.

"How about a dinner out?" Seth suggested. "Joe needs a night out."

I was happy it was Seth's suggestion and not mine, and I looked on hopefully.

"He won't leave the boat in the evening for any reason," Allen said.

"Why?" Jade asked, her eyebrows raised as she studied Allen.

But Allen never spoke much, and he never explained Joe. "He just won't leave."

"Maybe if I invite him to dinner, would that help?" I offered.

"I doubt it," Allen said.

But that night, after Joe returned to the boat, I poured us each a glass of wine and sat with him in the cockpit as he watched the world. "Today went well," I ventured. The sun had set, and the evening sky glowed in oranges and reds. Seth and Jade had gone to town. Allen was in his bunk.

"Yes, thank goodness it was a normal day." The hint of a smile peeked from under his stern and serious composure. Joe's eyes were piercing without his sunglasses, and I didn't like looking into them, afraid he would see the truth of my mission, my undercover job. I got right to the subject—no need to waste time or draw it out. I wanted to go to my bunk and lie down. "Allen says it's your birthday on Saturday. Can we go to dinner to celebrate?"

"Just you and me?" His eyebrows waggled, and a grin filled up his face.

"Is that what you want? I was thinking it would be fun if the whole crew went."

"I can't leave the boat unattended." He sounded almost ashamed to admit this.

"Why?"

He shook his head slightly and stared off into the distance. "I just don't like to leave her unattended."

"Even for a little bit?" I tried to flirt with him a bit, to see how it landed. "How about we all have one drink at the bar and toast you? Then you and I go to dinner, and the crew can return to the boat?"

"Hmm, it's an interesting proposition."

I went to my bunk to read but couldn't concentrate. I tried to sleep but tossed and turned all night. If only Joe would agree, we could finish this charade, and I could get off this boat. First, though, we needed to get through one more charter.

The next morning, I told Dad and Richard that Joe was considering drinks off the boat for his birthday Saturday night. "He's acting semi-normal again after that lady's heart attack. The charter yesterday was uneventful."

Dad studied me hard, looking for something in my face, maybe fear or doubt, but I hid it well. "Okay," he said. "Are you ready with a plan?"

"Yes, I'm ready," I said.

The charter went off without a hitch. When the cleaning had been completed, Joe called everyone on deck. "Let's get a drink at the bar tonight. I want to thank you all for such good work these last few weeks."

Tonight? I'd told Dad Saturday, which was tomorrow. Panic rose.

"I need a quick shower," Jade said, and I seconded that, wondering if I would be dining with Joe afterward. We gulped rum and Cokes while gathering our things, then headed to the shower. I wore a new long, spaghetti-strapped, clingy dress that showed off my tan and long blonde hair. The swirling orange color matched the sky in the evening. My white tennis shoes looked funny with the dress, and two long slits on either side seemed to accentuate them, but what could I do?

Dad and I had reviewed the plan multiple times, and I had reviewed it a thousand more. Would he be ready a day early, and could I slip that darn pill into Joe's drink?

How did Farrah do it? The ball in my stomach was so large I almost gasped for air. I couldn't fail now. I needed to finish this job.

At 5 p.m., Joe called out, "Is everyone ready?"

I packed the pills and my passport in my purse and left my backpack on the boat, abandoning everything I owned. I hoped Dad was watching from the shadows.

We closed the boat up, putting the hatches in the companionway and locking it. We walked together toward the restaurant. Seth and Jade were in a particularly happy mood. They had made an offer on a boat and would find out if it had been accepted on Monday. Allen was stone-faced as usual, and Joe watched everyone we passed as if they were thieves. I caught his eye while we walked. He flashed me a smile, and I wondered if he thought this would be his lucky night with me.

After ten minutes, we heard the calypso music coming from the crowded restaurant. We all huddled at the end of the bar and ordered drinks. I swayed to the music, forcing myself to relax and look like I was enjoying myself. My insides were hamburger meat. My stomach flipped and flopped so often that I thought I might pass out. I had no idea how to slip the pill into Joe's drink without being caught.

The crew said goodbye after one drink, Jade wiggling her eyebrows at me as they left. I hoped Dad had worked fast. I would need to work fast as well. Joe took the last swig of his rum and Coke and we were shown to our table.

"I didn't know if we were having dinner or not," I said.

"I'm starving, let's eat." He ordered another drink, and I ordered white wine. An awkward silence surrounded us. *What should I talk about?* The waiter handed us menus. I hid behind the menu for a few minutes, talking myself down. *You can do this. Pick something to eat, enjoy the music, and wait for him to speak.*

Time ticked by with a *thump, thump, thump* in my head. We ordered dinner and thank the good Lord above, Joe excused himself to the bathroom. *Please let me put this pill in his drink without anybody noticing. Please . . .*

I scanned the restaurant for anybody watching me; my mind flitted, and my hands shook. I reached into the small side pocket of my purse, took one of the pills out, carefully waved my shaking hand over his drink, and dropped the pill in as discreetly as I could manage while my ears roared from the panic that threatened to consume me. The music was a distant drumbeat, and I turned to look at the bathroom. There he was, smiling devilishly at me, walking toward me in his white linen pants and tropical shirt. His brown boat shoes looked newly polished. So far, nobody had said anything about my dorky white tennis shoes.

He sat down and took a big gulp of his drink. "What are your dreams, Leslie? What do you want to do with your life?" he said.

"I don't know. I love sailing, and I'd like to do more of that." I sipped my white wine, hoping the glass didn't slip out of my sweaty hands. "When did you start sailing?" I asked him, thinking, *I need to go.*

He took another big gulp of his drink and then steadied his eyes on me. "When I was a young man. My parents owned a powerboat, but I wanted a sailboat. When I was sixteen, they got me a Cal 25. I sailed through the Keys and Miami."

This was the most he'd ever talked about himself. But I needed to get out of there. "Fascinating," I said, grabbing my purse from the back of the chair. "Hold that thought. I'll be right back." I left through the back door, lifting my dress up to my knees and running to the tourist-populated Front Street. I could have flown on nerves alone. I hailed a cab and got in, and only then allowed myself to look back. Nobody was chasing me. I was alone and on my way to the airport. I hoped Joe just imagined I was taking a long time in the bathroom. Hopefully he'd be getting sleepy. Or maybe the crew had returned to the restaurant to tell him the boat was gone. Either way, I was out of there and so happy. It was almost over.

Twenty minutes later, I was at the small outdoor island airport.

It was hot and humid at 6:30 p.m. The flight board showed the next flight was to St. Thomas, the island I needed to get to. Lucky me. It left in thirty minutes. I shook and felt the ball of nerves in my clenching stomach.

After purchasing a one-way ticket to St. Thomas for $39 with the money in my tennis shoe, I waited in the corner of the airport, trying to calm down. Time crawled. I watched the small interisland plane on the tarmac come to life with mechanics and luggage handlers. Soon, I would be aboard, and the door would be closed, and I could lay my head back on the seat and close my eyes. Soon, I would be safe.

We boarded and when the plane's door finally closed, the sound was solid and secure. I sat in a window seat, looking out, half expecting to see Joe running toward me, waving his hands, screaming and calling me names.

The plane took off, and I laid my head back and closed my eyes. I was safe. I hoped never to see Joe Cohen again in my life. When we landed in St. Thomas forty-five minutes later, my head was pounding like those steel drums at the bar. I needed food and water and possibly a few aspirins. The taxi took me to the harbor hotel Dad had written on that piece of paper. The drive seemed to take forever, although maybe it was just half an hour. Exhaustion overcame me and I fought to keep alert, checking into the hotel without luggage. I ordered some bread and butter from room service, ate like a starving person, and fell into bed exhausted.

38

The next morning, I woke up famished with stomach cramps. I dressed, found a breakfast place, and ate until I was almost sick. The bathroom scale said I had lost seven pounds, but more importantly, I had quit shaking. My nerves were calming, and I could feel myself coming down from the stress. Outside by the pool overlooking the harbor, I searched the horizon for *Princess*. I knew it would be noon at the earliest before I saw them—if Dad managed to get the boat, that was.

I headed back to the hotel and fell asleep. A knock on my door late in the afternoon woke me. It was Dad in a floppy brown suede hat, holding his leather man-purse with a huge smile. I nearly jumped into his arms but instead wrapped my arms around him and laid my head on his chest. "Did you do it? Is the boat here, and everybody is safe?"

Dad wrapped his arms around me. "Yes, yes, everything went great." He sat down at the table.

"Where's Joe?" I asked.

"I have no idea. I never saw him."

"So you were ready a day early? I was so worried."

"Yes, we were ready." He checked his watch. "The guys are all starving. Meet us down at the restaurant when you can." He got up and, at the door, turned around. "You did a great job, Leslie. I know it was hard, but you did it! I'm proud of you."

I blushed, unaccustomed to receiving praise from this man I hated most of the time. "Thanks," I said, busying myself with straightening out the orange-swirl beach dress I had worn the previous night, glad I had picked up a pair of flip-flops in the hotel store. The dress would have to do double duty tonight.

Thirty minutes later, I arrived at the hotel restaurant—a group of tables on the edge of the sand. The afternoon was sliding into evening fast. Dad, the bag man Richard, and two other men I didn't recognize were already seated at the table. "Meet Kingston and Jayden," Dad said, standing up. "My crew on *Princess*."

I nodded to Kingston, who was very dark-skinned with bright eyes and a blinding yellow linen shirt, and Jayden, who was lighter-skinned and several years younger. I nodded to Richard, who eyed me up and down. The electrical charges again flew between us. The warm, humid night air fairly hummed with energy.

"Tell me what happened," I said, ordering a Coke and picking at the oysters and bread on the table, missing the rum.

"We watched you all walk away from the boat and were motoring out the bay within ten minutes," Dad boasted as he eyed Kingston and Jayden.

Richard said, "I am no sailor. I went below and waited for instruction from your dad."

"How'd you get into the boat and start the motor?" I asked.

Kingston said, "We had a bolt cutter and a duplicate engine key. It was a thing of beauty, I'm telling you." Jayden patted Kingston on the back in pride.

I shook my head in astonishment. "It was that easy?"

They all nodded.

Dad's eyes sparkled, and his face glowed like he'd had too many drinks. Or was that too much sun? He scanned me up and down, admiring my dress with his eyes. "Where'd you get that?" he said.

"Back on St. Maarten a few days ago."

He grabbed my hand. "Dance with me."

I reluctantly followed him to the dance floor. The song was "Feelings" by Barry Manilow, one of his favorites. I hated that song. I hated the way Dad sang it. He put his arm around my waist and pulled me close. "We did a good job, but it was too dangerous." He smelled like soap. His breath smelled like rum. His sky-blue eyes admired me and were soft and kind. I tried to avoid physical contact with him except for his arms around my torso and lower back as he guided me around the dance floor, but it was impossible to avoid touching him. He creeped me out.

"It was kind of crazy," I said. My skin crawled as we moved around the dance floor, me catching Richard's eye and wishing I were dancing with him.

"We make a good team, you and me. We deliver boats together, and now we've recovered a stolen boat," he said.

"Yes, we do." *Can I really be saying this?*

"I have to confess," Dad said, pulling away from me so he could see my face. "Motoring out of the harbor knowing you were still at the restaurant with Joe was one of the hardest things I've ever done."

Ahhh, he did care. As we resumed our dance positions, I told him the highlights of what had happened to Joe and the rest of us at the restaurant and how nervous I had been, especially when I put that pill in Joe's drink, left, and got in a taxi. I added, "*Charlie's Angels* isn't as fun as it looks."

"You mean Bjorn's Angel, right?" He chuckled.

I smirked and nodded, giving him the win. "I don't think I'm cut out for this work."

"Really?"

"I don't know. Maybe I'll feel differently later, but now I don't want to do another one."

"You won't be delivering *Princess*. You'll fly home."

I pulled back and looked at him. "Why?"

"I'll be sailing her to Miami with Kingston and Jayden. I want you home safe and sound."

"Okay." He pulled me close near the song's end, and I felt his hard penis rub against my stomach. I pushed back against him and broke the grip he had on me. "Dad!" I said, and looked down at his pants.

He threw his head back and boomed a laugh as I walked from him. *What a creep! Nothing has changed.*

I sat next to Richard and attempted small talk, trying to erase what just happened. Kingston and Jayden each had found someone and were out on the dance floor. Richard's penetrating eyes drew me in, and I went willingly. I sipped on my Coke but then took Richard's rum and Coke and guzzled it while Dad was still gone from the table. A warm, sweet feeling arose in my body as the alcohol spread out and made me relax. I danced with Richard and found myself filled with a new kind of anxiety—a thumping in my chest and fog in my brain. Richard was gorgeous with his dark eyes, beautiful white teeth, and alluring mouth. I didn't know I could feel that way about somebody I didn't even know. I guzzled another rum and Coke sitting on the table and felt the attraction solidify. I just wanted to be alone with him. His eyes said he felt the same way, but Dad wasn't having any part of Richard and me cozying up together, and at 11 p.m. he sent me back to the hotel room.

I flew home the next day.

39

I returned to school with a note that said I had been ill, as if nothing drastic had changed, except everything had changed. I'd met Richard, the most beautiful man in the world, and couldn't wait to see him again. The only obstacle was that he lived in Miami and I lived in Los Angeles.

My oceanography and photography classes were the only things that brought me happiness. I quickly caught up on the missed assignments. But losing ten days in my shorthand class made me want to pull my hair out. The squiggly lines weren't making sense anymore, and the teacher seemed to be dictating faster than my mind could comprehend.

An algebra test was scheduled for the following week, and I had two chapters of homework to finish before then. Math was just not my forte. It seemed to take double effort to learn it. I studied at lunch and after school, but nothing stayed in my mind. The information went in, then evaporated like water in the hot sun. I didn't know what was wrong with me. My thoughts drifted off to St. Maarten and Richard and running away to Simon, who I hadn't seen in nearly two years. Maybe the adrenaline from St. Maarten had changed my brain chemistry.

If all that wasn't enough, the date to take the High School Proficiency Test for the third time was only weeks away.

* *

Back at the house, the front door slammed, and a few seconds later Monica arrived at our bedroom doorway. I was reading a chapter in my oceanography book.

"Who do you know in Miami?" she said, waving the letter around.

"Never mind. Give it." I stood up and tried to grab it, but she hid it behind her back. "Ugh, you make me so mad!"

She laughed. "Why is it addressed to Leslie H. Johansen? What does the H mean?"

"Monica, give it!" She threw it at me, and it floated down and landed on the floor. "Get out!" I yelled, bending over to pick it up.

It was a business-size white envelope with no name in the return address, just a Miami address. I closed the bedroom door and tore it open, flipping the page to see it was signed "Love, Dick."

In the letter, Richard recapped our last evening together dancing to the Caribbean band in St. Thomas, reminding me of the dress I had worn and of having the "H's." He wrote he hoped we could take care of it soon.

I smiled, remembering us swaying together, his hand on the small of my back pulling me close, whispering in my ear "I've got the H's real bad." At the time, I didn't know what he meant, but now, reading the letter, I knew that "H" meant horny.

I reread the letter. He asked me to think of him and to visit so he could take care of the H's "on location." He closed the letter by asking for an 8 × 10 picture of me. Under his name was his phone number. I ran to the gas station down the street, clutching the letter, and called him.

The phone rang twice. "Speakeasy," he said in a velvety voice. R & B music played in the background.

"Richard?" I said hesitantly.

"Leslie?"

"I just got your letter." I put it down on the ledge in the phone booth, staring at the loopy lettering on the envelope.

"When can you come back to Miami?"

"I have no idea." I twirled and untwirled my hair on my index finger, hoping to think of something to say. My heart beat fast.

"You always have a place to stay if you ever return this way."

I blushed, remembering our bodies together on the dance floor. "Okay. Thanks. What are you doing?"

"Dancing to Boz Skaggs and thinking about you. I'm so happy you called."

"I'm glad we met." *Stupid. Why did I say that?*

"I've never felt such a magnetic pull to anyone before. It means something," he said.

My heart leaped. At least we both agreed there was enormous energy between us. "Really? I felt it, too."

I could hear him taking a drag of something. The song ended, there was silence, and another song started. My mind was blank. *Say something!*

"Hey, listen, keep me posted on your travel plans," he said.

"Why do you answer the phone 'speakeasy'?"

He laughed. "Why not?"

I nervously laughed but didn't understand. Why was everything in code with Richard? "Bye. I'll call you soon." I felt awkward and uncomfortable.

"I look forward to it. Until then, please send me a picture."

"Okay, I'll try." We hung up. I breathed deeply and wondered what was happening to me and who Boz Skaggs was.

That evening, Dad finally came home and was prickly when he walked in the door.

"How did the delivery go?" I asked at breakfast the following day.

"Fine." He was curt and distracted with some paperwork.

"I'm going to the library today."

He nodded distractedly, and I left.

Instead of going to the library, I called Jason from the pay phone.

"Let's go have fun today," I said. He was always ready for an adventure and we took off to Hollywood. We drove up Santa Monica Boulevard and back on Sunset Boulevard while I dreamed of seeing the bands and dancing at The Troubadour and the Whiskey a Go Go. Both places were shut tight during the day. At night, though, they came alive. The magazines showed pictures of people wrapped around the corner waiting to get in, women dressed in fringe miniskirts, headbands, and knee-high boots.

We spent an hour in Tower Records thumbing through albums. I found Boz Skaggs's album *Silk Degrees* and was shocked to see he was white. His music didn't sound white. I didn't say anything to Jason, feeling uncomfortable and not knowing if it would hurt his feelings that I was thinking of another man. We stopped at Bob's Big Boy for lunch before he dropped me back off at home a little before 5 p.m.

"Where have you been?" Dad asked as soon as I entered the house.

"The library, studying for my algebra test," I said, heading down the hall to my bedroom.

"Stop!" he yelled after me. "You were not at the library. Why are you lying to me?"

In a forceful voice, I said, "I was too at the library."

He came close, peering at me with those squinty blue eyes. "You were not at the library, because I had you followed."

"What?" I whispered.

"You got into a silver 240Z with a man and drove off."

I tried to recover the guilt on my face so he wouldn't have the satisfaction of winning. "You're wrong. I was at the library."

"Who was that man?"

The hint of a smile spread on my face at having the upper hand. The spikey fear evaporated, and for an instant, I felt powerful. "A friend. I'm seventeen now."

He turned and left abruptly. A sick feeling flamed up inside. Was he really having me followed?

40

On Monday, I took the dreaded algebra test, and when we graded each other's papers, I failed miserably, only getting two questions right. Once Dad found out, he would berate me endlessly, calling me names and humiliating me. I raged against his negative voice and wished I dared to yell "Shut up." A smaller voice also lived inside my head. It was much quieter than Dad's voice. It believed in me, defended me, and stubbornly refused to accept his opinion of my stupidity. But still, how would I ever pass the High School Proficiency Test and start my real life if I couldn't even pass a simple algebra test?

It was my day to be at Mom's. I dragged my feet from school the mile toward her apartment, heading down Prospect Avenue right past South Bay Hospital, where she would be getting off work soon. I bought a Coke at the gas station store and daydreamed about being an actor, going to Mexico to live on the beach—anything to help me escape my reality. Sailboats were visible in King Harbor, and I could almost rally some happiness at the thought of summer and freedom, but my failure overshadowed everything. I turned onto First Place, a steep street zigzagging toward the beach with million-dollar views. Fire trucks were parked in front of Mom's house. Black smoke poured out while firefighters unloaded their equipment and hooked up the hoses. A woman stood between the fire trucks. It was Mom—and she was fully naked!

I dropped my backpack and ran to her. "Mom!" I yelled, but she didn't hear me and began walking down the hill. Something dark dripped from her contorted hand. I rushed toward her yelling, "Mom! Mom!" She turned around but looked right through me. She didn't see me. She was gone, vacant. Her body was there, but her soul—or something—was gone. In a trance, she turned and continued to walk down the middle of the street. I saw now that her hand was dripping blood.

I ran after her. A car came around the corner and skidded to a stop. "Watch out!" I shouted. Robot-like, Mom turned and walked around the vehicle. The woman driving stared at us open-mouthed. I ran past her, continuing to yell, "Mom!" Rounding the corner, Mom stopped and stared in the direction of the ocean. Only a few feet behind her, I was afraid to see her vacant eyes. She cupped her bleeding hand with her other hand and held it in front of her. I reached for her arm.

"Mom! Where are you going?"

She turned to me, and something seemed to click. A presence that hadn't been in her eyes before suddenly came back with solid spirit and life, and she almost looked like herself. After her eyes focused, her body straightened, but her mouth was tight and drawn together in a pucker. I took in her small breasts and curvy hips, her black pubic hair, her shapely legs and bare feet. I looked around wishing I could cover her up. We were alone. The commotion was around the corner and up the hill. I felt embarrassed and ashamed our family's sickness was on full display.

"Lezlie," she said dreamily, "it got so hot in my room that I took off my clothes. I needed some air."

"Mom, the apartment is burning." I touched her arm, trying to lead her back to the house, but she yanked away and winced from the pain.

"God told me to light the fire. He said I should burn in hell."

"Mom!"

"He stood right before my window, outlined by the dark curtain, glowing in all his glory as he talked to me."

"Mom, what happened to your hand?"

"I punched out the window," she answered, looking like she was reliving the experience. "I'm not going back there. Evil lives in that apartment."

An ambulance pulled slowly up behind us, its lights flashing silently. Two men dressed in white got out. I didn't know what to say to them, but they knew exactly what to do. The mustached tall, thin paramedic with warm brown eyes and a kind smile approached Mom and, without gawking or staring at her nakedness, said, "It's time to go now."

"Where are we going?" Her voice was almost happy.

"For a ride. We need to get you some clothes and wrap up your hand. It's bleeding."

She gazed at her hand as if for the first time and then noticed the ambulance. She glared at me with a nasty face, all screwed up and distorted. "It's you. You and your father are the same. You tricked me."

Both paramedics held her arms, moving her toward the ambulance. Struggling against them, she twisted and bucked. "Oh no you don't. I'm not going in that thing. I'm not going back there."

"Mom! You need help." I was close to tears.

She stared at me with hatred, followed by an expression of fear. Then she pleaded, "No! I can't go back there."

The two paramedics held her arms. The second one was muscled like a bodybuilder, his shirt straining at the bulges. Mom writhed like a caged animal, yelling profanities. The men carried her to the ambulance, where they held her down and put a white jacket on her that tied in the back, restraining her arms. She whimpered and moaned, finally going limp and giving in. The muscled one wrapped her hand quickly in some gauze. They draped a hospital gown to cover her lower half and closed the door.

"Where are you taking her?"

"Probably Norwalk State Hospital, but you can call South Bay Hospital in a while and ask them."

South Bay Hospital? Where she works? Oh no!

The ambulance left with its lights going, but no sirens.

I ran toward the apartment to find the entire house engulfed in flames. Two fire trucks blocked the street, and the firefighters sprayed water from three angles. My backpack had been thrown across the road to the other side. I stood by it and watched the house burn. The sidewalk was crowded with neighbors talking and staring.

Damn my entire life.

A woman standing near me on the sidewalk, watching the flames, said, "Did you live there?"

I nodded and instantly knew what I should do. "Can I use your phone to call my dad?"

"Of course, darling, follow me."

Her clean and well-kept house smelled like chicken pot pie. Her big bay window, surrounded by sculpted Victorian curtains, framed the mayhem outside. I gazed through the window at the fire and the men working to put it out. I felt disconnected from myself and a trance-like stupor came over me as the adrenaline drained out of me. I needed to sit down.

"Here's the phone, dear." She stood by a desk.

I sat down and called Dad, telling him what had happened.

"I'm on my way to get you," he said, laughing uncontrollably.

41

The events of the following weeks were like shifting sand under my feet. I couldn't find my balance. Monica called Mom's work and found out they had taken her to Norwalk State Hospital. I called Norwalk and was told she was in confinement. They added, "You can see her in a week."

Dad kept saying, "She's where she belongs. Let it ride its course. She'll be out when she's better."

I shut down inside, replaying the incident until I was numb. My ears rang at times for no reason, and it felt like I would never smile again. Dad had no sympathy or compassion for Mom or me. It made me wish for his death regularly.

We had no other family around us, there was nobody to talk to, and Dad was unwilling to help us find out any information about Mom.

I returned to school the day after Mom was taken away, because Dad refused to let me have a day to recover. I didn't say anything about the failing grade on my math test, deciding to wait until the end of the school year for his wrath. Who knew, maybe I could leave before then? The proficiency test loomed large over me. If Dad knew I had failed that math test, he probably wouldn't let me take it. Nothing was going to stop me from trying to get away from him.

The numbness stayed for weeks. I studied the entire weekend

before the big test, trying not to think about Mom being tied to some bed in an institution. I took the test for a third time and hoped for the best.

Monica, Karen, and I talked, plotted, and schemed every day, trying to figure out a way to see Mom. It had been three weeks since the incident. We decided to ask Dad for a ride to Norwalk. I broke the ice during dinner one night; he didn't answer immediately but instead stayed quiet, studying us as he shoveled mashed potatoes into his mouth.

"Please, Dad, she needs us," Karen said.

"Girls, there's no reason to see her. When she's better, they'll release her. That's how this works. It's been like this since you were all toddlers."

Monica begged, "Please, Dad. She's the only mom we have."

"She needs us," Karen said.

"She needs a doctor and lots of medication." Dad laughed as he always did when he spoke about Mom's struggles, and it made me want to kill him.

"Shut up, Dad! We want to see our mom!" I yelled and took my full plate of food to the kitchen. When I turned around, the maniacal smile had disappeared from his face. I looked away quickly to avoid his eyes.

In a much lower and sweeter voice, Monica said, "Please take us. We won't ask you anything else for a long time."

"I know how that works. You girls always ask for more."

"Please, Dad," I whined, my voice softer now.

He finally relented and agreed to drive us the twenty-five miles to Norwalk on Saturday.

Midmorning, we filed into the car and drove in silence. Monica sat in front with Dad, twirling her hair and staring out the window. Karen and I kept eyeing each other in the back seat. I was anxious about what we would find.

My heart broke for Mom, and I regretted not helping her more when we were in Windsor. I could imagine her being consumed by the blackness and wondered if the doctors were helping. I had visions of her being tied down and her screwed-up face screaming for her freedom. Dad slowly entered the parking lot of Norwalk State Hospital.

"This doesn't look like the Hotel Dieu," Monica said.

The building looked like a prison, with barbed wire on top of the chain-link fence. Patients in matching brown pantsuits sat at picnic tables strewn around the grounds. A few big trees provided shade. The green grass was an insult, falsely promising happy times. We scanned the area for Mom, hoping to find her outside in the fresh air. Dad found a parking spot three rows back from the chain-link fence.

"There she is!" Karen said. "She's sitting at that table by herself. See her?"

Monica and I strained to see her as Dad turned off the engine and rolled down all four windows. Yes, there she was. She was staring into the distance. Her black hair was straight and lifeless. She wore a brown two-piece uniform. Her smooth and elegant face, with its usual red lipstick, was naked.

"Are you coming with us, Dad?" Monica asked.

I secretly hoped he wasn't, sure that all he'd do was make fun of Mom and irritate her. With a quiet voice that surprised me, he said, "No, I do not need to see her. I'll wait here. You girls go ahead."

Relieved, we walked across the parking lot toward her. She saw us and approached the fence, grabbing it like a prisoner who wanted out.

"Hi, Mom," I said.

Her face lit up, and her eyes raced back and forth between us. Her lips quivered, and she shook her head slightly, smiling. "Girls, it's so good to see you. Are you really here?" We put our hands on the fence and touched her fingers. She almost looked normal until her eyes darkened and her face suddenly changed. Her mouth twisted, her cheeks became tense, and her eyes focused past us to the parking lot. I turned around to see Dad smiling.

"Why is he smiling?" Mom asked.

"Ignore him," I said.

"He's a bastard," she announced.

"Yes, he is," Karen said. Monica and I agreed.

We heard his laughter, which stunned me for a minute. How could he be so callous? He was laughing so hard that his head was back and his belly shook under the strain.

"Stop laughing at me, Bjorn!" Mom yelled.

"Dad! Stop it!" Monica said.

But he continued to laugh in an even more sinister way.

"Dad!" Karen yelled.

"Dad!" I echoed and stomped my foot.

"Leave me alone, Bjorn!" Mom screamed, violently shaking the chain-link fence. Two orderlies came over and peeled Mom's fingers from the fence.

"Mom!" we called as they escorted her back to the building. Her twisted neck looked unnatural as she strained to keep us in sight.

One of the orderlies called to us. "If you girls are here to see your mom, go to the front desk and check in."

Mom disappeared inside, and we walked toward the entrance. Dad had finally stopped laughing and I stuck my tongue out at him as we left him behind. He gave me a big-toothed smile and a happy wave.

"Dad's a shithead," I said.

"I know. I can't believe he laughed at her like that," Karen said.

"I hate him," Monica said.

We reached the front door and were buzzed inside. After completing the paperwork, an orderly escorted us down a long hallway through the locked interior doors. The musty smell laced with antiseptic filled my nose. The lights from above shone on the brown linoleum. Shiny concrete walls were painted a nasty light green and echoed with every sound. We walked huddled in a close pack, trying not to see the patients along the walls. I kept my eyes on the floor, trying to avoid looking, but my curiosity got the best of me, and I glanced up a few times.

People sat on the floor and in wheelchairs down the entire length of the hallway. A middle-aged woman with long gray hair in conversation with herself shouted out occasionally. Another woman drooled, staring off into the distance, her shirt dripping wet as the saliva flowed from her mouth. One man said, "Hello, pretty girls," and when I looked, he had his hands down his pants, digging inside. I quickly looked away. A young man who looked like he belonged in college or a bank was pounding his head against the wall, chanting, "No, no, no." Poor Mom. Why did she have to come to places like this?

We turned a corner and entered a room with twelve or so twin-size beds lined up like in the story of Orphan Annie. Three or four people lay in their beds, including Mom, who was still with the orderlies. We stood at the doorway of the enormous room. Mom peeked around the orderlies and saw us. She began to scream. "Girls, get me out of here, please," she begged.

The other patients in the room began to scream in solidarity. Mom tried to get out of bed, but the orderlies restrained her. The nurse came toward us. "Today isn't a good day. She can't control herself today. Can you come back another time?"

"No. Our father won't drive us again," I said.

"I'm sorry," he said. "Please follow me."

"Bye, Mom!" I shouted.

"Yeah, bye, Mom," Karen and Monica echoed.

"Don't go, girls!" Mom screamed, but the orderlies restrained her and blocked our view of her.

The nurse said more sternly, "Follow me."

"Is she okay?" Monica asked.

"Why can't we hug her and tell her we love her?" Karen said.

The nurse didn't answer. He just kept walking.

When we got back to the car, Dad was composed. "What happened?" he said.

Nobody said anything. We sat shocked. None of us wanted to talk to Dad.

"What happened?" he asked again.

"Mom's not well, and we can't see her today," Monica said in a robotic tone.

"Yeah, because your laughing made her crazy," Karen sneered.

"I did not make her crazy, girls. She was born that way." He started the car and we drove out of the parking lot.

The truth was, Dad had been making fun of Mom for our entire lives, calling her names and provoking her into anger.

"The shock treatments she's had each time she goes into the hospital haven't worked," he said. "The medication she takes doesn't work either. And her drinking makes it all worse, especially when she reads that damn Bible."

"What shock treatments?" I asked.

"Your mother has had multiple rounds of electroshock therapy, girls. You must know that."

I looked at Karen and then at Monica. They appeared just as surprised as me. "No, we didn't know she had had that."

We drove in silence the rest of the way home. I had so many questions about electroshock treatments and that hospital, but nobody to ask.

Poor Mom—living in a horrible prison again. I hated Dad more in that moment than I ever had before. I wished he would die a violent death.

42

We couldn't discuss anything until we walked to school the following day. We never had any privacy. Dad listened to everything, read all our letters, and went through our things when we were gone. We crossed 190th Street and headed up Beryl Street. "We have to do something to help Mom," I said.

"She needs to get out of that horrible place," Karen said, "but how?"

Monica stomped on the sidewalk and punched the air. "I could just kill him for laughing at her that way." She punched the air again, kicked her foot, and yelled at Dad.

I wanted to do the same but stuffed it down. Karen looked like she was going to melt.

"She should be back in Windsor near Grandma," Karen said.

"Yeah, but how do we get her there?" I asked.

We walked silently for a short while. "What if we flew her back to Windsor and then checked her into the Hotel Dieu?" Monica said.

"How are we going to get her to the airport, let alone get her on a plane?" Karen mused.

"Let's think about it today and talk more on our walk home," Monica said as we arrived at school, adding, "Thank goodness I don't have basketball practice today."

I felt more solemn than most days, if that was even possible. Classes dragged as I tried to come up with a solution for Mom. Maybe

Jason or Pat could drive us to the airport, but then I felt too embarrassed to explain the whole thing and have them see Mom so sick. I met Monica and Karen in our usual place after school. "Well, did you guys think of anything?" I asked when we reconvened.

"Dad's our only option. We have to convince him to pick Mom up from Norwalk and drive us to the airport," Karen said.

"Oh God," I mumbled, but knew she was right.

"And what about the cost of the plane ticket?" Monica said. "You know Dad isn't going to pay."

After more discussion, we all decided to pitch in our saved money to get Mom the ticket, knowing that the biggest obstacle would be convincing Dad.

"He better not laugh at her. We have to get him to promise not to laugh at her," Karen insisted.

"Oh God, he's going to make us pay so badly," Monica said, shaking her head.

"You bring it up tonight, Leslie, you're the favorite. Let's get it over with," Karen said.

"Oh fine! Thanks a lot," I said, resigned to the fact.

When we arrived home, Dad was on the phone in the backyard office, yelling at somebody. When he hung up, he stomped out of the house and was gone until dinner. Monica went to study in her bedroom, and Karen typed reports in the office. I headed to the kitchen to prepare the food, since it was my week to cook. When we sat down that evening to cheeseburgers, I eyed my sisters.

"How was school today?" Dad asked. He loved cheeseburgers, and I made his extra big and cheesy that night. We all said school was fine, and the silence filled the room again.

"What's wrong with you girls tonight?" he asked. "Why the solemn faces?"

I launched right in. "We want to move Mom to Windsor to the hospital she was in before. It's so much better than Norwalk," I said.

Dad popped a chip in his mouth and looked intrigued, moving his head to the side and squinting his eyes like he was considering it. Monica and Karen jumped in with the details of paying for the ticket, and then we waited.

Dad said, "It's a good idea. I can make the calls to Norwalk and the airlines tomorrow. She can't fly alone, so which of you will fly with her?"

I could never guess what my father would say in any instance. I would have bet all the precious money in my wallet that he would say no.

"What do you mean?" Monica said.

"One of you needs to fly with her. She'll be sedated and need assistance," Dad said like he'd done this before.

"She'll be sedated?" Karen said. "Why?"

"So she doesn't jump out of the plane or act crazy," he said.

"I'll go with her," I said, thinking I could try to see Simon.

"Nope. Anybody but you," he snapped, looking at Monica and Karen. Then he looked back at me. "I know who you'll see when you get to Windsor, and I forbid it."

I didn't even try to argue.

"I'll go," Monica said in a low, resigned way.

Karen looked at Dad with a serious expression. "You'll be nice to Mom? And you promise not to laugh at her?"

"I promise to drive you. That's all I promise." He left the table.

We had a plan, and Dad was helping, but why? He bought Mom and Monica their tickets without asking for any money. Super suspicious. Why was he being so nice? Maybe it was just that he wanted her back in Canada, away from us. My stomach churned and rolled as

I thought about everything that could go wrong. We had no choice but to trust him.

Over the next several days, Dad made the arrangements, even calling Mom's sister, Melanie, to ask if Uncle Jack could pick Mom and Monica up at Detroit Airport.

The big day was set for Saturday. Dad sounded genuine about helping Mom get back to Canada, where we all knew she'd be well taken care of and near her mother, brother, and sister. I began to feel hopeful.

On the day of transport, we were quiet on the drive to the hospital. Dad met with the doctor and signed Mom out while we waited in the lobby. We had clothing for her from Goodwill, which she changed into with a little too much glee in her eyes. Walking to the Cadillac, Karen took Mom's hand as we left that godforsaken place. "Mommy, you're out of there," she said.

"Are we going home?" Mom said, almost skipping through the parking lot. She seemed so young and hopeful and not at all sedated.

Dad said what none of us could: "Paula, you're going back to Windsor to be with your family and to get help."

"But I don't want to go to Windsor. I want to go home," she sang out.

"You don't have an apartment anymore, Mom. It burned down, remember?" Monica said.

Mom looked confused, squinting like she was trying to remember as she got in the back seat of the car with Karen and me. Monica sat in front. As we drove, Mom looked out the window with the eyes of a woman being saved, drinking in the sights like we were on a fairground ride. "Can we put the windows down?" she asked.

Dad rolled down his window halfway. The wind felt nice and cool.

Mom looked young with her hair blowing around her face and innocent with wondrous eyes, not her reserved and coiffed self. She snuck peeks at us. I tried to smile and be friendly, but I felt weird. Who was this person? She wasn't our mother.

Thirty minutes into our drive to LAX, Mom said, "Who burned down the house?"

We all waited for an extra-long beat before Karen answered. "You did, Mom, don't you remember?"

But she looked out the window as if she were miles away from us, ignoring the answer. We drove in silence for a while longer.

"Where are we going?" Mom asked finally.

"We're going to LAX so you can fly home to Canada, where they have better hospitals," Monica said.

"What's *he* doing here?" Mom said with a sneer on her face for Dad.

"He's driving us. Leave him alone," I said. I didn't mean to sound angry, but this was ridiculous.

Mom reacted immediately. "He's the devil, you know. He's always in disguise, watching and waiting to inflict his pain on us."

Nobody responded, and Dad didn't laugh.

At LAX, Dad dropped us off at the United Airlines curb. "I'll park and meet you at the gate," he said.

Mom and Monica's plane was due to leave in an hour. I got Mom a wheelchair. She sat right down in it, and seemed content and cooperative, staring at the palm trees and blue sky. "Can I have something to write on?"

I dug into my purse and gave her paper and a pen. Neither Monica nor Karen carried a purse. We found her flight and gate number and since she had no luggage, there was no need to see the agent. Monica would get their boarding passes at the gate.

We wheeled Mom down the seemingly endless corridor toward the gate while she wrote furiously on the paper I had given her. Unexpectedly, she began yelling, "Help! I'm being kidnapped!" She grabbed the jacket of some man passing by and handed him a note.

"Mom! Stop it," I said, and smiled at the man, trying to act like it was a joke.

She looked at me and said, "You're the devil, just like your dad."

"Mom . . . stop it," I said. "If we don't get you to the gate, we'll miss the flight."

"I'm not getting on any flight. Nobody's going to kidnap me." And she yelled again, "Help! I'm being kidnapped!"

We wheeled her faster and faster until we were practically running. She kept yelling and people stared. We finally arrived at gate 39. All the other passengers were on the plane when Mom yelled her SOS again to the agent.

"She can't get on this plane," the agent said.

"What do you mean? She has a ticket, and so does my sister," I said.

Mom screamed again, "Help! I'm being kidnapped!"

We heard Dad's giant laugh behind us.

"Dad, don't laugh," Karen said, "it isn't funny. Mom doesn't want to get on the plane."

"No," said the agent. "She can't get on this plane. She isn't well."

Mom's face was all lit up and she looked like she might float away. Her eyes were glassy. God damn it! I thought she was supposed to be sedated! We turned the wheelchair around and faced away from the agent. "Mom, now you've ruined it, and you have to return to Norwalk," I said.

"I'm not going back there," she said.

The agent closed the doors, and the plane left.

Mom kicked, screamed, and scratched us for the entire ride back to Norwalk. When we arrived, I had no empathy left and couldn't wait for the orderlies to take her away.

43

My junior year ended, and Monica graduated, leaving Karen and me to fight the next year's high school battles alone. The Johansen trio was no longer represented at Redondo Beach High. When our report cards came, I somehow earned passing grades by racking up extra credit in most of my classes.

Mom was still in Norwalk, going on three months, and there was nothing we could do to help her. We hadn't seen her since the failed trip to LAX.

I half-heartedly looked for a job the first few days of summer even though I already had over $300 burning a hole in my pocket. The urge to leave, to get the hell away from Dad, consumed my every thought. With no plans for the summer and only the prospect of living under the microscopic eye of Almighty Bjorn Erling Johansen, I felt uneasy.

Quickly dressing one morning after discovering Dad had left for the day, I rushed to Cyndi's for a beach day. We smoked a joint, laughed, watched the boys surf for a few hours, then headed home. As I came up the driveway, Dad was pacing on the porch like he had on Valentine's Day. I had the thought that I should walk confidently. *Don't cower. Don't look weak or act high.* I had learned from the undercover work that walking tentatively or with a questioning face led to more inquiries. I marched up the three steps and said, "Hi," hoping my eyes weren't very glassy.

"Come here and give me a hug," he said.

I felt stunned when his arms wrapped around me, pulling me in so close I struggled to get away. "Dad! Get off me!" I yelled and pushed him away.

"You smell like pot and cigarettes."

He released me and took a giant step back. "No, I don't."

"You can't lie about it, Leslie. It leaves a definite odor on clothing." He eyed me up and down. "Why are you smoking?"

"I'm *not* smoking." I opened the screen door and headed for my bedroom.

Monica eyed me with a scared expression from the couch, where she was reading a book. *Man, am I high!*

"Come back here right now!" Dad yelled.

I stopped my retreat and turned around, feeling spiteful. "What? What do you want?" I spewed.

"You've been drinking, too, haven't you?"

"No."

"You're lying. I can smell beer, pot, and cigarettes on you." The vein in his forehead was bulging.

Karen came out of the bedroom in a cloud of soap and toothpaste, slithering past me in the hallway. The back screen door slammed. Dad's new secretary, Mary, looked distressed, heading for the coffeepot.

"So? What do you care? I'm seventeen now."

"Oh, you think you're old enough to do what you want?"

"Yes," was all I could manage.

"Do you have cigarettes and booze in your backpack?" He grabbed it and I tightened my grip, but he got the backpack. I swiped the air unsuccessfully. "Give it! It's mine."

He thought that was funny. "Nothing you have is yours. It's all mine." He opened the small front pouch and found a box of Marlboro Red and a book of matches. "I see you can lie straight to my face."

Wearing a smirk, I said, "Yes, and I'm getting good at it." My words stopped him. He bore down on me with his eyes. I held his hateful gaze. "My goal is to lie straight to your face without you being able to tell. I've been working on it a while now."

"You guys, stop fighting," Karen whined.

But I couldn't stop now. "Give me back my backpack. It's mine!" I reached for it, but he moved it away again.

"How many times do I have to tell you that nothing you have is yours? Your clothes, your money, your backpack, your cigarettes, your booze," he said. "It's all mine!"

"I hate you! Why can't you leave me alone?" I ran to the bedroom and slammed the door shut.

"If you can't follow my rules, don't let the door hit you in the ass on the way out!" he yelled outside my door.

I threw myself on my bed and screamed into my pillow, then realized I didn't need to muffle my screams, so I screamed as loud as I could. He opened the door, and I looked straight at him and screamed even louder. He threw the backpack at me, still holding the cigarettes.

"I hate you! I wish you would die!" I yelled.

In a calm and relaxed voice, he smiled, said, "I love you," and closed the door gently.

I cried for a long time, facing the wall with the pillow over my head, and woke in the middle of the night still in my clothes. Karen was asleep in bed. I hadn't even heard her come in. Lying in the darkness, I knew it was time.

I got up and retrieved the $320 hidden behind a can in our bedroom closet and shoved the money into my jeans pocket. I packed my backpack with a few pieces of clothing, tiptoed to the garage, got a small suitcase, and stopped in the bathroom for my toothbrush, hairbrush, and makeup. Back in my room, I packed my diary, poetry book, address book, and as many clothes as I could fit inside.

"What are you doing?" whispered Karen.

"Tell him I didn't let the door hit me in the ass on the way out."

"Where are you going?"

"Away from this place. Bye, Sis, I'll see you around." I squeezed her foot and winked at her.

It was 4 a.m. Slinging my backpack over my shoulder, I carried the suitcase and tiptoed down the hallway. A thunder of horses beat in my chest and my eyes strained to see the furniture so I didn't knock any pictures off the wall in the darkness. I grabbed an apple, a banana, and a sleeve of Ritz crackers from the kitchen. Out the backdoor, I carefully navigated around the trash cans, the farthest distance from Dad's bedroom, went through the side gate, and out to the street.

The night was silent, empty of the hordes of cars usually rushing past. The lights above lit the way to the gas station where my favorite pay phone lived. Refusing to breathe a sigh of relief until I was far enough away from the house that I couldn't see it, I called Simon. It was three hours later in Windsor, and I knew he'd still be at home getting ready for work.

He finally answered on the fourth ring. "Hello?"

"Hi! It's me. I didn't think you were going to answer."

"What's wrong? Why are you calling so early?"

"I left. I'm going to the airport right now and getting a one-way ticket to Detroit."

"What happened?" he asked.

"I'll tell you when I get there. I'm about to call a friend to take me to the airport. Should I call you at work later with my flight?"

"Yes, but use a different name, please. I don't want to raise any eyebrows." His voice was tentative and slow.

I gave him a name and said, "I'm getting the hell away from here today!"

"See you soon, I guess." His tone was tentative, but I couldn't let that stop me. I hung up and held the receiver to my chest for a few seconds, breathing, trying to calm down. Next, I called my most trusted and generous friend, Jason, and asked for a ride to LAX.

While waiting, I crouched inside the phone booth, waiting for the adrenaline to subside. Jason arrived fifteen minutes later. His mussed black hair proved he hadn't done anything but grab his keys and left. Overwhelmed with gratitude, I put my hand on his and nodded warmly. We drove up the coast through Manhattan Beach, El Segundo, and Playa del Rey, mostly in silence, watching daylight fill the sky. I rolled my window down. The ocean was calm, the waves small. He broke the silence. "Where are you going?"

"Back to a boyfriend in Windsor."

He nodded and returned his eyes to the road. We hugged at the airport and Jason looked deeply into my eyes. "Promise to write, or call collect anytime. Keep me posted on your whereabouts, and be safe."

I nodded and kissed his cheek. How did I deserve a friend like him? Watching him drive away, I knew God had given me a guardian angel in Jason.

Finally able to breathe, I felt giddy and screamed out in freedom. "I'm doing it! I'm actually leaving today!"

On the plane to Detroit, I promised myself never to ask Dad for help—not even if I was in jail or lying in a ditch somewhere. I would never give him the satisfaction of saying he won and that I was a ditz and a loser.

44

When I got off the plane, Simon was waiting for me. He grabbed me tight and embraced me hard, taking my breath away. His eyes were teary as he touched my hair, kissed my mouth, and looked deeply into my eyes. It felt like we were the only people in the Detroit Airport. Having expected him to be a little tepid about my impetuous decision, his intensity scared me.

In his familiar red sports car on the way to his house, I suddenly felt awkward and unsure about what I had done: I just ran away to Windsor, a place I'd always hated, on purpose.

"Tell me what's going on with your father."

"There's nothing to tell. I hate him. I've moved out. I will never go back."

"Does he know you came here?"

"No. I've never mentioned you once in the two years I've been gone."

Simon nodded, seemingly happy with my answer. He took my hand and kissed it. "Welcome home."

We crossed the Ambassador Bridge into Canada and my heart clenched at the sight of dirty, industrial Windsor. It was no California, that was for sure. Did I have any good memories here? The answer was a resounding no, except for Simon. Smog hung over the city in the summer heat, and I could see the Hiram Walker whiskey plant, where the same hops and barley smell from childhood filled my nose through the open window. We drove down Ambassador Bridge Road and turned onto Tecumseh Road. The gray cement buildings, the drab billboards, and even the people were all dressed in grays and browns. Didn't anyone wear colorful clothing?

Simon's gorgeous home welcomed me with its perfectly trimmed grass and tulips near the porch. Rushing inside like a child on Christmas morning, I ran upstairs to the bedroom hoping to find everything the same. I nodded to the shiny dark antique dresser and the single nightstand on the left side of the bed holding a small lamp. The perfectly made cherry wood sleigh bed that occupied so many of my memories sat in the middle of the room. The inviting mattress with its puffy squares of white down comforter beckoned me to jump and smash them down. I threw myself on it, stretching out like a cat. Simon stood at the doorway with a smile in his eyes.

"You're all mine," he said under his breath.

Our reunion was epic, everything I had dreamed about. Afterward, we cuddled in bed while he chatted about gardening, house maintenance, and clinic work. I told him about the boat recovery in St. Maarten, and he listened intently as he played with my hair and stroked my face.

A loose screen banged incessantly in the next room, and Simon went to the garage for tools to fix it. While he was gone, I noticed a large oak tree swaying outside the window as if waving to me. *Hi there, Mr. Oak.* A gust of wind made the limbs move frantically for a minute and a bad feeling washed over me. Was the tree warning me that I'd made a mistake coming here?

But as soon as Simon rejoined me in bed, the dark feeling was brushed away, and I focused on the man holding me in his arms with words of love. He made us soup and sandwiches, and I wandered slowly through the house, taking in his gorgeous mahogany dining room set gleaming from his meticulous attention. The living room had high-backed stuffed chairs, a cherry wood coffee table, ceramic lamps, and an English-style couch. Magazines on the coffee table were expertly placed. There were no extra knickknacks anywhere. The indoor plants thrived, the carpets were immaculate, and the kitchen looked like a picture, with no dish or spoon out of place. We spent a blissful amount of time in bed, and I was happier than I had ever been.

A routine formed as the weeks ticked on. I got up with Simon each morning and drank coffee as he prepared to leave for work. I had nothing to do during the day, so I would go back to bed after he left to read, write in my diary, and watch TV until he came home.

I wondered how Monica and Karen were doing and what had happened when Dad found out I left. I wished I could have seen his face when Karen told him I left in the middle of the night. Knowing him, he probably said, "Good. Glad to be rid of her."

Yeah, good riddance to you, too, asshole.

On our way to bed one night, Simon stopped at the bedroom's threshold. "What's this?"

"What?" I lay down, cozying up with my diary and scattered books.

"You didn't make the bed when you woke this morning?"

"No, I got up right before you came home, and here we are again. What a waste to make the bed for one hour a day."

He turned away from me and undressed.

"Come to bed. I've been keeping it warm." And he did.

The next day I made the bed an hour before he came home and was spread out on the couch reading when he walked through the door. He squinted at my bare feet on the sofa for a beat too long. I could read the signs. He was unhappy. I moved my feet off his precious couch. He scanned the room, taking inventory, maybe. I sat up and straightened myself as if I'd been caught doing something wrong. "Hello. How was your day?" I said in a cheery voice, hoping to distract him from my bare feet.

"Good. What did you do all day?" His voice was curt. He walked straight past me and into the kitchen.

I didn't answer.

"What's this in the sink?"

I followed him. "Oh, I had a cup of tea earlier."

He put his briefcase down on the table, then silently washed and dried the cup and saucer, putting them away in the cabinet. "The ashtray is overflowing on the front porch. Can you take care of that?"

"Okay, but first, let me tell you that I went to the bank today and opened an account."

He picked up his briefcase, stopped before me, said, "That's good," and left the room.

Slowly, with each passing day, he said more things that made me feel unwelcome, as if I were imposing on him. One afternoon, as I sat on the porch smoking, reading a book, and watching the neighbors, he came out and stood before me. "I would prefer if you didn't smoke on the porch. The smoke gets into the house and makes it smell." He went back into the house without waiting for my response.

Well, aren't we grumpy today?

Dinner together meant I watched him cook, which was fine with me, but I began to feel that it was because I didn't cook the "right" way for him. I started to feel like everything I did was wrong.

At breakfast one Saturday morning, I opened the refrigerator to get some milk for my tea and was standing there staring at the fridge's contents, half asleep, when Simon's voice boomed, "Leslie, you can't just stand with the door open. It's a waste of energy. You must have a plan before you open the refrigerator door so you can grab your items quickly and then shut the door."

Dumbfounded, I slammed the refrigerator door shut without

getting the milk. I sat opposite him on the horseshoe booth kitchen table with my black tea.

"When are you going to find a job? Or go to school?" he said.

"What do you mean? I'm not going to high school here in Windsor."

"Well, then maybe it's time for you to find a job," he said. "You'll have to start by applying for a work visa." He returned to reading his newspaper.

I looked past him out the kitchen window at the two bluebirds sitting on the telephone wire. *Jesus, what is happening?*

"Think about it. I'm going out to the garage for a while." The screen door slammed as he left, and the bluebirds flew away.

The thought of working in Windsor depressed the hell out of me. I could work at a fast-food place or typing in an office. Neither excited me, and it wasn't part of what I'd envisioned when I'd dreamed about living with Simon and being his girlfriend. Why did I have to work? I still had money.

I had talked him into seeing the latest summer movie, *Grease*, when we were in bed a few days earlier. The plan was to go for a picnic afterward and walk through the rose gardens at Jackson Park. He arrived in the kitchen as I was making sandwiches. I was about to ask him which movie time sounded better when he said, "I have to work today. Try not to get into trouble."

"What about the movie and our picnic?" I called after him. But he didn't answer.

Slouching down, I moaned, "We never do anything fun."

The hurt grew inside at the increasing slights and hostile remarks. I ran upstairs to bed and cried, not understanding why he didn't like me anymore. Grabbing my purse, I walked to the liquor store a few blocks away, bought a new pack of cigarettes, and sat on the Tecumseh Road curb and smoked. I stared at the traffic rushing past, the people walking to work, school, or someplace. *What is wrong with him? Why is everything I do wrong?* I smoked cigarette after cigarette until I felt sick to my stomach. Thirsty for a drink of some sort, I headed back to the house. It was 11 a.m.

A large rum and Coke with lots of ice in the backyard was just perfect. I smoked, drank, and wrote in my diary about my crumbling relationship with Simon.

He treats me like a child. I don't need another dad. Doesn't he know that's why I left California? He loves to have sex with me, but everything else I do is wrong. I need to leave. But where should I go? I'd rather die than go home to Redondo Beach.

Three rum and Cokes later, I was sloshed and heartbroken. Simon came home from work and didn't apologize, talk to me, or notice my sadness. He began dinner as I sat outside, finishing my drink. "Hello," he said from the kitchen window.

"Hi," I muttered.

"I'm cooking dinner, and then I'm going to bed early. I have a big meeting tomorrow."

I lit a cigarette and blew out a puff of smoke. "I'm not hungry."

That fact brought him outside into the backyard. "Did you eat late again and ruin your dinner?" I squinted at him but couldn't bring myself to say anything. He handed me a newspaper. "I got this for you." I nodded and sipped my drink, staring off at the oak tree waving at me. He went inside, ate, and went to bed. Crawling into bed late, I barely slept, knowing it was over and I had to leave.

The following morning, I stayed in bed pretending to sleep. Simon left for work after kissing me goodbye as usual, like nothing was wrong. I drank a cup of coffee and took two aspirins, went upstairs, packed my suitcase, and called a cab. I went to the bank, took out my $225, and closed my account. I would go to Miami and see Richard. At least he wanted me. I called him from the Windsor bus station feeling a bit better, thinking of our warm embrace in St. Thomas and his invitation to come and visit.

"You're really coming here?" I could tell he was smiling.

The buses were lined up outside the window. "Yes, I'm taking the bus, so it will be almost three days. Can I stay with you?"

"Oh man, I don't know. My girlfriend, Penny, isn't going to like it."

"You have a girlfriend?" Shaking my head, I let the receiver slip down my chest for a minute while my mind raced.

"Yes, I do have a girlfriend," I heard him say as I brought the receiver back to my ear. "But I'll try to figure it out before you get here."

We hung up, and I boarded the bus feeling a messy mixture of sadness, guilt, disappointment, and excitement.

What would Simon think when he got home from work? I should have left a note or called him at work, but I left the bed unmade and a cup and saucer in the kitchen sink for him to remember me by.

45

The bus drove through the tunnel under the dank Detroit River from the Windsor station. I'd never liked taking the claustrophobic tunnel, preferring the open sky view from the bridge always. In the tunnel's darkness, I closed my eyes and conjured the white sand beaches in Miami and Richard's welcoming lips. *Goodbye, Windsor.*

At the Detroit bus station, more people boarded, filling the bus up about halfway, but I still had a row of seats to myself. From Detroit, we headed south to Ohio, and I stared out the window, wondering what lay ahead in my life. Free to do whatever I wanted, where would I be in a year? Hell, where would I be in six months? Would I ever pass that damn High School Proficiency Test and get my diploma? Would Mom survive that cesspool Norwalk and be sane when she got out? Or would she be absolutely fucked up and unable to care for herself? I missed Monica and wondered if she'd moved out, hoping they were surviving Dad and all his craziness. I vowed to call them soon.

I knew I was making the right decision. Simon was treating me like a child. It occurred to me too late that I should have listened to the oak tree waving her branches at me in warning.

Riding on the bus into the unknown, I felt capable of providing for myself. After all, I'd sailed halfway around the world and back, been undercover on a boat recovery, lived on my own in San Diego, and saved enough money to leave home.

But just as day turned into night and the bus stopped at a diner, I made the horrible discovery that I had forgotten to change my Canadian money into American money. My funny-looking Canadian money was worthless in Ohio. I had no cash, no water, and no food.

Back on the bus, I wondered how I would make it two more days. The smell of food filled the air. A hippie couple one row ahead of me, clearly in love, giggled and laughed as they ate their carrots and brown bread peanut butter sandwiches. I smelled a whiff of delicious tuna fish and heard chips crunching a few rows behind me. I envied the bright smell of an orange. My stomach rumbled, and I buried my head in my sweatshirt. This was my punishment for leaving Simon without saying goodbye.

An odd selection of people got on and off the bus in various cities, or maybe they were all just ordinary people, and I was losing my mind from hunger. In Kentucky, a woman joined the bus with a newborn baby who wouldn't stop crying. Two teenage brothers sat across from me and played cards for hours, and in Tennessee, a young man with a guitar came aboard and strummed a few songs I didn't recognize. I sat as far back on the bus as my nose would allow. The bathroom in the back stank to high heaven, but I was grateful for it as we bumped along the road for hours and hours at a time.

Our stops were never in big cities where I could find a bank and exchange my money. They were only in small Podunk towns with a gas station attached to a small diner run by mean old women. At each stop, I dragged myself off the bus to the diner bathroom, cupping my hand to drink water from the sink faucet until I was waterlogged. Heading back to the bus, I tried not to breathe in the smell from the hamburgers and french fries people had ordered.

Reading was my only escape. I finished Jacqueline Susann's *Once Is Not Enough* and tried to sleep the next day away, ignoring my hunger cramps. I stared at grain silos in the vast open space outside the window through prairie country, and my negative voice reared its ugly head. "You're stupid, fat, and need to diet anyway," Dad would say. "Hunger is good," he'd add. "You need to lose a few pounds." I hated that he lived in my head—that booming Norwegian accent shaming and abusing me. My own voice now matched his.

There could be no doubt I was crazy to go across the country to see a guy I barely knew who already had a girlfriend. We'd only spent a few hours together five months ago.

An older woman with a floral dress and a perm climbed aboard the bus in Georgia and sat across the aisle from me. Her face was like soft dough, and her smile was warm. "Sweetie, you look so sad."

I forced a smile but couldn't manage to say "No, I'm hungry." Screaming inside were the words "Please don't be nice to me. I don't deserve it."

She adjusted her knitting, ready for a chat. "I'm going to see my first granddaughter, and seeing that I'm so happy, I can't stand it that you're so sad." Her eyes twinkled.

"What's your granddaughter's name?"

"Patricia. Isn't it just a beautiful name? So stately. I hope her mother doesn't call her Patty."

She chattered about her husband working on his cars at home, and I found myself enjoying the distraction. Eventually, I told her I hadn't eaten in two days. She was horrified and comforted me in ways nobody in my family had ever done. She patted my arm, and her eyes dripped sympathy and kindness as she dug into her bag and handed me an apple and a white bread peanut butter and jelly sandwich. After I took the food, she reached across the aisle and touched my hair with gleaming eyes. "Two days is a long time without food, darling." My chin shook as I nearly cried from embarrassment and gratitude.

"Thank you so much." I bit into the hard green apple. The juices filled my mouth and I laid my head back on the seat, swimming in the tang of it. I tried not to eat too fast. The sandwich dripped grape jelly, and the peanut butter was crunchy. I wanted two more apples and two more sandwiches to devour immediately.

When I finished, I tried to sleep. Why couldn't my mother be like this woman? If I ever had children, I would be like her: loving, kind, forgiving, and generous. My mother had moments of kindness and affection, but they had been spread thinly over the years. The empty well inside craved this tender affection and love, but instead, I had to keep my guard up around my mother. She saw me as a rival and competed with me for men's affection. She was jealous of the admiration I got from Dad and had made it clear she hated me for being his favorite. When I was six years old, standing on a chair doing the dishes while Mom and Dad fought in another room, Mom arrived in the kitchen crying and sniffling. "Look, Mommy, I'm doing the dishes and didn't break any."

Through her tears and snuffles, she yelled, "Leslie, get down from there. You'll fall!"

"No, I won't. I'm big now."

"Good girl," Dad said from the kitchen door, smiling generously at me before leaving the house. I beamed at him.

Mom stared at me from the kitchen chair. "Why do you have to be so good at everything?"

46

At 3 a.m. on the second night, the bus stopped and I startled awake as the bus driver called out, "Everyone off. Final stop, Miami."

I looked outside at the industrial neighborhood. *Is he going to throw us out on the street in the middle of the night? I can't call Richard at this hour.* The bus doors opened, sucking in a warm rush of hot, humid air that smelled like the tropics with a heavy dose of rotting garbage and engine oil. I grabbed my backpack and exited. Two men slept near their shopping carts on the side of the terminal. A line of cars waited for people exiting the bus. I lit a cigarette and waited for my suitcase to be unloaded as everyone scattered. *What should I do?*

Thirsty, I made my way through the double doors of the mostly empty bus station, past the closed ticket windows and the vending machines, surprised to see four men reading newspapers, talking, and drinking something like it was the middle of the day. My hackles went up. One wore a white fuzzy hat, another a beret and a thick chain around his neck. Another man wearing a red bandanna around his head stared me down. They didn't look like passengers waiting for the next bus but men conducting business. The heat and stickiness increased inside the building. A cloud of smoke hung over their heads. My eyes held for a beat too long on what looked like the leader, who had a nasty scar on his cheek and wore a black fishnet tank top. I quickly made my way to the women's bathroom.

In the corner stall, I heard two women murmuring. I took the stall on the other end as far away from them as possible. The door seemed like minimal protection and since I didn't have to pee, I used the toilet as a chair and sat down, clutching my backpack. I lit a cigarette and took a long drag. The back of the door was covered in stickers and graffiti. "Susan was here" was scrawled in loopy cursive. A sticker for a taxi company covered other writing. Too bad I couldn't call for a taxi with my Canadian coins.

A woman whined, "But I don't want to do this anymore." Then a long silence. "I just want to go home."

"I can't help you. It's too dangerous," said another woman matter-of-factly, as if she was bored of the conversation.

Wishing I didn't have to listen to these women, I shifted on the toilet seat.

"Hello?" a woman said, opening her stall door. "Are you peeing in there or what?"

I could see her glittery pink top through the door opening. "I'm waiting for my friend to pick me up."

"Come out here now," she demanded.

I hesitated for a few moments, flushed the toilet, then opened the stall door. *Walk like you own the place*, I thought.

Both women stood in front of sinks, waiting for me. The older one had her arms crossed and squinted her eyes to size me up. The whiny one had a ponytail and wasn't much older than me. They were both skinny and a little greasy, not from dirt but from life.

I walked to the sink to wash my shaking hands.

"Don't you think your ride would be here by now if he were coming?" the older one said.

"The bus just dropped us off. What do you care anyway?" I primped my hair in the mirror and pushed it behind my ears trying to find a hard attitude like I had on the boat recovery in St. Maarten.

"This is our place at night. You're crowding us," she continued.

I picked up my bag and headed out the door as if I knew where I was going, walking straight past the men again and out the double doors into the fresher night air. To my surprise, I heard an airplane and looked up to see the lights of a large jet in the near distance. We were near the airport and airports had foreign exchange booths. I walked to the end of the terminal driveway looking both ways. Trucks passed in both directions but there were no sidewalks in either direction. The purplish sky promised sunrise soon.

I walked back to the terminal and the main door opened. The man with the fishnet tank top came through the bus station doors. His eyes were hard black rocks. "Hi. What are you doing? Are you lost?"

I clenched my mouth, and my voice was shaky when I answered. "I'm just waiting on my ride."

"He's running late, huh?" He stepped a little closer, examining me and my suitcase and backpack. "I'm Whitey, what's your name?"

I moved a few steps away, but he followed. "What's your name?" he demanded.

"Patty," I said, hoping he would leave me alone. I considered crossing the street to get away from him.

He chuckled a little. "You ran away from home, didn't you?"

"No!" I said too quickly.

"Well, then, where's your ride?"

"He's on his way."

"He forgot you," he insisted, and then he added, in a quieter voice, "He fell asleep and won't be here for hours."

I glanced up at him as the fear rose inside. Then I looked straight ahead, using my peripheral vision to keep an eye on him. "Leave me alone."

"I can help you earn some money tonight."

"No thanks, I'm fine. I'll wait for my friend."

Headlights approached, and Whitey disappeared back in the building. It was a police car. I waved and walked toward the car, filled with relief and hope. The police officer rolled down his window. He was young with a thin blond mustache, barely visible.

"My bus got in a few minutes ago, I don't have a ride, and there's a man named Whitey hassling me." I pointed to the bus station doors. "I don't have any American money, so I can't call my friend for a ride."

After asking for my ID, he let me sit in the police car, where I picked at my nails while he went inside the station. Ten minutes later, he emerged with the young girl from the bathroom. She got in the back with me.

"Hi!" I said to her.

"Leave me alone." She scowled and turned away.

What a bitch. The officer drove us to the police station. At the desk, when the phone was offered to me, I dug out Richard's number and called him. It was 5:30 a.m. and I listened to the phone ring and ring until he finally answered, "Speakeasy."

"Hi, Richard. It's Leslie. My bus got in a few hours ago. Can you come and get me at the police station?" There was a long pause, and I added, "I'll explain later."

He cleared his throat and said, "I'm on my way."

He arrived less than thirty minutes later, tall and gorgeous, with chiseled facial features and body. *I remember you*, I thought. He winked at me and I got up and stood near him.

The desk officer greeted Richard and said, "She needs to make better arrangements next time. Arriving at the bus station at 3:30 a.m. isn't the smartest thing to do when you don't have a ride or money to pay for a cab."

"You don't have money?" Richard said, staring at me.

"Can we talk about this later?" I turned and headed for the door.

Richard followed me as I pronounced, "I'm starving. I haven't eaten in three days. I forgot to change my Canadian money before I left Canada."

He looked at me sideways with a grin. "Let's get some breakfast. You've got a lot of explaining to do."

47

Banyan trees lined U.S. Route 1 as we approached Richard's modern apartment building. A smile filled up my entire face. We drove past a cluster of six-story buildings called Village at the Falls, with a community pool and tennis courts. Richard parked and we got out.

"Can you believe I'm here?" I said but I didn't wait for him to answer. "I can't!"

He carried my suitcase and backpack toward the building. "I was surprised when you called. I never thought you'd actually come."

"Is it okay? Are you sure it's okay for me to be here?"

He pushed the button on the elevator. "Yes, it's fine."

We traveled up to the sixth floor and down a long, narrow hallway. He unlocked the door. "Come in and make yourself at home." He set my backpack on a dining room chair. "I have to jump in the shower and get to work."

A blast of air-conditioned air hit me in the face. "Thanks, it feels so good in here."

I walked directly to the balcony and opened the door. Hot, humid air rushed in, and I quickly closed it. The view was of Coral Gables in the distance and beyond that, the blue-green Atlantic Ocean beckoned. The place was small but well furnished.

I sank into his navy couch, hugging an overstuffed pillow, drifting off into a light sleep. The bedroom door opening startled me awake. Richard was dressed in a dark-blue linen suit with a blue open-collared shirt. *Man, he's handsome.* His spicy-sweet cologne wafted through the room.

He sat next to me on the couch. "The only thing you haven't explained is why you couldn't go home to California."

"I hate him. I can't go home yet. I have to prove I can make it on my own without his help."

"Does he know where you are?"

"No. And I don't care . . . he doesn't deserve to know where I am."

After Richard left for work, I showered and fell asleep on the couch for the entire day, waking only to get a drink of water but quickly falling back to sleep again. Richard came home as the sun was setting. I was on the balcony trying to wake up when familiar music began playing inside. I turned around to find him smiling at me from the kitchen. I came in from the balcony.

"I like Boz Skaggs," I said. *Especially now that I know who he is*, I thought.

"Me too. He's been an obsession for a long time now." We listened for a few minutes, and I sank into a beanbag chair by the window.

"Would you like a soda or juice?" he asked as he lit up a joint, took a long draw, and then offered it to me.

"Orange juice, please." I took a short toke.

The music was velvety, the high from the pot was soft and wonderful, and the pizza we ordered was delicious. We laughed and danced and relaxed together for hours. His laugh was infectious, and his sense of humor was biting with a hint of sarcasm, just like I liked it. The sexual energy I'd experienced in St. Thomas was still palpable. My skin tingled, and my heart kicked. His lovely full lips tempted me, and he made the first move, pulling me up to dance like we had in St. Thomas. "We're All Alone" played, and we swayed, fitting together so naturally. He kissed me and led me to his bedroom, and we made love. It felt so right, as if I'd always known him. As we lay together in bed, I interlaced our fingers and counted, "Black, white, black, white." He kissed my hand. Higher than I'd ever been, everything seemed to glow. I traced my fingers down his chest.

Being high broke down all my walls of insecurity and self-doubt. He liked me, and I liked him. We fell asleep nestled in each other's arms, and by the time I awoke, he had left for work again.

After a few days of Richard and I hanging out and continually making love, Penny stopped by, bringing dinner on a Friday night. Her blonde bob swayed with every step between the kitchen and dining table as she laid out a fried chicken dinner for us. I mentally pushed my relationship with Richard away and became seventeen-year-old Leslie from California, whose tyrant father worked with Richard. We drank white wine from the most enormous glasses I had ever seen. Fish could have lived in them.

"So, how long are you visiting?" she asked, her big brown eyes shining.

"I'm not sure."

I felt the need to share my complicated relationship with my father so she knew I was a refugee needing help, hiding out until it was safe to go home. I hit the high notes of my angst and suffering. "Sounds complicated for sure," she said.

Richard shook his head in an "I can't believe it" way, never having imagined I had such a storied history with my dad. "I only worked with Bjorn on that one job in St. Maarten, so I don't have any references with his personal life. He's a demanding guy, though."

Penny offered, "I also had a difficult relationship with my father, so I can relate."

Penny and I discovered we were only eight years apart, and each had two sisters. I liked her. We played a few backgammon games, and the evening wrapped up around midnight.

She spent the night in the bed with Richard while I slept on the couch. I lay there alone, hoping not to hear them having sex. Jealousy and envy rose in me but were thwarted when I reminded myself that I was not the girlfriend but instead the visitor and traitor. A stab of pain had me smoking the leftover joint in the ashtray and falling asleep alone.

In the morning, the door opened to the bedroom as I was sipping my orange juice in the kitchen. "We're running some errands, so we'll see you later," Penny said.

"Okay, see you guys later," I said, trying to sound chipper. My stomach clenched, unsure of what was happening.

Richard nodded, smiled, and closed the door behind him.

I waited for them to return for the entire weekend. I wrote, read, and missed Richard. Sharing him didn't feel good.

When he finally returned at the end of the weekend, the magnetic energy between us reignited. We put on Boz Skaggs again and I fell under the spell of this incredible man. I couldn't get enough of him. Like the tides, our carnal connection and rhythm made me feel destined to be with him. We got high, drank rum like pirates, danced naked, and then made love on the bed, in the shower, on the couch, and partially covered in whipped cream on the kitchen floor. We watched HBO movies while eating mac and cheese and pizza in bed.

I had been staying with Richard for almost two months when Penny began questioning me about my plans as we played backgammon one Friday night. A routine had developed as the synergy built between the three of us. We cooked together and played in our own backgammon tournaments, keeping the teasing and competitiveness alive.

Whenever Penny came over, Richard and I reverted to "just friends." The sexual energy became a switch I could flip. We never breached the thin separation by flirting if she went to the bathroom and left us alone. When she was there, we were just friends. Period. I whined and complained to Penny about my parents, school, and boyfriends while she listened like a big sister. She gave me advice, and I considered it. Richard and Penny were not often affectionate in front of me, which made it easier to believe we were all friends.

One night, Penny threw the dice in backgammon and asked, "So you've failed that high school test twice, right?"

"Yes," I said, taking my turn and moving the pieces.

"You need to finish high school," she crooned as she shook the dice.

"I know. I'm waiting on the results from my third attempt. They should be out in a few weeks."

She moved the pieces around the board. "If you pass, what are your plans?"

"I don't know," I moaned. "I need to pass that fucking test. Other than that, I don't know."

"What about a job while you wait?"

I shook my head in frustration. *Why is she pushing me so hard?* "Just hand me that joint so I can forget."

She handed it to me, and I took a hit. I believed she was sincere in her concern for my future, but also imagined she wanted me to stop living with her boyfriend. I felt guilty about sneaking around with Richard, but he never asked me to consider my future.

Richard brought cheese and crackers to the table and took the joint from me. "Take it easy, ladies. We have the whole evening to talk." A knock on the door diverted our attention. Richard answered, and I heard a familiar voice say, "Is Leslie here?"

48

I came to the door, heart thumping in my chest. Simon stood in front of me with pleading eyes and his familiar bushy walrus mustache.

"Hi," I said reluctantly, "how did you find me?"

Ignoring my question, he demanded, "Why did you leave without saying goodbye?"

I was so high, nothing came to mind. I stepped out into the hallway and closed the door behind me, trying to calm down and gather my thoughts. He was wearing his usual outfit: beige cords, a brown striped shirt tucked in, and Wallabees.

"Simon, you shouldn't have come here."

"I love you, Leslie. Please come home with me." His face was earnest and begging.

"No," I said quietly, focusing on the floor.

"Why? What did I do?"

"You treated me like a child. I am not a child, and you are not my father."

"I'm sorry. I love you and didn't want you to make any mistakes."

"Go home, Simon. I'm staying here."

"With the Black guy?"

My head snapped up to look him in the eye. "What does that mean? He's a friend of our family, and who cares if he's Black?" Standing in the hallway was awkward, so I walked to the elevators at the end of the hall, desperate to get rid of him. He followed me. I pushed the button on the elevator.

"Simon, I'm not going back with you. I'm sorry you came all this way. It's over."

The elevator doors opened, and he got in. Tears welled in his big brown eyes and threatened to spill over. His bottom lip quivered. The doors closed, and he was gone.

I felt nauseous, and my knees were weak. I wobbled my way back to Richard's apartment, holding on to the wall as I walked, sinking onto the floor before his door.

The elevator dinged at the end of the hall, and I stood up quickly and went inside. Richard and Penny were eating dinner when I came in. I went straight to the balcony and stared at the ocean.

Reality slapped hard. The whole damn world seemed to be telling me to get a plan. I moped around for a few days, drinking too much rum and smoking too much pot while Richard went to work.

Already the magic and sweetness was evaporating between Richard and me, just like it had between me and Simon. "If you're going to stay, it's time to get a job," he told me.

"Yeah, yeah, yeah," I mumbled. "I get it." Where had I heard that before? Jesus!

Typing was my only "real" skill, and I decided to become a legal secretary. If I was going to type for money, it might as well be legal briefs and complaints instead of letters and memoranda.

After scouring the paper, I landed my first interview in downtown Miami. On the test they gave me, I typed eighty-nine words per minute error-free, and I was hired at the law offices of Reginald M. Hayden Jr., as a legal trainee making $75 a week. It was so simple to get a job that it shocked me.

Penny came over for dinner to celebrate my job. I made spaghetti for them. The three of us laughed and joked about the backgammon count as we outwardly celebrated, but inside I felt unusually sensitive and found it challenging to play the innocent charade any longer.

After eating and drinking our fill, Richard put his hand over Penny's and said, "We're so glad your job is going well. We think it's time for you to find your own place."

Everything was "we" now. They were banding together against me.

"Yes, you're probably right, but I don't want to. I love it here with you guys. Can't I pay rent?"

Penny shook her head. "It's time, Leslie. You need to make some decisions about your life. You're just hiding out here."

As the passion between Richard and me had cooled over the weeks, Penny had begun eyeing me differently. She wasn't nearly as accommodating, kind, or keen to talk about our lives.

The next day, I searched the *Miami Herald* for a room to rent and found several to choose from. I decided to rent from an older woman who had a furnished room with a bed, a dresser, and a small television for $120 a month. I got kitchen privileges, and she said she liked to share dinners she made.

Richard was adamant that I write to my father and tell him I had a job and a place to live. I protested, but he insisted.

With the song "What Can I Say" by Boz Skaggs playing in the background and a joint burning in the ashtray, I typed a letter on Richard's Corona typewriter, sitting at the dining table.

> *Dear Father,*
> *I am fine. I am in Miami. I make $75 per week and rent a room.*
> *Leslie*

I did not sign the letter but typed my name. I even typed the envelope without a return address. There was no personal handwriting on anything. I hated him and only sent the letter to keep Richard happy.

* *

Moving out from the beautiful high-rise apartment building into a shabby old house with a shabby older woman meant losing everything fun and happy in my life. Simon was gone, and now so was Richard. I imagined Dad laughing at me, which made me redouble my efforts to become independent.

My job at the law firm was challenging and fun. The people were friendly and accepting of me. I learned about filing, typing pleadings, copying, and answering the phone. I had thirty minutes for lunch daily and always went outside for fresh air. I discovered street vendors selling delicious small pastries with spicy ground beef inside for seventy-five cents. The first time I bought one, I was running late and starving. Expecting fruit inside, the flavor was pleasantly scrumptious—and within my budget. From then on, I ate the meat and potato empanadas for breakfast and lunch. At home, with the small amount of money left over, I ate popcorn for dinner. I was broke after paying the first and last month's rent and buying a used bike to ride to work.

The depressing weeks dragged on. I ate with my landlady once or twice when she made chili or scrambled eggs, but the silence was heavy at the dinner table. I was conflicted about so much in my life that I didn't know what to talk about. What was I doing in Miami? Proving that I could support myself wasn't as fun as I had imagined. Nobody was cheering me on. Life was hard and I needed a plan.

49

My only solace was writing in my diary. I went to work, came home, and stayed in my bedroom with the door closed, eating popcorn, writing in my journal, writing poems, and pacing around my bed with old movies playing. Something was wrong in my life. I began thinking about home, school, and getting my high school degree. It was October, and my head had been buried in the sand the last few months, so I didn't know if I'd passed the proficiency test I'd taken back in April.

The next day, I called Monica from a pay phone. "It's so good to hear from you," she said. "Where are you?"

"Miami, can you believe it?" When I asked about Mom, Monica said she had gotten out of the hospital a month after I left.

"She has an apartment in Torrance and works at Harbor General Hospital."

"That's so great! How's Karen?"

"She's in Kenya for a semester."

"What? Lucky girl in Africa."

Monica explained that Karen had gone to her "Outward Bound-type" experience called Interalp, a semester-long educational program. "I get letters from her telling me all about the program. There's a stack of letters here for you, too."

My heart softened at the thought of letters from Karen at home. "Have you seen my test results?" I asked.

"No, I haven't seen them. I moved out. I'm living with some girls from church. I'm only here now to pick up my bike. But I can try to find the letter in Dad's office. Hold on."

I waited and hoped, praying to a god I didn't believe in. She returned to the phone. "You didn't pass, Leslie. I'm sorry."

It was my third fail. My voice shook as I fought back tears. "I've got to come home and finish high school."

"Come home, Leslie. You can live with Mom. She'd love it."

"Ugh, I guess that's my only option."

When I got back to my bedroom, I had a good cry. It was time to give notice at work and go home.

50

Seeing Monica with a big smile at the gate as I disembarked from the Miami flight skewered me. Her gazelle-like frame, long blonde hair, big brown eyes, and thick curly eyelashes shone before me. Her smile and awkward way of doing everything, including walking toward me, touched someplace deep inside. I'd missed my sister.

"Hey, Lez," she said as I ran to her and threw my arms around her neck. "Hey, hey, are you okay?"

I pulled back and looked at her scatter of freckles. "I've missed you so much."

We talked nonstop on the drive to Mom's apartment. I confessed the disastrous end to my relationship with Simon, my job as a legal secretary in Miami, skimming over what had happened with Richard and Penny.

"I'm glad you're done with Simon," she said, then pausing slightly, she added, "Now on to a better topic." She handed me a stack of letters from Karen in Kenya. I flipped through the thin blue airmail envelopes that doubled as paper. "I'm seeing Mike from Redondo High. Remember him?"

I nodded. She explained their connection in that church, Faith of Our Fathers. "Just in case you wanted to know, Dad is gone. He's traveling for his new business, so you can go to the house and get your stuff if you want."

"Does he know I'm coming home?"

"Yes, I told him. I hope that's okay."

I nodded. "It's fine." But after a minute longer of silence as I felt the bruises of being in a fight with life, I added, "Will you come with me to the house, please?"

She agreed, and we made plans to go the following day.

Mom now lived in a densely populated two-story concrete apartment building on Western Avenue with very few trees. We entered her one-bedroom cave-like abode, where all the windows were covered in black sheets, and tried to act normal. I put my suitcase and backpack down near the couch.

"Hi, Mom, it smells so good in here. How are you?" The smell of garlic bread and Mom's famous spaghetti nearly knocked me over. I was starving.

She came around the corner from the kitchen, skinnier than I remembered, with red lipstick on her tight smile. "I'm fine, girls. I hope you're hungry." She wrapped me in her usual airy hug and kiss, barely making contact. The wear and tear of that horrible place, Norwalk State Hospital, was visible up close. I could tell she struggled every day to get out of bed, and that this dinner had been a Herculean effort.

"Of course, we're starving," Monica said, licking her lips. Nothing had changed; Monica was always hungry.

It felt good that my return was a moment to mark. Spaghetti was the dish Mom served on most special occasions. She had perfected it since our childhood, even though she didn't have an Italian bone in her body.

"Lezlie, it's so good to have you home," she said, directing us to the neatly set linoleum table.

I hated when she pronounced my name like that, but I didn't say anything, wanting to keep the peace and enjoy the reunion.

She placed heaping plates of pasta before us, hovering and doting with offers of more parmesan cheese, sauce, or another slice of garlic bread.

"Aren't you going to eat?" I asked.

"I'm not hungry right now. I'll have some a little later," she said as she washed the dishes.

Monica left after dinner, and I inspected the old brown-and-green plaid couch that would be my bed while living with Mom. She had made it up with fresh sheets and a blanket, and I was grateful. Exhaustion hit me like a truck, and I fell into bed with a smile and a full stomach.

Over the following few days, raw and weepy feelings overwhelmed me, surprising me each time they ballooned. I chalked it up to feeling like a failure for having to come home to finish high school. When would I ever be free of this nagging obligation to graduate?

Even after a week of watching television all day and sleeping all night, I couldn't get a handle on myself, feeling sensitive and tender-hearted. Mom stayed in her room most of the time, calling into work some days, and other days rallying and heading out the door in her white nurse's uniform with a sullen, sad, and depressed feeling about her. She and I barely spoke. I had nothing to say; apparently, she had nothing to say either.

I devoured Karen's letters about Kenya: her studies, the boys, hiking, the big city of Nairobi, and language classes. Africa felt so unfamiliar to me. My only reference was *National Geographic*. I couldn't imagine hiking Mount Kilimanjaro.

After several weeks, I forced myself to enroll at Narbonne High and reluctantly attended classes, feeling more like an alien than ever before. This was the fourth high school in three years and the most challenging. I counted myself among only a tiny handful of white girls. It wouldn't have been a problem except the Black girls hated me, sneering and pushing me at my locker and in the hallway for no visible or plausible reason.

Complaining to Mom or the office administration about being bullied and intimidated was pointless. I just had to hold out for the proficiency test in March, and I prayed I'd make it until then.

Every morning, I felt more nauseous than the day before. The four-day Thanksgiving break gave me leave to stay home and sleep, trying not to moan or groan when Mom was around. Scared that it might be a tropical flu from Miami, I kept the apartment dark and couldn't bear to eat. I was doing a version of Mom, and that scared me too. Monica called to invite Mom and me to some special Thanksgiving thing at the church. We declined, neither of us wanting the crowd. We both subsisted on soup and saltines, but she still drank heavily, hiding the liquor in her bedroom.

By early December, things were not improving with my health. Barely able to keep anything down, I called my old friend, Cyndi, who suggested a pregnancy test. I had not even considered that a possibility and felt foolish for being so naive. When the test came back positive, I called her back and begged for her help.

The nasty flu from Miami was a baby growing inside me.

Cyndi took me to the beach for a long chat at our old stomping grounds, the strand in Hermosa Beach. I cried about the pregnancy and that the rest of my life would be dictated by the choice I made at this moment. How convenient that Richard was utterly unaware of the dire situation I found myself in. *Oh, to be a man in this world.*

Having the baby was not an option. Richard would never marry me or be a reliable person to have a child with. He loved Penny and lived in Florida. My life and family were here in California. I'd have to raise the baby alone, which sounded impossible. I envisioned a happy, successful life, certainly not one as a single mom ostracized and shamed by society. Abortion was the only choice, but I needed to keep it very quiet. Mom couldn't know. With her Catholic upbringing, judgment and condemnation would be the only things I could expect from her.

Cyndi took me for an appointment at the free clinic, where we discovered an abortion cost $225 and that being knocked out during the procedure cost $75 more. I called Richard. When he answered "Speakeasy," I gave it to him straight.

"Oh God, Leslie. How did that happen?" I rolled my eyes, shook my head, and waited for him to catch up, twisting the phone cord around my finger. "If your dad finds out, he'll fly to Florida and kill me. I'm sure of it."

"That's what you have to say first . . . really?"

He paused and finally said, "Sorry. It's what I thought of."

"Well, don't worry. He won't find out. I haven't even seen him since coming home. My friend will take me to the appointment, but I need three hundred dollars."

Without hesitating, he said, "Of course, I'll put the check in the mail today."

I hung up the phone and cried my eyes out. How could I be pregnant? How would I get through this? Now, I would always be a person who had had an abortion.

51

On the appointed day with the $300 in hand that Richard sent, Cyndi drove me to the clinic, where nurses dressed in operating room scrubs led me into a room. I tried to think of something else, to envision myself in a forest of redwoods along the Northern California coast. Still, the whiteness and sterility, the antiseptic smell, and the squeak of the nurse's white shoes on the white linoleum made it impossible to pretend. She handed me a white gown to change into, and when I climbed up on the table, she said the words I dreaded most: "Put your feet in the stirrups and slide all the way down." Another nurse inserted an IV into my arm, and everything went black.

I woke up groggy with my legs flat on the table. The nurse said, "Whenever you're ready to get up, darling, you let me know."

Staring at the white tiles on the ceiling for a few minutes, I sat up. The nurse rushed to help me. I dressed, and Cyndi took me home. We didn't speak on the drive. I wanted to cry but didn't allow myself. I stuffed it down. This was punishment for being a stupid, irresponsible, bad girl. I deserved to be punished.

I was told to stay off my feet for forty-eight hours. I bled heavily for the first three days. If I had had a bedroom, I would have crawled into it and locked the door to cry and sleep forever. But my bed was on the couch, and there was no hiding my medical condition from a professional nurse. Mom studied me with big eyes, searching my face to find a hint of something.

"What's wrong with you?" She put her cold hand on my warm forehead. I rolled away, but she put her hand on my back and rubbed gently. Having her study my face for an answer made everything worse. If she found out what I'd done, she'd decide things about me that would make me cry.

"Did you have a procedure?"

The way she said the word "procedure" meant she knew. Burrowing my head into the couch, I nodded. She cried, yelled, and paced around the apartment, saying that we could have moved to Windsor, lived together, and raised the baby. Peeking out from under the cushion, I saw her cross herself while mumbling something incoherent. I rolled over. "No, Mom. I couldn't live in the shadows and be ashamed my entire life. I'm only seventeen." I buried my head in the covers again. She finally left me alone, and I cried myself to sleep.

Damn Richard. Damn men in general for never having to go through this kind of thing. I silently swore to myself that I'd never let this happen again. I'd take responsibility for my own birth control. Never trust the man to take care of the birth control—never!

As Mom began to feel less depressed and I healed from the procedure, we made our way into the world again: she at work and church with Monica, and me back to dreaded Narbonne High. The Black girl contingent still tortured me, and I lived in fear of them finding me alone somewhere.

A few days before Christmas, I received a card from Dad. I had yet to talk to him since returning from Miami. The front of the card showed two children in a wintry scene: a girl bundled up in a jacket, handmuffs, and a hat, and an older boy bundled up in a scarf and hat, both staring up at a bird cage on a pole with two birds. The front said, "Hi, Daughter! It's a nice Christmassy feeling...". Inside, it said, "... to wish you the Merriest!"

The card was signed in a woman's cursive hand: "Love, Dad."

What was this? He would never sign a card that way. He never signed "love." What a scam. He'd ordered his secretary, Mary, to send me a card! How thoughtful! How sincere!

A typed letter on A-1 International Marine Recovery stationery fell out, containing a $100 credit at Holiday Photo on Hawthorne Boulevard for photo equipment and film development. It was also signed "Love, Dad." Damn him for ordering Mary to be nice to me. Damn him with this olive branch. I used the credit to develop a half dozen film canisters of pictures I'd taken in Miami.

Karen and I had been trading letters, but the mail service from Kenya took weeks, sometimes more, so I was surprised a few days before Christmas when I received a letter dated December 12, 1978. She wrote that she was meeting Dad in Norway for Christmas but was alone stuck at London's Heathrow Airport, having missed her flight to Oslo. Envy and jealousy rose in me. *I want to go to Norway for Christmas.* It sounded so much nicer than Narbonne High.

Reading this letter ten days after the incident made me panic for my sixteen-year-old sister, all alone in the world. But, the next day, a postcard came from Karen with Ingemar Stenmark on the front, relating the good time she was having in Norway and Sweden.

Dad and Karen came home in early January, and Monica and I couldn't wait to catch up with our sister. Mom made her delicious Salisbury steak with mashed potatoes and gravy, and we sat around the square card table while Karen regaled us first with fabulous stories of Africa and then with family stories of Norway and Sweden, including that she'd stayed at our grandfather's home in Oslo with Dad.

My heart pinched with envy. Monica and I hadn't seen our bestefar (Norwegian for "grandfather") since 1971, when he had lived with us for six months on our ranch in Paradise, California. Bestefar had helped Dad build the house on our property. He barely spoke English, but Monica, Karen, and I didn't need many words to have fun. We loved him and laughed with him. He showed us Norwegian music and dances. Language was inconsequential when it came to getting to know our Norwegian grandfather.

"I have news," Karen said suddenly as we all ate.

"What?" I said, surprised she had waited so long to say something.

"Don't be shocked, but we have a brother."

The news landed with a thud. Stunned and silent, Monica and I stared at Karen. Mom had an almost imperceptible smile on her face. I leaned toward her. "You knew?"

"Yes, I knew. I'm sorry I didn't tell you girls, but I promised your father."

Without missing a beat, Monica jumped in. "Like you promised not to tell me about my real father?"

"Now, Monica, calm down," Mom said. She let her fork drop with a clang.

I rushed in to support Monica. "You promised to keep a secret to a man who's been horrible to you," I said. "Since when do we keep promises to them?"

Mom just smirked at us. She seemed to enjoy shocking us and the attention of it all, her face open and wide-eyed with that terrible grin that reminded me we were only beats away from her mental illness.

I turned back to Karen. "Tell us."

She ran it down succinctly. His name was Rune. He was twenty-two, lived in Oslo with his mother, and looked a lot like Dad if

Dad had hair. "He's coming to visit us next summer." But that news didn't land.

"He's only a few years older than me," Monica mused, her voice trailing. Another bombshell in our fucked-up family.

As we said goodbye to Karen after dinner, Mom said, "Girls, never mind about the details. You have a brother, and he's coming to visit."

52

I was only weeks away from my eighteenth birthday and two months away from taking the proficiency test—again. Fear of those girls at school consumed me as I counted the days by X-ing out squares on the calendar I hung on the living room wall.

I rushed to class one day and slipped into the girls' bathroom. Luckily, there was no one in there. While I was reading the etched-out graffiti on the back of the door, somebody entered the stall right next to me. This girl reached underneath the wall more quickly than a jackrabbit and swiped my leg with a razor blade. The flash of the metal caught the edge of my eye. I felt nothing at first, but saw the blood gushing from my shin. The girl ran out of the bathroom, hooting and hollering in happiness. I covered the gash with a gob of toilet paper and rushed to the office, where I had an emotional outburst so loud it beckoned every administrative staff member from their office to see the commotion until the nurse fixed me up and sent me home.

Fuck high school! My life was in danger at that school!

While I was at home recovering, Mom doted on me and tended my wound as I studied for the proficiency test from a workbook I had found in the school library. It broke down the test by section, with practice questions at the end of each chapter. *If I fail for a fourth time, I should be certified as the stupidest person alive.*

I took the test again in March and never went back to that damn school. If I failed the test again, I didn't know what I would do. The school called many times but eventually gave up. I was eighteen and legally didn't have to go to school anymore.

Richard wrote frequently, checking on my progress, feeling guilty about everything I had endured. When I said I needed a car, he sent me money. I found a used two-toned white-and-orange 1971 VW van that was hollowed out inside, so it only had a driver's seat and passenger seat. I paid $800 for it and imagined putting a mattress in the back, driving away, and never coming back. The dream of escaping my life was never-ending.

Grateful for the freedom only wheels could provide, I found work at a Vietnamese restaurant, seating people and packaging food to go. I saved every cent. I called Raine in Oceanside and begged her to come and visit. She spent one night with me on the couch at Mom's apartment, but it was too small for us. We dreamed out loud together of earning enough money to be independent. She was still living with her crazy mom, Myrna Loy. We even talked about selling ourselves to respectable men to make money fast. We talked out each step. We would move into my van, hit the road, and find some paying customers in Hollywood or Venice Beach. But when it came right down to it, we both chickened out. I returned to work at the restaurant, and she went home to her mom.

I found a second job typing documents for a real estate company through a temporary agency. On my way from the office job to the restaurant one night, while waiting to make a left turn on Western Avenue, I stretched to look around a car coming in the opposite direction. The car was stopped and making its own left-hand turn. I determined it was clear, so I put my foot on the gas and let out the clutch. The van jerked and sputtered as usual, and by the time I got out onto Western Avenue, everything had gone black. Later I was told that another car had hit me with such force that I flew through the front windshield and landed in the McDonald's parking lot on the corner. My van was bent in half, and I was unconscious, splayed out on the sidewalk.

I woke up completely disoriented to a blond paramedic standing over me. I tried to sit up, but my right arm fell away from my body. I screamed out, grabbed it, and hauled it close to me, fearing it would break off. "Looks like you fractured your clavicle," the handsome blue-eyed man said while wiping the bloody gash on my forehead. "Let's get you loaded up into the ambulance." They transferred me to Harbor General Hospital, where Mom worked.

The doctors reset my clavicle, taped my arm to my body, and put it in a sling. They wrapped my head in white gauze and sent me home with pain pills. I couldn't lie down, so Mom fashioned a pillow chair on the couch for me to sleep sitting up. "This is going to take a while to heal," she said, adjusting my pillows and changing my sheets every few days.

"Thanks, Mom. I'm sorry I'm such a pain in the ass." Her full and generous smile let me know she was kidding when she said, "Some things never change." The pills took the pain away from my shoulder and also, thankfully, took me away from my life. For a week, cocooned in a haze, I dozed in and out, feeling happily free from the churning ball of hurt that lived in my stomach like a twenty-four-hour washing machine. Coming out of the Vicodin fog, I realized both jobs were history and my van was totaled.

I didn't have car insurance, and neither did the guy who hit me.

I was back to square zero.

53

Near the end of my recovery, the phone rang, and Mom answered it in the kitchen. She talked low, but I heard her say my name. A few minutes later, she called, "Leslie, your father is on the phone."

Perplexed at what those two could have to talk about for several minutes quietly, I picked up the living room receiver. "Hello?"

Without any introductory pleasantries, he launched into the conversation. "I have some good news for you."

"Okay," I said hesitantly. Mom watched me from the kitchen. I turned my back to her.

"Can you come to the house this weekend?"

My stomach clenched. I didn't want to see him. He continued, "Karen can come and pick you up. How about Saturday at 3 p.m.?"

"Um, okay, I guess. What's going on?"

"It's a surprise. You'll be happy. See you Saturday." He hung up.

Mom came out of the kitchen with a beaming face.

"What is going on, Mom? Please."

She moved her fingers across her sealed lips and made a grand gesture of throwing away the key.

Karen also refused to give me even a hint of a clue when she picked me up. "I promised him I wouldn't tell."

We arrived at the 190th Street house in Redondo Beach and found

Dad working on a sailboat rudder in the garage. He met us in the driveway. "Hello."

It had been a year since we had seen each other. He looked thinner, tanned, and had a kinder smile. He took my arm and led me to the street, where traffic whooshed by. Sweeping his hand over a baby-blue Chevy Chevette, he said, "This is yours," like we were on a game show.

"Mine? Really?"

He handed me the key and returned to the garage without further fanfare. Flabbergasted, I watched him walk away and wondered what made him tick.

I took Karen on a shakedown ride to the beach. "What is with him? This car surprise thing is so wonderful but also crazy." We turned north onto Coast Highway.

"I know you don't believe it, but he loves you."

"Stop talking right now. I'm grateful, but please . . ." I had to turn my head away from her, my voice trailing off, afraid I might start crying and never stop. Now if I could just get a passing grade on the proficiency test, my life would be headed in the right direction again. The results were due soon.

I was summoned for dinner at the Portofino Inn in King Harbor a few weeks later. Karen, Monica, and Dad greeted me in the parking lot, standing next to a tall fair-haired man I didn't recognize. "Meet Rune, your Norwegian brother." Dad beamed.

"It's nice to meet you," I said to Rune, whose pudgy baby face reddened.

"Nice to meet you too," he managed in a thick Norwegian accent.

He appeared shy and entirely out of his element. I could tell he didn't know our loud, boisterous father.

Hang tight, Rune, the fun is just beginning.

Dad looked relaxed and happy. His bald head always made him stand out in a crowd. Karen beamed, watching us all get acquainted. She was the only one who still lived at home with Dad.

Inside the restaurant, I sat directly across from Rune, watching him and wondering so many things, trying not to stare. I studied my food, looked at Monica and Karen, and tried to eat normally in a very awkward situation. Silverware clinked, and eyes darted. None of us girls knew what to say. Did he speak fluent English? Dad filled the silence by sharing plans he had to fly Rune in his plane all over the West Coast.

After we ate, Dad led us out to the jetty, and we watched the ocean. I wished we spoke the same language, or that I had time to talk to Rune away from Dad. I had so many questions. Did he sail? Was he in college? Did he work? But I didn't get a chance to ask.

"I'm running back to the car for the camera," Dad called as he walked toward the parking lot.

I knew it would be the only time I'd have to ask Rune the one burning question I had held on to since I was twelve.

"Will you translate something Dad says to me in Norwegian, if you can?" I asked.

"I will try," he said sincerely.

"I don't know if I'm saying it correctly, but here goes: Freska bona sloshe por tre leggin."

His quizzical face looked out toward the ocean, concentrating on the words. Anxious, I kept talking. "Dad would say these words every time he slapped my thigh."

I repeated the phrase and slapped my upper thigh. He listened and watched me, then shook his head. "Say again."

I repeated the words a third time, but he shook his head again. "I do not know. I never heard those words before."

Dad returned just as Rune finished talking, and we all posed for the camera like a happy family. "I have to get to work. It was nice meeting you, Rune." I was back at the Vietnamese restaurant after having recovered from my car accident.

"I'll walk you to your car," Karen said. I nodded and began walking.

"I'm saying goodbye, too," Monica said. "It was nice meeting you, Rune," she added. We left Dad and Rune on the jetty.

"Man, I'm glad that's over!" I said, feeling relief at the letdown inside.

"Me too," Monica said.

Karen took our elbows as we walked, talking deliberately. "I have something to tell you both. I don't want you to be shocked. Dad has a Swedish girlfriend at the house now, and her name is Elisabeth."

"I mean, who cares?" I said, dripping attitude.

"She's only twenty-four years old," Karen added.

"She's one year older than Rune?" Monica said, incredulous.

"Yeah. But they are so happy. And I like her very much."

All I could think was, *So that's why he looks so relaxed and happy.*

54

"Come down and visit me in that new car of yours." Raine sweet-talked me through the phone. "There's a party in Leucadia this weekend."

That was all I needed to hear. I got the weekend off, packed up my little Chevette, and headed south. The party was in a three-bedroom condo in a guard-gated community called Monarch Shores. Twenty or so people were on their way to the beach with a volleyball when we drove up. The smell of pot wafted through the air as The Rolling Stones blared. *Yes! I need this*, I thought.

A tall, thin, very sexy older *GQ* man with thick dark hair ran up to Raine and lifted her in a bear hug. Her dark-brown hair swayed to the side. "Hi, Raine," he exclaimed louder than the music. "Introduce me to your friend." He winked at me, put Raine down, and bowed exaggeratedly.

His name was Mark Stanton. He promptly kissed my cheek, enveloping me in his sandalwood scent. "Nice to meet you, gorgeous." His cobalt eyes danced. A woman with a hint of a scowl appeared out of nowhere and took Mark's arm, pulling him away. My nasty self decided she was too average-looking for such a slender, foxy man.

"Come on, we're up in the tournament," she said.

He winked as she whisked him away. "Make yourself at home," he said. "There's food and drink inside. Come to the beach and watch us play volleyball."

We found the wine, put on our bikinis, and followed the crowd. "Mark is a family friend from way back," Raine said as we walked toward the beach. "He's a handful, so be careful." We rounded the corner and saw the sudden-death tournament raging, with Mark and his girlfriend nearing match point. The crowd of partygoers cheered, and we sat down behind them.

Over the next hour, Mark and his girlfriend fended off challengers until they finally lost and the crowd headed to the pool. Straggling behind, Mark yelled back to us, "Hey, girls, come in the pool!"

Raine's freckles popped off her sunburned face. "In a minute."

He ran after us and threw his arm around my shoulders. "Where did you come from?" He threw his other arm around Raine. "Where have you been hiding Leslie?"

His glassy eyes slid up and down my body. I looked away from his intense stare.

"Don't you have a girlfriend here at the party?" Raine said.

He ignored the question and massaged my shoulders. "I ask again: Where did you come from?"

"Torrance," I said.

"Leslie and I went to junior high together," Raine added.

"Come and join us!" he said, running back to the crowd.

When we got to the pool, it was full of people on floaties, drinking and smoking pot. The music was so loud I couldn't hear anything. We didn't know anybody except Mark, but Raine and I waded into the middle of the mayhem in the pool. Mark tossed a ball in the air, watching me intently. He waved to me just as the song "Kiss You All Over" by Exile began playing. He moved his shoulders to the beat, then floated toward me. He was staggeringly beautiful. His thick chest hair, long dark eyelashes, and bushy eyebrows looked like he belonged in a magazine, but his dark, azure-blue eyes melted my defenses. He studied me like a painting.

"Gorgeous," he mouthed. He danced around me, moving the water in small waves, rubbing up against me.

"Where's your girlfriend?" I rolled my eyes at Raine, trying to downplay Mark's antics around me.

"Over there," he said, indicating a table in the corner. When the chorus began to play, he stood behind me, kissed my neck and shoulders, and swayed, whispering, "This is our song today." I swam away, trying to regain my space and composure.

"One of These Nights" by the Eagles played and I gently swayed to one of my favorite songs. I motioned for Raine to join me. Mark offered us both a floatie and we climbed on. He circled me, spinning me, singing, and kissing my neck.

"I'm going to marry you one day," he whispered in my ear.

I laughed. "You don't even know me."

He continued dancing and repeated, "I'm going to marry you one day."

"Mark!" His girlfriend's voice cut through the music and the laughter. He spun around and went to her. Raine and I got off the floaties. "Man, Raine, who is this guy?"

"He's a friend of Aunt Sande's."

We found a place on the side of the pool. "How old is he?"

"Early thirties, but don't you think he looks younger?"

I shrugged. Here was the third man in his early thirties inexplicably drawn to me. Did I have a sign around my neck saying AVAILABLE ONLY TO MEN IN THEIR EARLY THIRTIES?

At the condo, several people did lines of cocaine on the coffee table and offered us some. I had never tried coke and was reluctant. "It's good," Raine said, and she did a line. I watched how she did it with a rolled-up $20 bill. When she handed it to me, I took the money straw, held one side of my nose, and sniffed hard on the line. Man!

Instant glory. Instant euphoria. Nice! And that deliciously odd taste in my throat—yes, please! Everything fell away, and all the questions in my life were answered. More, please!

The evening disappeared as I hovered near that pile of cocaine, talking and doing lines with my new best friends. The crowd from the pool arrived and the party got louder and more coke came out. Mark found me in a beanbag chair with a vodka cranberry balancing on my knee, relaxing with my head back after dancing to twenty or more songs. It was so nice to feel good and not be worried about anything. Freedom and euphoria were welcome companions. Nothing could ruin my mood. I didn't have to be back to work until Monday night.

Raine disappeared somewhere with a surfer friend, and Mark slid into the other half of the beanbag chair with me. I scanned the room. "Where's your girlfriend?"

He put his hand on my knee, helping himself to a sip of my drink. "Want to do a line?"

I nodded yes with a big grin on my face.

"Follow me," he said, pulling me up from the beanbag chair. "Bring your drink."

I followed him to the bedroom, even as warning bells went off in my head. I wanted more cocaine. That was all that mattered. He opened the dresser, took out a neatly folded paper triangle, and laid a thick line. Then he took out a $100 bill rolled into a straw and handed it to me with a gaze that pierced my soul. I sniffed up my line. He did his line and then studied me up and down. "Where did you come from, sweet Leslie?"

"I thought I already told you, Redondo Beach." A flash caught my eye at the doorway. His frowning girlfriend wore an orange bikini, eyeing the dresser and the cocaine. Mark fixed her a line, and I left the room.

When I returned to the living room, Raine was cozied up in the corner with the surfer, looking very happy. We waved to each other.

It was late or very early, depending on how you looked at it. The party was thinning out and I sat on the couch watching everyone, happier than I could ever remember being in my entire life. I didn't want to ever leave this magical place. Mark sat down beside me.

"Stay the night here on the couch. I'll talk to Raine. You two shouldn't drive back to Oceanside tonight."

I nodded okay, and he disappeared.

Restless, I walked to the beach by myself. I wandered through the condo complex to the stairs to the beach, sitting on the last step with my feet in the sand. The moon was half full, and I watched the waves break on the sand one after another. My mind was clear of all thought and I felt light and euphoric. I finished my drink and headed back to the condo. Everyone, including Raine, was laid out on the floor like beached seals when I returned. I passed out and didn't wake up until I heard screaming and crying.

Mark's girlfriend stood at the threshold of the living room. "It's over!" Mark said at the door. "Get out." She left in a river of tears, slamming the door behind her.

He came to the couch and took my hand, leading me to his bedroom, where he shut the door, and I allowed him to ravish me. I must have passed out again, because we woke in the afternoon groggy, hungry, and thirsty. His dark mustache and warm hands slid over my body, leaving me in a trance. His beautiful smile mesmerized me, but his money, nice clothes, and sexy dark-brown Camaro parked out front wooed me best. He seemed successful, like people who lived in Malibu or Marina del Rey—rich people. Money and freedom enticed me like nothing else.

When Raine left with her guy friend, I stayed for the rest of Sunday and Sunday night with Mark. By the time I woke up relatively sober Monday afternoon, it had been three days, and Mark and I had been intimate many times. It felt good to be adored. He laid out the morning line, delivering it to me on a small, round mirror with a $100 bill.

He got me coffee and Bloody Marys, made me food, brushed my hair, and laid out my clothes when I was in my swimsuit so they wouldn't get wrinkled. He doted on me, and I savored it. He told me over and over again how beautiful I was and how he would marry me one day. I laughed each time, but I lapped up his attention.

We lived at the beach, lounged in the sun, jumped the waves naked at sunset, making love until we hurt. I willingly became his captive lover. We looked good together. People stared at us for just a beat too long and we reasoned that they did this because we glowed. We deserved to be on the cover of a magazine as the pure representation of love. Over the course of a few days, I had fallen completely under his spell, adrift in the world, lost, without purpose or direction except to be with Mark, completely willing to leave my other life behind without a second thought.

55

Two weeks later, we moved to Orange County to conquer the world. Newport Beach was monied in the way we dreamed for ourselves, and we intended to work there and hobnob with the rich. We found a two-bedroom apartment in Laguna Hills, a newly designed suburb for up-and-coming young professionals. That's how we saw ourselves. We were talented, ambitious, and beautiful, we told ourselves, worthy of great success and fortune.

Every wealthy person needs to start somewhere, so I found a job with my only valuable skill: typing, being hired as an executive secretary at Far West Services, the corporate headquarters for Coco's, Baxter's, and Reuben's restaurants. Mark found work as a restaurant manager at Baxter's in Newport Beach. Nothing could ruin our high. Every single week, without delay, he asked me to marry him.

Over the next month, we worked hard, drank, and partied harder. High on cocaine, I could focus intently at work, organizing the filing system and impressing my new boss. I lost weight, which was always on my mind. My father's voice in my head continued to berate me. There was no turning off that droning sound. Cocaine was the answer. It made me skinny and feel whole, loved, and energetic.

We tried to only use it on the weekends at parties, but the absence of coke led to drinking heavily to take the edge off.

On the way to Los Angeles to pick up some cocaine one day, the sunroof open and the blue sky shining her happiness down on us, he said once again, "Marry me, Leslie. Why won't you marry me?"

"I'm only eighteen. Let's wait, okay?"

He pouted and gave me puppy-dog eyes.

"I'm not saying no."

"Do you want kids?" he asked, leaning over to my side of the car.

"Eventually, yes."

He kissed my hand and sang to the song on the radio at the top of his lungs. I raised my hands out the sunroof, grabbed for the blue sky, and screamed in euphoria as loud as I could, thinking, *Maybe I should marry him*. He seemed dead set on it. *Maybe it's the right thing to do.* I was so happy. Everything was working out beautifully.

When the song ended, he said, "Should I ask your father for your hand in marriage?"

I thought, *Oh God, he'd lose his lunch for sure*, intrigued with the idea.

I nodded. "Yes, you should ask my father for my hand in marriage."

The following day, after Mark had reminded me a thousand times to call my father, I did. It had been months since I'd talked to anybody in my family. Taking my cue from the King himself, I got right to the point and didn't waste time with pleasantries.

"Hi, Dad. I met a guy and want you to meet him. It's getting serious."

"*Reaallly?*" he said, drawing out the word.

"Yes, *reaallly*," I echoed.

"Bring him to the Torrance airfield Sunday, and we'll take a short flight before we have brunch with your sisters and Rune."

He was playing nice, so I decided to play along. Mark was ecstatic at the offer.

On our drive to Torrance Airport on Sunday, my nerves ate me like a nasty germ. We had each done a few lines of cocaine that morning, and I felt jittery and unmoored from anything solid. Mark stopped and bought a pint of vodka and a carton of orange juice, and we alternated swigging each liquid while laughing about making screwdrivers in our mouths with each gulp. The vodka made me feel anchored to the world, settling my stomach and nerves so I wasn't floating free.

We met at the airfield, where Dad and his Swedish girlfriend stood by his four-seater Beechcraft Bonanza. *A double date—how nice.* Introductions were awkward as I struggled to relax. It was my first face-to-face meeting with Elisabeth. She was young, very pretty in that Swedish way with long flowing blonde hair, just as Dad liked it. She was demure yet smiling when he introduced her to Mark and me. While we were growing up, Dad had always insisted my sisters and I keep our hair long and flowing. Cutting it was a crime worthy of punishment.

Dad wore jeans and a Mexican shirt with a red-and-blue ascot tied around his neck. I hadn't seen him wear an ascot since he was dating a Tahitian girl years earlier. It must have been serious with Elisabeth. I watched him scowl as he secretly shot glances at Mark while performing his pilot checks.

Mark and I loaded into the back seat and we took off for an hour-long coastal tour. It was just as well that there was no talking over the engine noise in the plane other than Dad yelling, "Put your seatbelt on" and "Hold on, we're landing."

Thank God we drove to the restaurant separately. Mark and I made more screwdrivers in our mouths, and Mark had a surprise line for me. Maybe I did love him after all.

Brooding as he drove, he said, "Your dad doesn't seem to like me very much."

"It's not you. He doesn't like anybody, and he especially doesn't like guys I'm dating."

"Well, I'm not some guy. I'm your future husband."

I stared out the window, not knowing what to say.

We entered the Portofino Inn for their champagne Sunday brunch and saw my sisters, Rune, Dad, and Elisabeth sitting at a round table in front of a big bay window. They all had drinks in front of them. I hurried over to the table. "Sorry we're late. Everyone, this is Mark Stanton."

Mark presented well, and I held on to his arm, proud of how we looked together. My pink strapless summer dress perfectly complemented Mark's light-tan summer suit. He was model-worthy. This was our big entrance, and I focused on being the perfect couple. Mark pulled the chair out for me, and I sat. My life had officially begun, and I felt immensely grown up until I had to order a Coca-Cola while Mark ordered champagne like the other adults. At least I had had the screwdriver in the car before we arrived.

The view of the harbor, the boats' masts, and the fishing boats was spectacular. We ordered and ate. The air was thick and uncomfortable. I tried sharing some details of our life to break the ice, but no one had much to say, and no one asked Mark any questions.

Finally, I turned to Rune and asked, "When do you go back to Norway?"

"Next week," he said.

"And you?" I looked at Elisabeth. "Are you staying or going back?"

"I'm here for good," she said.

I nodded and tried to smile genuinely. I didn't like Elisabeth even though I had no real reason. Dad paid the bill and we all headed outside.

"I'll be right there," Monica said, heading for the bathroom.

"I'll join you." I rushed after her.

In the bathroom, I grabbed Monica by the shoulders and shook her gently, smiling, nervous, anxious, and needing to release some tension. "Do you like Mark?"

"Yes. He's very handsome. He seems nice," she said.

"He's asking Dad if we can marry."

"What? Really?" Her brown eyes were as big as pancakes while she stood frozen. "You're getting married?"

"Yes, I think so."

"How long have you known him?" she asked, drying her hands.

"Three months." I cringed a little inside, knowing it wasn't much time. She didn't respond.

When we arrived outside, Mark's face was red and twisted.

"Leslie, can I speak with you?" Dad said on the way to the parking lot, motioning for me to follow him.

I gave Mark a questioning look and followed Dad away so we could speak privately.

"He's a loser, Leslie. Don't marry him."

My heart beat loud in my chest. "That's what you have to say to me: He's a loser? Jesus, Dad."

"Let me add that he's a huckster and you shouldn't marry him." His voice was commanding and authoritative.

"How dare you? Why can't you be happy for me?"

He laughed and looked away.

I continued, "What about you? Elisabeth is almost my age. Why are you dating somebody so young? You look foolish."

He took a step back and squinted at me in anger. "Don't marry him, Leslie. You'll regret it." He walked away quickly, getting into the car and skidding a little in the gravel parking lot.

Tears welled up, but I pushed them down. Damn him ruining my happiness like that.

Monica stood by her car with a concerned look on her face. I waved goodbye to her and went to Mark, who was already in the car. "What did he say to you?" I demanded.

"He said no, I do not have permission to marry you."

"Jesus! Really?"

I couldn't tell him what Dad had said to me, so I edited it. "He told me our relationship won't last."

Mark shook his head. "All he did was quiz me on my life, work, and plans while you were in the bathroom."

"I hate him. I've always hated him. I wish he would die."

Mark started the car, and we drove home silently, all the joy gone.

Dad called me at work the following day, his voice bright and pleasant. "I have the results from the proficiency test."

"And . . ." The familiar bile bubbled up at the sound of his voice.

There was a ripping sound. "You finally passed after four stupid tries. Congratulations." His voice was sarcastic and spiteful.

My heart soared, but I controlled my voice and said, in the same commanding tone, "Thank you for calling."

"Are you going to marry that loser?" he said before I could put the receiver down.

"That's none of your business." I hung up just as a big ball of hurt floated to the top of my throat and I had to run to the bathroom.

56

A few weeks after the brunch, Mark asked me again to marry him while driving home from a party. "I love you and want you to be my wife."

It was probably the thousandth time he'd asked me. I thought, *I haven't tried marriage yet, so why not? Let's do it.* I found his eyes and said, "Sure, I'll marry you." We were the perfect couple, and soon we'd be joined in matrimony.

He kissed my hand as he drove down the 405 freeway. "Since we don't have much money, can we have the ceremony at the apartment?"

The half-dream of a white dress, a supportive family, a strawberry wedding cake, and a loving father walking me down the aisle vanished before it ever appeared. I was never the kind of girl who spent time planning my wedding. I knew this: Dad would be pissed. He would be so mad. That pleased me. I'll show him. I'll marry Mark and be happy despite him!

"Sure, that sounds nice," I lied. A heavy feeling enveloped me, and it felt like I'd walked into a new room in the world. The room of the bride and groom. The room of a married couple.

I knew marrying Mark was a mistake, but I shoved that feeling down hard, ignoring the warning bells. The little voice inside kept saying, "No, no, no, no," but I didn't listen. I ran right over that stupid voice and said, "Yes, yes, yes, yes."

"Will you invite your parents?" I asked, trying to focus on the positive.

"Sure, Mom and Dad will love you. She'll do the wedding cake, I'm sure."

"And I'll invite my sisters and Mom."

He grabbed my hand again. "I love you, Leslie, and want you to be my wife."

The date was set for September 15, 1979—the following Saturday. Mark hired a preacher from a local church. After the invitations were made, Mark's parents, John and Colleen, were kind and gracious about the whole shotgun aspect and offered to bring the cake. The regrets from my side of the family rolled in. Monica couldn't come because of church commitments. Mom was working, and my best friend, Raine, was visiting her grandmother in Louisiana. Karen came to our apartment and helped me with my hair and cocktail dress, which I had purchased the day before at May Company.

The ceremony lasted ten minutes, and I wondered why I had bothered to put on a dress. We ate sandwiches in the apartment, toasted with champagne, and cut Colleen's cake. Nothing felt like I thought it would. I wasn't even happy to have defied Dad. I wasn't excited to be married. *What in God's name am I doing?*

Karen, Colleen, and John left shortly after eating the cake. As soon as the door closed, Mark removed my dress, took me to bed, and was rougher than he'd ever been with me. In the coming weeks and months, Mark's sweet, loving attitude and doting nature would change into a possessor of my body. He would demand sex without regard for my wishes, forcing me into submitting to his pleasures. He would watch my every move, and I would recognize that paranoid look from years of seeing it on my mother. He would study my body and took pictures of me, as Dad used to do on the boat as if he was entitled to have whatever he desired. At first, I'd try to make it fun and do what he said, but as I'd refuse him, his attitude would become rougher. I would cower, scared and helpless to make him stop. My objections would only make him angry—and meaner. His personality would change so dramatically in such a short time, and it would not be lost on me that Dad had been right.

57

The phone rang. I was expecting to hear from Raine. She was planning a visit to our new apartment, so when I answered, breathless from hurrying from the kitchen where I was making dinner, my voice was happy when I said hello.

His voice answered low and gruff: "Hello."

Adrenaline surged so fast I thought the rush would knock me over. My face flushed and I sat down on the couch. I hadn't spoken to Dad since I married Mark two months earlier. I refused to be the one who called first to "make nice," and now that things had turned dark in my life, I didn't want to talk to him. He continued, "It's nice to hear your voice."

"Did you need something?" I whispered.

"I'm calling to invite you on a family Christmas trip to Scandinavia with Monica, Karen, Elisabeth, and me. We will spend time with Bestefar and see family in Sweden."

"Oh," I whispered. I sat gingerly on the edge of the couch, with my eyes fixed on the blue slice of sky out the sliding glass door. I had missed seeing Bestefar last year when Karen and Dad were in Oslo. My heart tugged.

"Think about it. Call me back tomorrow. I need to book tickets immediately."

"Okay. You're inviting Mark and me?"

"No. Just you," he said firmly.

"Oh." My voice trailed off.

"Goodbye, Sweetie."

My lips quivered at the word "sweetie." He used to call me that when I was little. I fell backward on the couch and stared at the ceiling, letting the phone slip to my chest. The loud *beep, beep, beep* from the receiver brought me out of the trance, and I put it back on the hook.

Mark came out of the shower and found me on the couch, staring at the ceiling. "What's the matter with you?"

"Dad called to invite me to Norway for Christmas with my sisters." I stared at a big gouge in the bumpy ceiling. The ice clinked from the kitchen as he made himself a drink. "But he didn't invite you."

He arrived at the couch. "And what did you tell him?" His voice was challenging.

"I didn't tell him anything yet." I got up to make room for Mark to sit down. He took the space and squinted at me over the rim of his gin and tonic, taking a large gulp.

"If I can't go, neither can you."

The drink looked good and I fixated on the beads of water collecting on the side as he set it down. He laid out two lines on the coffee table. "You can't say that. You don't get to decide for me."

He snorted in his line. "You would go without me?"

"I didn't say that. I'm just saying you can't decide for me." I did my line and went to the kitchen to make my own drink. "I'll call tomorrow and decline."

After Mark went to work, I called Dad's office and told Mary that I couldn't go on the family Christmas trip. "You should tell him yourself, Leslie."

"No. You tell him," I said, and quietly hung up, fighting back tears. My whole face quivered, and an ache inside felt like it would split me open. I made a drink and did a line.

58

A knock on the door woke me from dozing midmorning a few days later. Mark had left for work, and I had called in sick, needing time to plan my escape. I put on a robe and cracked open the door a slit to see a middle-aged man in a suit.

"Hello?"

"Hi, does Mark Edward Stanton live here?"

"Yes, but he's at work."

Consulting his clipboard, he asked, "Are you Leslie?"

"Yes, but who are you?"

"I'm Parole Officer Johnson. Can I come in, please? I have an appointment with Mark." He pushed a business card at me.

I took it, my grip on the door steely, looking around to see if any neighbors were near and if he was alone. "He's at work. Go there and talk to him."

"He said he was married and gave me your name. We really should talk."

My mind whirled at the fact that Mark had a parole officer, and he knew my name. "Let me get dressed." I closed and locked the door and rushed to the bedroom to put the cocaine paraphernalia away. I put on a pair of jeans and a T-shirt and opened the door a few minutes later to see Officer Johnson leaning against the railing, waiting patiently. I went out to the landing and closed the door behind me.

"Don't you want to talk inside?" he asked, staring at the door.

"I don't know you. Just tell me what you have to say."

"I'm Mark's parole officer and he missed his regular appointment last week, again."

I searched his face for a clue. "Parole officer? He never said anything about a parole officer. Are you sure you have the right Mark Stanton?"

The man chuckled, and his expression turned serious. "I am sure. Are you sure you have the right Mark Edward Stanton?"

"Please, come inside."

We sat on the couch, and I listened while he told me that Mark had been in Lompoc Prison, maximum security, for the last five years for selling heroin to an undercover cop. He stopped talking momentarily, waiting for me to move from my statuesque position, staring at the floor. When I didn't move, he added, "He was just released in June and hasn't missed an appointment so far."

"June? Are you sure?" That was right before we met at that weekend party in Leucadia. Tinny fear filled my mouth, and I swallowed hard.

Officer Johnson also revealed that Mark had an ex-wife and two children living in Illinois, who hadn't been receiving their support payment for the last two months. "It's part of his parole to send child support payments every month."

I shook my head in disbelief. I went to the kitchen. "Do you want anything to drink? I need some water."

"No thank you."

I came back to the living room. "Let me get this straight: Mark was in prison for five years and has a wife and two kids?" I drank half the water.

"Yes, that's correct."

After Officer Johnson left, I paced around the apartment, switching from water to a Bloody Mary and doing a fat line. *God damn it!*

How could I be so stupid? Dad was right. He's a huckster. Why did Dad have to be right?

That evening in the kitchen, after making him a drink after work, I said in my best carefree voice, "Officer Johnson came by today."

"Yeah, I meant to tell you about him," he said, his voice flat.

"That's kind of a big thing not to tell me." I handed him the rum and Coke.

His eyes were hard as copper. "It's no big deal. Drop it." He took a large gulp from his drink.

On the way back to the kitchen to freshen up my drink, I said, "And you have a wife and two kids in Illinois?"

"An ex-wife! Also, not a big deal." His angry, loud voice filled up the room.

Too scared to push it further for fear of retribution, I dropped it until he had finished his drink and had a line. At the turntable, I put on *Chicago*. We needed a happy distraction. The mood immediately lightened. Mark changed from his work clothes, calling from the bedroom, "I got us an eight ball for the weekend."

"How old are the kids?" I called back.

"The boy is seven, the girl is nine." He came back to the living room in jeans and a T-shirt.

I nodded, trying to keep calm, glad he didn't say their names. I didn't want to know their names once I realized I was a stepmom, only ten years older than his daughter.

I retrieved the baggie of coke from his jacket pocket and brought it to him in the reclining chair. My mind flitted all over the place, considering what it all meant, including mulling over why Raine hadn't told me about Mark's prison life. He put down two large lines, and we started the weekend partying.

"Let's start making babies. I'm ready to be a father," he proclaimed like some king.

I shook my head. "You're already a father."

"But I want to have babies with you," he decreed.

I stood up from the couch, feeling the need to assert myself forcefully. "We're not having children until you start taking care of the kids you already have." I bent over, did a line on the coffee table, and gulped my drink.

His voice turned sweet. "I will take care of them. I promise. I just forgot to send the payments a few times." He grabbed my hands and pulled me down on the couch with a mischievous look. "We can practice now."

Thank goodness I had an IUD.

59

My secretarial job at Far West Services got very interesting when a hunky guy from Facilities named Adam began hovering near me—tall, with dark hair, big muscles, and a winning smile like the actor on the new TV series *Magnum P.I.* I felt this magnetic pull to him, like with Richard. My body had a mind of its own as I silently responded to him. Adam somehow knew when I was in the copy room alone. He bumped against me, sliding his hands over my stomach and waist while I made copies. I froze like Bambi in the forest when the lion came, staring at the wall, knowing it was wrong but unable to do anything about it. He whispered in my ear, "You're gorgeous. We should get to know each other better." I didn't know how to respond at first, but eventually, I relaxed, giggling and squirming when he touched me.

He sauntered by my desk multiple times a day, smiling, stopping to visit, and showing up unexpectedly in the coffee room. I liked him best when he'd stand next to my desk and talk to me like a fellow employee, a real person, even if he was admiring me with his eyes. The teasing and flirting went on for months as a crescendo built. At night, when I'd leave, he'd sometimes walk me to my car and ask me out for a drink. I never accepted. Once he even invited me to go away with him on a weekend business trip. I declined all his invitations, but he intrigued me. It was nice to be admired by a man who could have easily been on the cover of *GQ* or *Playgirl*.

I also became quite close to a coworker in Accounting named Cher. She helped me with my employment paperwork and took me under her wing. She dressed smartly and worked hard, and I admired her kind heart. We regularly ate our lunches together. As I opened up about my life, she was shocked to find out I was only nineteen yet married to a thirty-one-year-old.

"Join us for a drink," she said one day after work. "We're going to a bar near my house."

"But I'm not twenty-one."

"It's okay, we're all regulars, and you look twenty-one. Stick close to me. Nobody should card you."

The place looked like an English pub. I studied the carved wooden sign of a headless Dutch woman hanging in front of the ivy-covered brick building and wondered what twisted man had designed it. I opened the heavy door, and my eyes took a minute to adjust to the darkness. The dark wooden walls felt like a warm hug, even if the logo was offensive. The barstools stood like soldiers at the ornate mahogany bar with small tables behind them. A low wood-and-brass railing separated the bar from the restaurant, where booths were ready for customers with red lamps on white linen tablecloths. We headed to one of the small tables next to the bar.

Cher ordered her wine from the waitress in the short flouncy skirt, and I ordered the same. No questions. No problem. A few people from the accounting department joined us, and I was grateful to be in this group. Once I started going with Cher regularly, I ordered other drinks and nobody questioned me.

A few weeks later, we decided to meet at the bar after work. Mark and I had traded cars that day so he could get some maintenance on my Chevette. I drove his Camaro, and met Cher and my new work friends just as they were getting ready to leave. "Last one buys a round." I groaned with a big smile, happy to have these new friends and buy them a drink. Adam and a few guys from his department congregated at the other end of the bar. He winked and watched me. When Cher and the others left, Adam swooped in and put his arm around me, leaning in close enough for me to smell his whiskey breath. His chiseled face and beautiful white teeth mesmerized me. He ordered me another Canadian Club and Coke and a whiskey neat for him, and we had our first genuine conversation away from work. Drunk, I confessed immediately that I was married, and he admitted he was married and had three children. *Yikes.*

The warning bells rang, but I was good at ignoring those. It felt nice to be wanted again. Our barstools faced each other—his knees around mine like parentheses. He caressed my legs and arms, his face hazy around the edges as I tried to focus. I put a cigarette in my mouth but couldn't find the end with the flame. He helped without saying one bad word. When it was very late, he walked me to my car, and I shivered in the chilly night air. He wrapped his corduroy jacket around me, and I put my arms around his warm body and looked up, falling hard into his velvety brown eyes. We fit together so nicely. We kissed until I pulled back against his magnetic force. Adam was delicious and kind and being with him felt good. He kissed my neck and said goodnight. I drove away glowing and happy, watching him in the rearview mirror.

Bam! The next thing I knew, I woke up parked in a strange gas station. The clock on my dashboard said 3:15. Slowly, I got my bearings and realized that I was two exits past my usual exit in Laguna Hills. I shook my thick head and started the car. When I rolled forward a *thump, thump, thump* sound stopped me. I had four flat tires.

Scared at what Mark would do to me, I tried to remember what had happened to me, to understand how I had ended up there. My mind was blank. The last thing I remembered was driving away. Finally, I called Mark from the gas station pay phone.

"I've been waiting hours for your call. Where have you been?" he demanded.

Crying and scared, I blubbered the location of the gas station, then went back to the car and laid my head on the steering wheel. *How did I get four flat tires?*

I was startled awake when Mark opened the car door. He took me home, yelling and raging at me about the damage I had done to his precious Camaro.

Still very drunk, I shook from either fear or cold—I wasn't sure which. I could barely walk. I had the uncontrollable urge to lie down everywhere. I just wanted to stop moving but couldn't stop crying, sniffling, and whimpering.

"You sleep on the couch tonight," he said as he helped me through the front door of our apartment.

I fell asleep, grateful for the world to stop moving, and woke up to Mark standing over me, sipping his coffee, the sunshine in the room bright enough to be a spotlight. Covering my eyes with the back of my hand, I peeked at Mark. He sneered at me. My head pounded. "Tell me where you were last night and who you were with."

I shook my head. "I was with girlfriends; we lost track of time." I sat up, continuing to shield my eyes from the sunlit room.

He huffed and puffed, shaking his head and pacing around the apartment. He stormed out a few minutes later for his shift at the restaurant.

I staggered to the phone, called in sick, and fell into bed for more sleep.

60

A few days later, after Mark left for work, I packed my things and left him behind like a bad habit. I refused to have a knock-down-drag-out fight with him about a divorce. Yet again, I slipped away without a word. The first time was with Dad in the middle of the night, then with Simon in Windsor, and now it was Mark's turn.

I drove to Corona del Mar and found Cher's house. I knocked tentatively. Her boyfriend, John, answered. He looked Swedish, with light-colored hair and eyebrows. Craning my neck around him, I said, "Is Cher home?"

Seeing my suitcase, she rushed to me and wrapped me in her arms.

"I left," I whispered to her.

"Good," she whispered back.

She ushered me into their spare bedroom, which had impossibly bright yellow curtains. She moved the boxes and books off the bed and placed my suitcase near the closet. We stood on either side of the bed and made it up with fresh sheets as I told her everything.

The first week at Cher and John's was difficult. I worried Mark would show up unexpectedly and drag me back home by my hair. It was like anticipating a slap that never came. I hadn't told him much about my friendship with Cher, but Mark was possessive, smart, and motivated. It wouldn't be long before he found me.

I hated being a burden. My plan was to take my next paycheck, open a checking account in my name, and start saving to move into a room near work. A knock on the door interrupted my planning and figuring. "Leslie, we're having London broil tonight. Would you like to join us?" John said from the other side of the door.

"Yes, thank you. I'll be right out."

"Great! You can make the salad. I'm going downstairs to barbecue."

My heart filled with immense gratitude. I lowered my head in a slight bow as I passed Cher, who was lounging on the couch reading a magazine. Her generous smile warmed me.

The front windows were open, and the jacaranda tree was blooming. Lettuce, tomato, cucumber, and avocado lay washed in the sink, and I closed my eyes briefly, taking in their scent. Sharing that first meal forged a bond between the three of us. Cher and John let me into their lives, probably saving mine.

Over the course of the next few weeks, I drove to work with Cher in her audaciously colored orange Corvette, leaving my little blue Chevette behind in case Mark came to the office and scoured the parking lot. He called me at work a gazillion times, and I learned to hang up on him professionally. "No, I'm sorry, she can't talk right now. Would you like to leave a message?" Then I'd wait a beat or two. Mark would usually be yelling at me about how I needed to listen to him. Then I'd conclude the call and say, "Okay, I'll let her know. Goodbye."

One day his angry voice was replaced by a depressed and pleading one. The resigned tone shook me just a little. "We need to talk. I know you're mad. I'm mad too."

I still answered in the same voice. "No, I'm sorry, she can't talk right now. Would you like to leave a message?"

He hung up without another word, which was new. What game was he playing?

On the drives home with Cher, I'd watched the side mirrors. Agitated and depressed from my withdrawal from cocaine, the only thing that smoothed things over and took away the nerves was lots of alcohol. John fancied wine and beer, and Cher and I liked mixed cocktails at the bar. I learned about tequila sunrises, margaritas, piña coladas, grasshoppers, White Russians, Black Russians, and CC and Cokes. I tried them all. Cher and John generously included me in their Sunday routine, starting at the Rusty Pelican for oysters Rockefeller, champagne, and a few Bloody Marys, then to Blackie's for beer and pool. We always ended up at Mutt Lynch's for burgers before returning to the apartment for an afternoon nap. Sundays quickly became my favorite day of the week.

My life was fun again, at least on the surface. Cher and I shopped together, and I upgraded my look at work. I loved fashion and spent most of my money on making myself look better. Cher taught me how to put on eyeliner and lipstick properly. I curled my hair and had long acrylic nails painted bright red. I wore nylons with three-inch heels and was amassing quite a few gorgeous dresses. Adam still accosted me in the copy room but now it was mutual. We saw each other very casually, hanging out together a few times but usually only when the group drank after work. I just couldn't invest anything in him. My life was a mess, and he was married with three kids!

One day, Cher surprised me by signing me up for the 1980 Miss Newport Beach Pageant. Technically, the contestants couldn't be married, and I hoped not to get found out. My sponsor for the pageant was a law firm named Virtue and Scheck. When I wore my pageant banner, only VIRTUE was visible, as the SCHECK went below my breast and around my side. We laughed about that one. Me virtuous, what a joke. Self-conscious and unsure of myself in every way possible, I struggled to participate in each of the events, but especially the talent contest, where I channeled my sailing days and sang a Carole

King song and played the guitar. I didn't win or even place, but I finished it and swore never again!

After work, Cher and I continued to stop for a drink before going home, but I could never totally relax, wondering what hole Mark had fallen into. My eye would catch a shadow in the corner of the bar, or I'd see a tall, handsome man backlit as he came into the dark bar, and I'd flinch, straining to see if it was him. I hadn't heard from him in weeks and knew it was only a matter of time.

One Saturday morning, I decided to go to the Laguna Beach craft fair, giving Cher and John some privacy, but when I went out to the street my car was gone. I ran back to the apartment, crying to Cher and John, who were having morning coffee on the balcony, "Somebody's stolen my car. It's gone. Nowhere to be found."

"Call the police," Cher said.

"The police?" Skeptical about involving the police, I hesitated.

"Does your husband have a set of keys?" John asked as I flitted around the balcony and the apartment in a tizzy.

I stopped cold. "Yes, he does."

The phone rang not fifteen minutes later; it was Mark sounding smug and confident. "Can we meet for a talk?"

"You stole my car!"

"You keep avoiding me." His voice sounded defeated, even sad.

"Bring my car back now. And how did you get this number?" I demanded.

Cher and John were sitting nearby watching the entire exchange, being my witnesses.

"Can we just talk? I'll explain everything."

"Okay, but it better be good."

I waited for him on the street, away from our house, and he drove up in his Camaro, motioning for me to get in. He was wearing new clothes and looked as suave as ever.

"Where's my car?"

"Around the corner. I'll take you there. Just get in." I left with him and saw that he had parked my car two streets away. "Can we have a cup of coffee and talk?" he said as we sat idling next to my car.

"Fine."

We drove south along Highway 1 with the windows down. The ocean breeze mesmerized me. He took my hand. "You look good, Sweetheart. I've missed you so much."

I didn't recoil from him but instead found my heart thawing at the edges. He seemed humbled somehow, full of regret and remorse. We got margaritas on the patio at Las Brisas in Laguna Beach, and slowly my defenses melted away. He quietly slipped a small plastic bullet filled with cocaine. I went to the bathroom and did a few toots. The rushing in my head was instantaneous. *Glorious!* It was like going home and finding the softest blanket to snuggle in. I felt joyous, connected to the world, like I was glowing from the inside.

Shades of the old, fun Mark came back, the one who'd admired me and considered my wishes. I craved more coke instantly. He was generous and sweet. We enjoyed another drink, staring off into the Pacific Ocean elated and euphoric. Mark tooted from the bullet right at the table, discreetly holding it in his hands. It felt dangerous so I copied him, fumbling the first try but having success on the next. Adrenaline rushed in my ears and I felt alive.

"Come back to me." He studied me, pushing the hair away from my face.

"No. You lied to me about so much. And you're so mean."

"I know, I'm sorry. There was so much stress."

"What stress? You never said anything to me."

"I know. I'm sorry. Give me another chance."

"I like where I'm living. I'm happy."

Thin white clouds filled the sky, and I suddenly wanted to go home to my own bedroom, safe at Cher's house. I didn't want to be with

Mark any longer. His chameleon-like ways scared me. His colors were beautiful now as he wooed me and gave me cocaine, but I knew the ugly colors would return as soon as I let my guard down. I didn't want to be around him any longer. He drove me back to Corona del Mar.

I got out of his car and bent over to look in the window. "Do not ever take my car again or I'll call the police." He laid his head on the steering wheel, and I thought he nodded. "Let me go, Mark. It's over."

61

A few weeks later, my dad and Elisabeth came by Cher's house unannounced. He knew where I was living from Karen, but still—what the hell was going on? The day felt warm for early June. Elisabeth wore a summer dress and sandals. Her long blonde hair hung straight and glossy. Dad looked radiant in his Hawaiian shirt, happier than I had ever seen him. We descended the stairs and headed back to the street for some privacy.

"Can you come to dinner? I have a proposition for you."

"I can't come to dinner. What's your proposition?" I wanted him to leave.

"I'm flying us to Acapulco. We leave this weekend, and I want you to come."

"In your plane?" I asked.

"Yes, with Elisabeth and Rune. We have an extra seat just for you. Come with us," he pleaded, his eyes kind and welcoming.

"I can't just up and go. I have a job." I felt instantaneously irked at his assumption that I would drop everything to go with him and her.

This time it was easy to say no and not feel jealous. This time his invitation didn't entice me at all. Elisabeth and Rune were his adventure buddies now.

"Why are you living here?"

"Mark and I separated."

A grin of victory bloomed on his face. His eyes danced while he gloated at my misfortune, and it burned me up. He'd predicted it, and I hated him for that.

Part Two
After

62

Ten days later, I picked up the phone at work. "Far West Services, Executive Office. This is Leslie."

Karen's voice was frantic on the other end. "Dad's plane crashed in Mexico. He's dead. We have to go down there now. Elisabeth survived, but she's hurt."

"What?" My mind could not take in the words she'd just uttered.

She repeated herself, and a tiny seed of happiness grew inside. I couldn't stop a small smile that he was dead, yet at the same time, I was utterly shocked. "Dad's dead, really?"

"Yes. Pack a bag and come to the house now."

"I'll be there soon." *Could it be?*

At home, I threw some clothes into a bag and headed north, feeling a slight twinge of guilt at being happy. Would he ever stop springing things on me unexpectedly, changing my life instantly? *Wait, what was I thinking? This can't be real. And still, the Mexican authorities must have gotten things mixed up.*

When I arrived, Mom and Monica were at the dining room table with files and papers spread out before them, Mom still in her nurse's uniform and Monica in her Alpha Beta attire.

"*Lez*lie, you made it," Mom crooned, getting up and air hugging me in her usual way. Monica nodded her head at me in a *hey-there* motion. "Lez."

I nodded back at Monica, using her childhood nickname, Pooh. I searched the room for Karen. "Can this be true? I'm in total shock."

Monica shrugged and shook her head. Mom folded her long-fingered hands on the table.

"So, where's Karen?"

The back screen door slammed. "I'm here. I was just getting the details of our flight. We leave tomorrow."

I needed a glass of wine but decided not to ask for one. "I need to hear all the details. Who called and what did they say?"

Karen launched into the story, probably her fifth or sixth telling since it had happened just four hours earlier. When she was finished, we sat at the table and ate leftover lasagna together in silence.

"Does anyone else think Dad is playing a joke on us?" I asked.

Monica instantly answered, "I do. He's played bigger tricks on us."

Karen nodded her head. "Yeah, I agree. It's crossed my mind, but we have no choice but to go down there. If it's a joke, we'll know immediately."

"If it's a joke, I'll be so pissed. I told him I couldn't come on the trip. If this is his way of getting us down there, I'll kill him myself," I said, raising my voice in anger.

"He invited you on the trip?" Karen said. I nodded.

"Like being pissed at Dad is anything new for you," Monica said.

"Girls, don't fight," Mom pleaded.

I asked, "How was it decided that Karen and I would go to Puerto Vallarta?"

"I'm terrible at red tape," Monica said. "And he isn't even my real father," she added under her breath.

"Monica!" Karen and I said in unison. "He is, too, your father," I added.

"Yeah, Monica, he loves you, and we're sisters," Karen insisted.

Monica shook her head and went to the kitchen.

"Okay, girls, we all agree that you two should go," Mom said, looking back and forth between Karen and me.

Nineteen

"We'll stay in touch with you guys once we find out what's happening," Karen said.

We cleared the table, and I mused out loud, "Dad can't be dead. He can't be the first person I know who's died."

"I know," Karen said, placing dishes in the sink.

"Girls, let's take this one step at a time," Mom said, and she and Monica gathered their things and left.

I carried my bag to Karen's bedroom, planning to sleep in my old twin bed. "Monica is still harping on the different dad thing?" I put my pajamas on and climbed under the covers.

Karen turned off the light and crawled into her bed. "Did you know Grandma helped her contact her biological father but that he didn't want to talk to her or even acknowledge her existence?"

I shook my head. "No, I'm sorry. I didn't know that."

The house was so quiet. Dad's room sat eerily empty across the hall. I did not venture there, feeling like a stranger in this house. "So you stay here all alone?"

"Yeah, I've been here alone since Dad, Rune, and Elisabeth left."

"Did you hear anything about Rune?"

"No. I guess we'll find out when we get down there."

"Yeah. So, Dad didn't invite you on the trip?"

"No, he wanted me to stay here and help Mary while he was gone."

"I'm sorry."

She rolled over, facing the wall. "Good night. I set the alarm for 5 a.m."

"Goodnight," I said. "Thanks for making all the arrangements."

Monica dropped us off at LAX early the following day and promised to stay by the phone. On the plane, Karen and I stared out the window in silence, shell-shocked, stunned, trying to make sense of the mess. My mind flooded with images of Dad laughing his big laugh, throwing back his bald head, standing like the King of Siam on the foredeck of our sailboat, or yelling at me with his twisted-up face. The most recent image was of him standing in front of Cher's apartment with Elisabeth a few weeks ago, asking me to go on this trip, his piercing blue eyes gleeful when he realized Mark and I had separated. The stewardess broke my trance when she brought roast beef sandwiches and fruit cocktails for lunch and offered us a drink.

I pondered the situation again while picking at my sandwich silently.

He couldn't be dead. He was larger than life, invincible, indestructible. He was probably laughing hard now, drunk on tequila, and this was his way of getting me to Mexico without risking my job. But geez, faking his own death? No, it wasn't possible.

My mind flirted with scenarios: *Maybe he did something with the Mexican authorities or the drug cartel in Acapulco and they killed him. Maybe it was Interpol who was involved because of the last recovery he did overseas somewhere.* He traveled quite a bit to Australia and New Zealand. I could only assume it was to recover boats. This plane crash had to be a story he had concocted. Maybe he needed to disappear for a time to keep the heat off. Perhaps he was hiding out in South America, laying low on some beach.

God knows I'd wished him dead for years. It had become a mantra, a rut in my brain where hatred for him grew like a weed. Every time Dad interfered in my life, mistreated Mom, or was inappropriate with me, I wished him dead. Maybe when enough people wish you dead, the universe grants it. Maybe my wish had been granted.

And still, who would I be in this world if he never came back? My whole life had existed to fight against him. I could already feel the vacuum of where he used to be beginning to suck me in.

We landed in Puerto Vallarta and went to the closest American hotel, the Holiday Inn, located on a white sand beach only minutes from the airport. "It has to be ninety degrees," Karen said, handing Dad's company credit card to the front desk clerk.

"And ninety percent humidity." I walked across the marble-floored lobby and looked out toward the ocean. We dropped our bags in the room and hired a taxi to take us to the police station.

When we arrived, we introduced ourselves to the police officer at the desk, and tried to speak English slowly while he rattled on in Spanish.

"Mañana," the police officer said. We understood that word.

"Where is Elisabeth Brolin?" Karen asked. He handed us a card with an address on it, and we went there immediately.

The Sanatorio Emiliano Zapata maternity hospital was located in a residential area on the corner of two quiet cobblestone streets. It was a white one-story adobe building with very few rooms. "Why would they bring her here?" I wondered as we walked in.

"It is strange," Karen said. We asked the first nurse we saw for Elisabeth's room. She pointed down the hall. "Habitación diez."

We headed down the hallway, passing several women sitting in a line of chairs, some of them looking ready to give birth. At room 10, we found Elisabeth in a bed looking smaller than usual, pale, and drawn. Her blue eyes were matte, and she had bruises on the left side of her face. A strained smile came over her face when she saw us, and she stood tenderly to hug Karen.

"Don't get up," Karen said, rushing to her. Two fans blew air around the hot room.

Elisabeth wore shorts under her hospital gown, but I saw the purple and black bruises peeking out from a bandage covering what I imagined was a gash in her leg.

I didn't know whether to hug her or not. She looked broken, so I stayed at the foot of the bed and strained to smile. Karen took stock of Elisabeth's injuries, gently touching her face and arm. Her most serious injury was a dislocated shoulder and broken collarbone, which was tied up with her arm in a sling. She looked delicate, beaten, and afraid. I felt pity but my stubborn nature and lack of connection with her kept me behind an emotional wall. I didn't know her. We had spoken just a few times as she hung on my father's arm, but we had never had a meaningful moment alone.

Karen said, "What happened?"

Her eyes glazed over and she stared down at the floor. "Bjorn's gone, and Rune too." Her face clouded over. Karen glanced at me with a sympathetic look.

There was our confirmation that Rune had died with Dad. I felt numb and void of any reaction. "Can you tell us what happened," I said gently.

Elisabeth shook her head and quietly said, "They're gone."

She was traumatized. That was obvious. I stood by the foot of the bed and said, "I'm going back to the police station to see if I can get something from them. I'll meet you back at the hotel."

"I'm staying here." Karen sat down on the edge of the bed and took Elisabeth's hand.

I stared at her. "Okay, I'll be back in the morning." I smiled sympathetically at Elisabeth.

The shock of the past twenty-four hours was replaced momentarily with a sharp pain of loneliness. A twinge of jealousy rose inside at Karen's tender feelings for Elisabeth. She had obviously become close with her over the past months.

63

The cab bumped along the cobblestones from the hospital to the police station while every part of my body sweated. The driver took me past a street market bursting with pineapples, mangos, avocados, and carrots, then a taco cart doing a brisk business, filling the street with the aroma of cooking meat. An old Mexican woman sat behind a shaded table filled with candies and chips for sale. Dogs ran in and out of houses and stores, barking and chasing each other.

I pondered what could have happened in the plane that Dad couldn't handle. He could handle everything. Dad was great in an emergency—invincible, indestructible. He could never die. Besides, he was the luckiest guy ever.

A slight sense of relief washed over me again that he might truly be gone. It was late when I arrived at the police station. The front door was locked. I peeked in the window to the empty office. "Shit!" I hailed another cab and returned to the Holiday Inn, exhausted and spent. What little cash I had brought was dwindling fast.

Entering the lobby again, I noticed for the first time the pool, the palm trees swaying in the evening breeze, the sweet smell of flowers blowing through the lobby from the beach. Tahiti came flooding back, another tropical paradise Dad had brought me to. The intoxicating music, the lush greenery, and the happy vacation people were familiar, and I could feel myself relax. There was nothing I could do until morning.

The beach and pool were filled with people as far as the eye could see. I found the bar and took a seat. Dad's credit card guaranteed that I could charge everything to my room. The legal drinking age in Mexico was eighteen. I was nineteen. The door to adulthood swung right open for me, beckoning me to come in.

At home, I would never dare waltz into a bar alone and order a drink. Never. Nobody drinks alone at home except for desperate people, right? But here, the vacation vibe, the tropical breeze caressing my shoulders, the waves rolling into the beach, and the flow of tequila made it okay. I desperately wanted a margarita—felt I needed it to calm my mind and heart. I deserved to be at the bar. I deserved a drink. I deserved some respect, God damn it. My father just died. I ordered a margarita from the cute Mexican bartender.

The emotional heaviness of my life melted away like this hot, muggy day ending with a sky filled with oranges and reds. I was free and anonymous. Free of Mark and work, free of Dad and his judgments and criticisms. Nobody knew me. I could do anything I wanted. I could order three margaritas and drink them all myself. I smiled at the beachgoers, the ocean, and the cute bartender. Nobody would say no to me, no matter what I ordered.

The margarita came like the slushy answer to my prayers. The salt around the rim of the wide, shallow glass slid down my throat and mixed with the sweetness. I smiled again. The tequila spread out in my stomach and traveled up my torso into my chest, where it settled in and assured me all was right at the Holiday Inn in Puerto Vallarta. I ordered chips and guacamole, drank several more margaritas, charged everything to the room, and stumbled upstairs hours later.

Sleeping fitfully, I woke early with my mind running at full pace as if it were sitting on the bedpost, thrumming its fingers, waiting impatiently until I opened my eyes. There were so many tasks to be completed and thousands of questions to be answered about Dad, Rune, the crash, and the bodies at the funeral home. My head pounded but I dragged myself up and found some coffee.

Dad had been dead less than four days.

64

Back at the hospital, I found Elisabeth on the edge of the bed, perched like a bird with a broken wing. Her face was strained and pinched. She rocked back and forth ever so slightly while Karen sat in a chair reading paperwork.

"Good morning," I said from the doorway.

Elisabeth half smiled and walked to the window. In front of her was a thick vine of orange bougainvillea crawling up the building across the street.

"Good morning," Karen said, watching Elisabeth with pinched eyebrows.

"Did you two have a good night?"

Karen squinted at me like Dad had used to when I said something stupid. "Can I bring you some food?"

"We ate," Karen said briskly, then added in a softer tone, "They have delicious food here."

Elisabeth went back to the bed and sat down. "I've been released from the hospital and want to go home."

"What? So soon? How is that possible?" I searched Karen's face, and then Elisabeth's.

Karen said, "She doesn't have a passport, so according to the man who visited us early this morning from the American Embassy, she needs to travel to Mexico City, where there's a

Swedish Embassy. But she can't go alone." Desperation swirled around her.

There was a pause as Karen and Elisabeth made eye contact. "I can't take her because I'm only seventeen. She needs an adult with her."

"So, me? I should take you to Mexico City?" I didn't want to leave Puerto Vallarta until we found out where Dad and Rune were.

"No. You and I need to stay here and figure out the plane crash. We've been thinking maybe Mom could fly down today and go with Elisabeth to Mexico City tomorrow," Karen said.

I hesitated. "Yeah, that might work, but right now, I want to go to the police station and find out where Dad and Rune are. Come with me, okay?"

"Yeah," Karen said. Elisabeth nodded, and we left her, saying we'd return soon.

Walking down the hallway, I said, "Isn't it weird to have Dad's ex-wife helping his fiancée?"

"What choice do we have?"

She was right. We called Mom collect from the pay phone in the hospital lobby. She agreed to fly down that afternoon.

In the taxi, we were bumping silently along the cobblestone streets when Karen began speaking. "Elisabeth says she saw a huge black cloud ahead of the plane. Dad changed flight paths and tried to avoid the huge cloud but as they approached it, it became bigger and blacker. She thought it was a mountain and wondered if Dad was flying too low. She checked the instruments, as Dad had taught her how to read them in many previous flights. The altimeter said ten thousand feet and she looked again at the wall of black clouds. They entered the cloud. It began to rain, and the wind was throwing the plane around in the sky in what Elisabeth has recounted as severe turbulence. Dad called to the Puerto Vallarta tower and declared a Mayday."

I stared at Karen unable to blink. She continued, "The next thing

Elisabeth remembers is that the front of the plane had disappeared. One minute, the plane was there with Dad and Rune, the next minute it was gone. The wind whipped and the rain drenched them. She looked at where Julia had been and saw an empty seat."

"Wait, what?" I interrupted Karen. "Who's Julia?"

"An Australian woman who hitchhiked a ride in Acapulco."

"Okay, go on."

Karen continued, "She was alone but says she was calm. She didn't have any sensation of falling. She knew she would die and the last thing she remembers is a piece of the wing flying at her."

Karen stopped for a minute, allowing me to take it all in.

She continued again, "The next thing she remembers is hearing Dad calling for her, but then waking up to men yelling, 'Hola? Hola.' A group of boys from a nearby village found her. She had landed in a tree, still strapped into her seat. They carried her out of the jungle, and then she remembers being pulled on a board by a horse. All her memories are fragmented. She thinks she was in and out of consciousness." Karen stopped.

I couldn't believe how lucky she was, or that three other people were dead.

Karen continued, "The next thing she remembers is being in a house where two older women cleaned and bandaged her the best they could. Then she was in the back of a truck, bumping along slowly, aching with pain. Finally, she woke up in the hospital in Puerto Vallarta."

"Wow, that's an incredible story," I said, and then added, "so Dad flew into a storm cloud." That didn't seem like something the great Bjorn Johansen would do.

Karen nodded.

"It must have been a huge storm cloud. Otherwise, he would have flown around it."

* *

Nineteen

We were given the address of the funeral home at the police station. Karen and I took another taxi there, but nobody spoke English, so we returned to the hotel to get help finding a translator. While we waited, Karen ran upstairs and took a shower and I went to the bar and ordered myself a margarita and a shot of tequila, which I downed in a few large gulps. By the time Karen was ready, the alcohol was taking the edge off my anxiety.

A translator named Hector arrived in the hotel lobby a short time later, and we returned to the police station and then the funeral home. He translated official details from the police report: "The plane crashed around 1600 on Thursday, June 26, 1980, sixty-eight kilometers south, southeast of Puerto Vallarta in the jungle near a town called Cabrel. One person was found alive, and the bodies of three other people were recovered, along with a flight bag and some clothing."

He looked up from the paper, at Karen and me. "Should I go on?" We nodded. "They found a white man with no hair, a young white man with blond hair, and a young girl also with blonde hair."

Karen and I nodded again. "When can we have the personal items?" I asked.

"Soon," was the answer translated.

At the funeral home, the director talked rapidly in Spanish, and Hector's jaw tightened. He looked at the floor and translated. "They need somebody to identify the three bodies."

I said, "We don't know the young woman. But the other two people are our father and brother."

It felt weird to say the word "brother." I had only had a brother for two summers and now he was gone. We would need to call Rune's mother in Norway soon and let her know about the plane crash. As far as Julia, we had no idea how to find next of kin for a girl we'd never met. We would ask Elisabeth for help, if she could manage it.

Hector glanced at Karen and me for an answer to identifying the bodies. We held a gaze. I thought, *No way, not me.*

He continued, but I struggled to hear. "The bodies were found in pieces scattered over the mountain."

Karen shifted her gaze away from mine.

I held on to Karen's arm, even though the humidity made our skin slick. The words tossed around in my head: *The bodies were in pieces.*

My mind went into overdrive. *This can't be right. Dad is indestructible. And, if they found body pieces, they were probably not his or Rune's. They could be anybody's. Dad could be drinking a mai tai in South America by now, laughing at his great escape, just like James Bond.* Dad had loved James Bond and his chaotic life with beautiful young women falling all over him. But reality intervened—escape from what? Dad had been happy with Elisabeth, and she had witnessed the plane break in half. Bjorn Erling Johansen, man extraordinaire, lover of young women, world traveler, insurance detective, adventurer, and world sailor, was surely dead.

"Can you make a positive identification now?" Hector asked.

I looked at Karen. She backed up toward the door. "I'm not doing it. I'm going back to Elisabeth."

"I'm not doing it either," I said. "I want to go back to the hotel."

65

Mom disembarked the plane on the tarmac, carefully walking down the steps, glancing up every few seconds, looking for us. We waved. She was dressed to the nines with red lipstick, black glamour sunglasses, and a yellow chiffon dress cinched tightly around her petite waist. As she approached us with a big smile, we air hugged as usual, ensuring not to wrinkle or muss anything on her. "It's hot and humid here," she said, handing Karen her square powder-blue makeup case and taking my arm.

On the short ride to the hospital, we caught Mom up without mentioning anything about needing to identify the bodies. She had never even met Elisabeth face-to-face, so that was our first hurdle.

We entered the maternity hospital and found Elisabeth rocking back and forth on the edge of the bed, her long white-blonde hair hanging around her face. Her pained expression seemed permanent. She wore a Mexican blouse and skirt, which the nurses must have given her. They hung off her slight frame, making her look even smaller.

Karen rushed to hug her, making the introductions. Mom took Elisabeth's hand with both of hers. "How are you doing, dear?" Her voice was warm and friendly. She studied Elisabeth like a nurse for a moment and then moved to the foot of the bed next to me. Karen explained to Mom that Philip Ober from the American Embassy had set an appointment at the Swedish Embassy in Mexico City for the next day. "I've made the reservations. You fly out tomorrow morning at 9 a.m."

Elisabeth looked relieved but her shoulders slumped a bit. She smiled at Mom and nodded. Looking at Karen, Elisabeth spoke more forcefully. "Bjorn sold a boat in Acapulco. There was ten thousand dollars cash on the plane."

Karen and I looked at each other with solemn expressions. "Wow! We'll never get that back," I said. Karen nodded.

Nothing of Elisabeth's had been recovered from the crash site: no clothing, no suitcase, no identification, no money. She lay back on her bed, her peasant blouse deflating like a balloon.

"We're going to get Mom checked into the hotel and I'll be back soon to stay with you again tonight," Karen said. "You rest."

In the hospital lobby, we stopped. "There's one other thing we need help with," I said sheepishly. Mom looked at us with sculpted eyebrows raised. "Yes, what?"

"Can you identify the bodies?" Karen said quickly.

I quickly added, "We told the funeral director we'd do it today."

Mom watched us closely, considering the request.

"You're a nurse. You've seen dead bodies," Karen said, trying to convince her before she answered.

"Okay." She nodded.

Impressed and slightly shocked, I felt cautiously grateful. Then fear shot through me. She could change her mind at any time without warning. Mom changed her mind all the time. We'd be wise to get there quickly. We hailed a cab.

Once at the funeral home, we waited a long time in the small sparsely furnished lobby before the director brought out Polaroid pictures, holding them close to his body.

"Why am I looking at pictures? Aren't they going to take me into the back?" Mom asked, but the man shrugged and put the pictures down on the counter. He didn't speak English.

Karen nudged me with her elbow ever so slightly. A long moment passed as Mom stood over us, waiting for an answer. I shrugged, unable to explain that Dad and Rune were in pieces. It felt like we were duping her by not telling her, but we had no choice.

Mom walked to the desk. My imagination conjured a bloody and bashed head like in a horror movie. I looked at Karen and grimaced. She grimaced back, and we held each other's gaze. I dove into her velvet brown eyes and saw streaks of gold and a black pupil. I held my breath.

Mom gasped, and I flinched, turning to stare at the back of her yellow dress. "Yes, that's my ex-husband, Bjorn Johansen." She turned around with a strained expression, mouth pulled tight, trying to smile reassuringly at us. He pointed to the second photo, and she identified our Norwegian brother, Rune Hansen.

Mom shook her head at the third Polaroid, saying she didn't recognize that person.

"Gracias," the man said, taking the pictures and leaving us.

The funeral home was closing for the night. Mom looked exhausted, and I took her to the hotel while Karen returned to the hospital to spend another night with Elisabeth.

For the first time in my life, Mom led us through a crisis. It was nothing short of a miracle. I couldn't remember any other time when Mom did the hard thing the rest of us couldn't do.

Mom and Elisabeth flew to Mexico City the following day.

66

On our third day in Puerto Vallarta, Karen and I returned to the police station, where we received some of Dad's belongings: a flight bag with files and papers and Dad's brown leather clutch purse he had carried since we were kids. Inside were his checkbook, green card, pilot's license, aviation insurance card, various receipts, and business cards. His suitcase and his clothing were still missing. His Norwegian passport was gone. Nothing at all that belonged to Rune, Elisabeth, or Julia was recovered. And, of course, no $10,000.

Through the translator, we told the police about the duffle bag of cash, but they said they knew nothing about it. It wasn't surprising. We would never see that money.

Next, we returned to the funeral home to find out about taking the bodies to California. Hector translated back and forth. The funeral director told us that the bodies were too decomposed and needed to be cremated.

"How long will that take?" I asked.

Hector asked and translated, "They can cremate the bodies tonight."

When we asked how much it would cost, the funeral director tried to get us to claim Julia, but we didn't have the money to pay for her. It was sad, but they needed to find Julia's next of kin. When that was settled, Hector translated, "They can cremate both bodies for two thousand American dollars."

"Two thousand dollars! Really? That's a lot of money," I said to the funeral director and hung my head, knowing we did not have it.

"Okay, we'll return to get the urns tomorrow morning," Karen said.

We couldn't speak freely on the ride back to the hotel with Hector in the car. Once at the hotel, Karen and I agreed that $2,000 sounded like a lot of money to cremate two bodies. Everything in Mexico was cheap. A cab ride was $2. Dinner was $3. A margarita was $1. Why would cremation be so expensive?

Karen phoned Monica and asked her to call funeral homes in Los Angeles to find the going rate for cremation. Monica called back less than an hour later. "On average, it costs four hundred dollars," she reported back.

The funeral home director saw us as wealthy Americans. Of course, they thought we were rich. Our father owned a plane and was flying his friends around.

We went downstairs for something to eat. "What are we going to do now? We don't have two thousand dollars," I said, drinking my margarita while Karen eyed my glass. "Order one. Nobody's going to stop you."

She ordered one, and nobody stopped her. When dinner came, we decided I would write the funeral home a check for the cremation and hope they took it. I ordered two more margaritas and drank them, mesmerized by the ocean and tourists.

The following day, we took a taxi to the funeral home, where I wrote the check for $2,000, and they took it without question. With urns heavy in hand, we returned to the hotel, checked out, and flew home.

67

Elisabeth was sitting on the front porch when the taxi dropped us at the Redondo Beach house. Her face lit up in joy, and she hugged us and asked how it had all gone. The warm feelings between Karen and Elisabeth spilled over on me and I embraced them. We filled her in on the details of getting the urns out of Mexico, and she told us that in Mexico City she had got her passport easily. "Your mother was generous and kind," Elisabeth said.

Here was Mom's second act of saving the day. Amazing! I tried not to be outwardly shocked.

Elisabeth made Swedish chicken with heavy cream and ketchup, which sounded horrible when Karen described it to me, but tasted fantastic. She served it with rice and vegetables. Monica came to dinner, and Mom joined us after she got off work at the hospital.

In the coming days, Monica flew Rune's ashes to Norway. I returned home to Corona del Mar and stopped payment on the check I had written to the funeral home in Puerto Vallarta, rationalizing that those men were greedy and uncouth.

After months of discussion and deliberation, we all agreed to charter a sailboat in Oceanside and spread Dad's ashes outside the harbor, since our family's sailing adventure had begun there seven years earlier in 1973.

On the appointed day, the sun hid behind white puffy clouds and the wind was still when we loaded the boat. Dressed mostly in black, we all looked solemn, me feeling a bit nostalgic and soft inside at returning to the harbor where it had all started. I brought a poem by Merrit Malloy to read, hoping we could mark the moment enough for it to feel final and like he was dead.

We sat quietly in the sailboat's cockpit as the captain motored out of the harbor. Monica instantly felt seasick. Elisabeth looked a bit green as well. Karen looked mad as she clutched the urn in her lap.

It was a confusing mix of emotions. We had not agreed ahead of time to a specific order of events in the ceremony. When the captain stopped the boat, nobody said anything. Nobody took charge of the order of things, so I did. "How about we each say something and then we spread the ashes?"

Monica nodded. Karen said, "I don't have anything to say."

"I don't either," Monica said.

Elisabeth nodded her agreement.

"Really? Nobody's going to say anything?"

Monica shrugged. Karen and Elisabeth stared off at the horizon.

"Okay, I want to read a poem."

"Why are you reading a poem?" Karen said. "You hated him."

"Shut up. I'm reading this poem, and then we can spread the ashes." I pulled out my book, opened it to the page, and read Merrit Malloy's poem "Epitaph," about love and death and felt foolish.

I looked up to see both sisters roll their eyes and look away. "Are you done?" Karen said.

I squinted at her in hatred. "Yes, I'm done."

"Girls, let's get along," Elisabeth said.

I rolled my eyes at her. "Our father is dead."

"Leslie!" Monica said.

I looked away, feeling angry and embarrassed that I had read the poem out loud and that they didn't like it. "You guys do the ashes."

Karen went to the stern of the boat with Monica and Elisabeth, and they spread the ashes while I brooded in the cockpit. When they finished, we returned to the dock, and Monica, Karen, and Elisabeth drove away, returning to Redondo Beach.

I walked around the harbor filled with sadness but not understanding how I could be sad. Karen was right. I hated Dad. I'd wished him dead at least a thousand times. Shouldn't I be happy?

Instead, I felt lost. A storm brewed inside. How could Dad be dead? How was that even possible? A complicated mix of guilt, love, hate, and terror for the future filled me up.

After driving home, I began to feel a tiny bit free and tried to relax, but two realities emerged—one was that Dad and Rune were actually dead, and that made me hyperventilate, and the other that Dad and Rune were very much alive, laughing and drinking rum in Belize or Costa Rica, on the run from Interpol or MI6. Dad was just waiting for the right time to walk around a corner in his Mexican straw hat, tank top, and pair of OP corduroy shorts, and say, "Gotcha!"

The first reality was gradually sucking me in, but I wasn't quite ready to believe it all the way, and it would take months before any of it felt real.

68

As the weeks ticked on, Dad did not appear. I was living my life, but not fully present. I felt like two people, one who was going through the motions, and one who watched Leslie from afar. It was easy to sit to the side of myself and watch things happen in my life. I'd stare in the mirror, looking deeply into my own eyes, wondering who was in there. Could I see my soul if my eyes were windows? Were there two of me in there?

Unmoored and adrift, I ran back to Mark. I wanted somebody to take care of me. I did things I didn't want to. The other me was in charge. Mark dealt coke from the apartment, and I looked the other way because a line of cocaine made me feel better and let me forget.

"Do you want to go to LA with me to pick up some coke?" Mark asked one day.

"Okay," I said, even though all I wanted to do was go to bed and cry.

As the separation inside became bigger, I drank and did cocaine until the confusion went away.

I quit my job at Far West Services and partied continually, drinking and drugging until we ran out of money. I looked for another job, interviewing high, with just the right buzz, for multiple legal secretary positions, cavalier and uncaring about what anybody thought of me. It wasn't until I walked into an interview with John

Moravek, General Counsel at Century 21 International Real Estate, that I landed a job.

Mr. Moravek was my father's age, I guessed, with a kind smile and a weathered face. We talked about sailing and cruising for the entire interview. I regaled him with my crazy stories about sailing to Tahiti, surviving a life-threatening storm, the sinking of our boat in the South Pacific, and then Dad dying in an airplane crash the previous year. My harrowing stories riveted him.

"I have a Peterson 44 docked up in Long Beach and have dreamed of sailing away to French Polynesia."

"You should do it."

His smile was long and dreamy as he gazed out the window, his words trailing off. "Maybe someday," He snapped back, "Start tomorrow, 8 a.m."

As I headed out his office door, feeling the drain of energy from so much storytelling after the bump I had done in the car before the interview, he called to me, "You do know how to type, don't you?"

I smiled. "As well as I sail." I could type one hundred words per minute error-free in my sleep. On cocaine, I'm sure it was more.

At first, I functioned well enough at work, but after a while, things began to crumble as the world closed in on me. I hid it with drinking because everybody drank to excess. The handsome guys in Accounting and the cuter guys in Trademarks always invited me to drink with them.

Arriving home from work one particularly bad day, I entered the bedroom as Mark was putting a needle into his arm. I stopped in the doorway and stared, speechless, as I'd never seen anybody shoot up right in front of me. "Is that heroin?"

I had always promised myself I would never do heroin because that meant I was a "real" addict.

"It's coke," he said. "Do you want to try? It's the best high."

A voice inside yelled "No!" but I said, "Sure, as long as it's coke and not heroin."

He nodded. "It's coke."

Inside, I screamed "No, don't do it," but was paralyzed. I was two people cracking in half.

I wanted to die. And if I couldn't die, I wanted to quit my job and run away. Dad had been dead for six months. Maybe I could find him in Belize on a beach somewhere.

Before I knew it, I was sitting on the side of the bed, and Mark put the needle in my arm. *What heaven!* I flew in the clouds. A surge of love, a big ball of serenity, connectedness, and freedom filled me up. *What a feeling! What a trip.* I fell back and rolled in the sloshes of our waterbed, glowing inside and serene for the first time in forever.

Mark stood over me with a grin. "Didn't I tell you?"

The tightness in my chest melted away. All my pains and fears disappeared. I felt elated and happy and so grateful to Mark for showing me this wonderful place. "Thank you, darling. Thank you for this," I mumbled as I stared at the intricate pattern in the wood beams on the ceiling. The two people had merged into one person. *Thank God!*

A short time later, Karen discovered Dad had a stack of Krugerrands in his safe deposit box and when Karen got access, we split them up. Mark and I used two of my Krugerrands, which were selling at nearly $1,000 apiece, to buy a big order of cocaine. The more you buy, the bigger the discount. Mark got so much that it scared me to see it downstairs in a pile on the workbench, like a heaping mound of mashed potatoes.

"Promise me we won't use all my Krugerrands on cocaine. Let's take a trip."

He promised, but it wasn't long before we spent the last two Krugerrands on cocaine as well.

Mark always sent plenty of coke with me to work. But I couldn't wait to get home and use the needle. I felt numb and drained but hid it with new dresses and shoes, hiding the gray skin under foundation, eyeliner, and red lipstick. When I looked in the mirror, my father's voice made fun of me. "There she is all prissy in her makeup and high heels. Can't you see her taking down the sails in those red pumps?" I ignored the voice. He didn't know anything.

Being thin was the most important thing. Dad couldn't make fun of me then. No more slapping my thigh and saying those Norwegian words, which I was sure meant my legs were triple-size. Men liked skinny girls and I made waves at work because I looked so good.

After the Krugerrands were gone, hiding what was underneath the clothes and makeup became increasingly challenging. I looked drawn and bony, with black circles under my eyes, and shook nearly all the time. In one last gasp of desperation, I swindled two Krugerrands from Monica. She wasn't even using her coins for anything. They just sat in her jewelry box in her apartment, and I didn't have any compunction unloading them off her.

"Mark! Can you come and help me, please?" I called from the bedroom, where I was sitting on our waterbed. He was downstairs doing something with the latest supply. He always packaged up the coke in one-gram packets, although he left a few eight balls for larger orders.

"I'll be right there. Do you need a bump?" he called back.

I mumbled, "Why else would I call you?"

The needle tip lay in the tiny piece of cotton in a spoon.

Mark arrived in the bedroom. His dark eyes were pinpoint, and he was ready for business. "Tie off your arm, at least," he said, irritated, as he prepared the dose in the needle.

I tied my arm off, pumped my fist, and held it closed. I looked away to the wall, where a large poster of a rainbow dripping into the ocean with a dolphin jumping through it hung at the end of our bed. He eased the needle in.

I woke up in a tunnel. Mark was yelling, "Leslie! Wake up," but his voice was faint, as if he were way down the beach, and the wind was roaring. I couldn't open my eyes all the way, but could see through my eyelashes. We were in the shower. I saw the tile. Mark kept yelling, "Leslie!" I felt myself falling. He slid down onto his knees. The water sprayed his hair and it hung around his face. He shook me and wiped my face. Why couldn't I feel his hand? My bones were liquid. I couldn't feel Mark holding me up, but I could see his arms around me. I opened my eyes wider, but Mark was still far away—down a tunnel—and I could barely hear him screaming at me. "Leslie! Come back!" His mouth was wide open, his eyes frantic.

In one instant, I zipped back into my body and could feel the cold water pounding on me. Mark yelled my name again, but I still couldn't move. He lifted me, and this time, my knees locked and I could stand, leaning against the wall. He wrapped his arms around me and lifted me out of the shower. Fully clothed and dripping wet, I leaned on him.

"What happened?" I murmured.

"Oh, thank God, oh, thank God you're back." He hugged me tightly and kept saying, "Thank God."

Dad had been dead for more than a year.

69

We needed a fresh start away from California, the dealers, and the cocaine. We were out of Krugerrands, and Texas had so many opportunities for young families, especially in Houston, where the city was expanding, and employment was easy. We left cocaine behind and went there to reconnect as a couple. I reminded myself to believe in the dream of marriage. After all, I had said "until death do us part" in my wedding vows.

We found a nice house in a suburb called Sugarland. A three-bedroom that was only a few years old. I dreamed of decorating it, of having my family come for Christmas, and of all the happy times ahead. I found a job as a legal secretary, and Mark found a job on a nearby oil field. We drank and did quaaludes occasionally, trying to combat the withdrawals from cocaine.

A few weeks after moving, we were invited to the home of one of Mark's coworkers. I prepared a dish to share, my macaroni and cheese, which Mark loved. I dressed for a barbecue in a pair of jeans and a blouse, wearing my flip-flops because the humidity and heat nearly had me passing out.

To say I didn't fit in would be an understatement. The other four women at the party were decked out in formal attire—for a barbecue! Hair coiffed, heavy makeup, push-up bras, tight dresses or jeans with low-cut tops, and cowboy boots in a rainbow of colors. The twang in their voices grated as the hostess welcomed us into her mansion. Mark tried to imitate their accent and it drove me crazy. Culturally, I had never been farther away from the beach girl in me. Even Windsor wasn't this bad.

Most of the women had grown up on cattle ranches nearby, and their fathers and brothers were real cowboys herding cows. They swarmed around me when we arrived, eager for any bit of California knowledge I had. Once again, my status as a "California girl" initially made me popular. But my stories of the beach, sailing to Tahiti, and living on the boat had them cocking their heads to one side and twanging out, "Oh darlin, you're just too much." They quickly lost interest in me, and I resumed my familiar role as an alien.

Mark assimilated quickly and began drinking whiskey in a short glass, wearing a black cowboy hat and boots, Wrangler jeans, and cowboy shirts with snap buttons. From the first day we arrived, he yearned for a truck, almost whining when he'd tell me about the other men's trucks on the job site. His Camaro was not Texas-cool. He wanted a couple of rifles in the back window and a handgun in the glove box, just like other guys.

Meanwhile, I was trying to play the role of the good wife. I'd rush home to make dinner for Mark, who would invariably not show up or show up late, having already eaten with his new friends.

One night the front door opened at 11 p.m. Mark had gone out with his cowboy buddies after work again. "Where's dinner?" he yelled from the kitchen. I startled awake. The bedroom door flew open with a thud. "Where's my dinner? I'm starving."

He looked like he'd been sleeping somewhere or rolling around fighting, maybe. His hair was mussed, which was unusual for him. His face was contorted, and he slurred his words.

I rolled over to face him in the doorway. "I left it in the oven because dinner was hours ago."

"Get up and heat it up for me, woman," he demanded, actually calling me "woman."

I lifted myself on one elbow to look at him more closely to see if he was serious. He was. "Just put it in the microwave for a few minutes," I said.

He stormed out of the bedroom, voice booming, "Leslie! Get out here now!"

Mumbling to myself, "What the hell?" I put my robe on and arrived in the kitchen just in time to see Mark take the plate of lasagna out of the oven. "I deserve to have a hot meal when I get home."

He threw the lasagna against the wall. The crash was deafening. The cheesy noodles slid down the wall in slow motion.

"What the hell, Mark! It's after eleven," I said. "Dinner was five hours ago."

"Damn you, why can't you just be like the other wives and perform your duties without back talk?"

"Because I'm from California, where women are independent." I returned to the bedroom, grabbed a blanket and a pillow, and took them to the couch. "You sleep here tonight," I said. "I will not be treated this way."

He grabbed my arm hard and squeezed as I walked past him and shoved me up against the wall. "Clean that mess up in the kitchen."

"I will not clean up that mess. You made it. You clean it up."

He lifted his hand as if to hit me. I ran to the couch, grabbed the pillow and blanket, and covered myself in it. "Leave me alone, you monster."

Mark went to the bedroom and slammed the door. I slept on the couch.

I dozed and considered a plan. I'd left him once, and I could do it again. When the bedroom door opened the next morning, I sat up and faced him. He stared back at me for a long second, eyes squinting like he was sizing me up, then stepped over the lasagna on the floor in a big, exaggerated motion to make the coffee. He left without saying goodbye, slamming the door behind him.

I waited fifteen minutes until I knew he was gone. I got some boxes out of the garage, packed all my clothes and papers, and called work. "I'm coming in to pick up my final check. I need to get back to California for an emergency. I'll be there in an hour."

I called a cab and then called my mother, asking her to pick me up at the Orange County airport that evening.

I was a failure at marriage. My father was alive and well inside me and his horrible words came back with force and I couldn't stop berating myself. I wondered, *Will I ever amount to anything?*

Once I was back in California, John Moravek hired me back in the Century 21 Legal Department. I moved in with a friend and filed for divorce. Then, I found a cocaine dealer of my very own.

Dad had been dead two years.

70

Six female friends surprised me on my twenty-first birthday with an evening in a white stretch limo. Money flowed like water, and cocaine and alcohol flowed in rivers that night. ABBA's "Dancing Queen" blared, and we all sang as loudly as we could. The side windows were down as we cruised Sunset Boulevard and watched all the famous sights go by: Whiskey a Go Go, Tower Records, Griffith Observatory, and the Hollywood Bowl. I drank double CC and Cokes, with a thick line of cocaine as a back. The mood was festive. The women laughed and grooved to the music. Standing up in the limo, head and shoulders out the sunroof, we hooted and hollered at people on the sidewalk.

I joined them for a while, but then felt far away from myself. One part of me laughed, sang, and hooted at the boys on the sidewalk, while the other part shook her head and glared at me. I sat down on the leather seat, leaned my head back, and closed my eyes. I didn't want to be in the limo. I was so tired. I felt forty-five—as old as my father when he died. I had seen more things, done more things, and survived more things than most people my age. How would I survive the rest of my life?

"Hotel California" played and the girls belted out the words. I snapped back into one person, came back into my body, smiled at my crazy friends, and started singing along.

* *

It was increasingly hard to keep my shit together. My life ripped and frayed at the edges. I gave all my money to my cute cocaine dealer, Mike. He kept me in blow and gave me credit when I needed it. Sometimes my heart raced so fast it felt like I was having a heart attack. My breathing was short and labored, as if I were being chased and needed to run faster. When I was sober at work, the racing feelings and anxiety couldn't be controlled except by guzzling alcohol at lunchtime.

At first, I'd go to lunch with my coworkers at the Royal Crown or the French restaurant across the parking lot from our building, but eventually I skipped out from the crowd, needing to drink more than was appropriate at a work lunch. I'd take myself to Coco's for lunch and drink three glasses of wine quickly, which made me feel somewhat better, except for the stares from the waitress. After I had done this a few times, the waitress approached me with piercing eyes and a knowing look, saying loudly enough so everybody could hear, "Do you need the bottle?" After that, I ended up at the liquor store at lunch and guzzled booze in my car instead of eating.

Mark showed up in the lobby of my work one day. He looked all tanned and healthy and *GQ* again in his slacks and dress shirt. His face lit up as I warily greeted him. "Hi."

He whispered back, "Yeah, hi! I need a divorce. I've met somebody."

I nearly burst out laughing. The papers had been in my glove box for more than a year. "Follow me." I led him out to the parking lot, where he signed the papers on the roof of my car.

He looked into my eyes trying to make a connection. "How are you doing? Are you happy?"

I stared at the ground, avoiding his eyes. "Do you have a bump for me?" I felt low and strung out and embarrassed to beg him.

"No, sorry. I'm not using anymore."

Damn him for looking so good.

"You look tired, Leslie." He said it with concern in his voice and that pissed me off.

"Fuck you, Mark," I snarled and went back to work.

Six months later, the judge approved the papers, making me a twenty-four-year-old divorced woman.

A month or so later, on my way to work after not sleeping the night before, I felt euphoric from the massive amounts of drugs still in my system. I must have reeked of cigarettes and alcohol, so I dabbed on some perfume from the glove box. Feeling hopeful for no reason whatsoever, I drove to the office with a sense that everything would work out. The hope was like a flower fighting its way to the surface of heavy snow. At a stoplight, a man in the red Jaguar next to me tapped his horn and rolled down the passenger window.

"You are glowing. You're gorgeous."

I looked at myself in the rearview mirror. He was right, I was glowing. My skin shone and my eyes were bright. I wished Mark could see me now. I smiled at the man in the Jaguar, saying thank you.

Arriving at the office, everybody stared. *Is it my imagination? Why are they staring at me?* As I sat down at my desk, Sue and Kathy, who worked next to me, looked at me in a strange, new way. "What?" I said, sipping my coffee, my hand shaking slightly. "What are you staring at?"

"I don't know. You look so good. What kind of foundation are you wearing?"

"Jesus! Are you joking?" They both looked at each other perplexed.

I knew I'd crash soon but wanted to avoid it for a little while with the cocaine I had stashed in the car. It was going to be a long day and I would need some alcohol at lunch to calm my nerves. It was only 9:30 a.m.

I worked for the only woman attorney in the company, Margaret, and when I walked into her office, I said, "Good morning, do you need anything?"

Margaret looked up from the papers on her desk in her business suit and white blouse. "Good morning," she said haltingly, tilting her head to the side.

"What?"

"I keep being reminded how pretty you are. You're glowing."

What was happening? Was I in a dream? Baffled, I returned to my desk, where I came down on a slow-motion slide over the course of the next few hours. The shine wore off. I went to the bathroom to see my face; it was gray, drawn, and strained. How utterly strange to go up so high and then fall into the pits, like a flower born and wilted in a day.

Two weeks later, I was fired. Nobody was surprised but me. I thought I had them all fooled.

Dad had been dead for more than four years.

71

It hurt to be fired by my friend John Moravek, who had been my biggest supporter and fan. He was a surrogate father to me in many ways. We'd shared meaningful moments over the previous four years. He'd taken me on weekend sailing trips to Catalina with his partner, Lisa.

I was restless, irritable, and discontent with everything in my life. The pain inside threatened to consume me. I couldn't think of one thing I cared about. After being fired, I headed into a dark place, moving in with my cocaine dealer, Mike.

Hatred and shame bubbled inside. I worked for Thor Temporaries at different law offices around Irvine and Newport Beach on short assignments if I could get out of bed. I barely functioned.

Men filled me up. I would go anywhere with anybody to escape myself. Most were good-hearted men who saw something in me. There were so many men I played a game with, acting like I was a princess granting their wishes. The problem was that I wanted them one minute but not the next, evidence of another split inside me.

While drinking alone one night at a bar in Newport Beach, I met a businessman who wore a suit very well. His kind eyes pleaded with me to go home with him. His warm smile won me over and I granted his wish. The next day, we flew to Atlanta for the fun of it, but on the plane something happened. A switch flipped inside, and I didn't want to be there any longer. We arrived in Atlanta and the shine had disappeared, along with my patience for granting wishes. Stuck with him for the next twenty-four hours, I was completely shut down. The withdrawals from coke were intense and I drank heavily to combat it. He gave me a pill that took the edge off. I was grateful but not grateful enough to sleep with him again. He got mad when I refused, and I slept on the pullout couch. We didn't talk on the plane home, going our separate ways at the Orange County airport without so much as a goodbye. I didn't even know his last name.

The gulf inside of me grew in proportion to my pain. I listened to "Wasted Time" by the Eagles on repeat. The Grand Canyon–size space separating the two Leslies became so large I feared splitting in two. My father's voice yelled in my head: "loser" and "stupid girl!"

I was at a pool party in Newport Beach in a string bikini in the sunshine one minute, the next minute, *poof*, I woke up naked in a Jacuzzi in Palm Springs. Three days later? I don't know. People smiled at me. Somebody handed me a drink. I felt nauseous but happy and fuzzy. *How did I get here? Where are my clothes? Who are these men touching me?*

I was being led through life by a line of cocaine. If you had cocaine, I would follow you. The pain and chasm inside threatened to overtake me. I was nothing, worthless, all alone in the world. Fatherless. Rudderless.

Mike locked me out of our apartment one night. I found all my things outside at midnight when I got home. I had a complete kicking, screaming meltdown at his door. I had become *that girl*.

Dad had been dead for five years.

72

Sleeping in my car that night was the beginning of the end. For the first time in my life, I didn't have a husband or a dealer. Men were not lining up to grant my wishes anymore. I didn't have a job or very much money.

I turned twenty-five while living in my car, drinking alone. I was homeless. The ache pulsed inside me—son-of-a-bitch emotional pain that hurt like an open sore, festering and oozing. It had a heartbeat of its own. The world was closing in on me like a pack of hungry wolves.

I reluctantly drove through Hermosa Beach early one moonless morning toward my little sister's house. I dreaded going there and stalled as long as I could. I had been driving around town for two days. Karen was my only hope for help. I couldn't live in my car anymore, but I couldn't force myself to face her and the disgusted look she would have for me.

Blocks from her house, a red stop sign glared at me. I glared back at the red octagon. A voice inside said "Leslie, stop!" I laid my head on the wheel, heart racing, palms sweating, my whole body revolting. How had I ended up here? My car idled roughly. Black smoke poured out the tailpipe. I held both feet hard on the brake so it wouldn't lurch forward.

At the sound of another car, I raised my head. My eyes blurred from the pressure of my hands against them. I tried to focus. All I could see were headlights blinding me in my rearview mirror—two big spotlights shining on me. I took my feet off the brake and the car lurched forward. Black smoke poured from the tailpipe as I pulled to the side of the skinny beach road, waving the car past. He honked his horn at me, but I didn't look. The gas gauge read a quarter tank. The cloudy dawn was silent and still, the streets deserted. Just hints of light began to show in the sky. I rolled down my window and heard waves crashing on the beach.

I parked in front of Karen's studio apartment, probably reeking. I hadn't showered in days. Minutes ticked by as I tried to muster the courage to knock on the door. It opened and Karen stepped out looking clean and fresh, her hair bouncing and a red scarf around her shoulders. Our eyes locked, and she stopped. I got out of the car and walked toward her. "Hi. I need a place to crash for a few days."

There it was, the disgusted look I was expecting. She tossed the keys to me as she got into her car. "I'll be home by six."

"Thanks," I murmured as she drove away in her sky-blue Karmann Ghia to her squeaky-clean life as a college student at Long Beach State.

Her small and clean studio apartment smelled like lilac shampoo or lotion—a sanctuary with beer and wine in the fridge and a bottle of tequila on the counter. I popped open a beer, sat on her wicker loveseat, and turned on the TV. It was so strange to drink beer after years of downing champagne, CC and Cokes, White Russians, and gin and tonics. Plain old beer was now what quenched my thirst.

The Today Show was live broadcasting from Cape Canaveral, Florida. A banner at the bottom of the screen flashed January 28, 1986, 8:30 a.m. The Space Shuttle *Challenger* was being launched into space with the first ever civilian, Christa McAuliffe, a teacher.

As I drank the beer and watched the coverage, I wondered what it would be like to be good enough, smart enough, and capable enough to be chosen as the first civilian to be flown into space. Her parents must have been so proud.

Then a tiny, almost imperceptible voice whispered, "You are capable and intelligent." I lay my head back and closed my eyes, willing that voice to become louder. But it faded away when the commentator said, "It's time for the countdown. Let's listen."

As they counted down from ten, I got another beer. I took a long drink as the Space Shuttle lifted off in a roar. And then, seventy-three seconds later, Christa McAuliffe and all the other astronauts died in a fiery blaze. Stunned and speechless, I, along with the entire world, watched pieces of the shuttle float down to earth in slow motion.

Christa McAuliffe, the hope for the future of space travel, was dead.

Hope was dead.

73

I disappeared for a while, drinking and finagling cocaine from friends of friends by hocking the gold watch Simon had given me, but was back at Karen's in a few weeks. Again she met me with the expected look of disgust. I deserved it. I was disgusting. I fell onto her wicker loveseat, exhausted. She said, "Mom's checked herself into a treatment program to get sober off the pills." She was wearing a pencil skirt, pink blouse, and black pumps, looking so put-together.

"Wow," I said, thinking about the beer in the fridge.

"She's been there for eight days, and today is her birthday," Karen said. "She's forty-seven."

"She's stopped stealing pills at the hospital and is getting sober?"

Karen grabbed her purse and straightened her hair in the mirror. "Yep, she's getting sober."

"Let's see her tonight and bring her a birthday cake," I said, feeling a sudden surge of happiness for Mom.

She hesitated at the door, studying me. "Okay. Can you bake the cake today?"

I nodded. "Do you have a cake mix?"

She opened the door. "Yes, in the cabinet." She paused and added, "Please take a shower," before closing the door behind her.

* *

We drove to the Century City New Beginnings with a chocolate cake that evening. On the drive north on the 405, I said, "Maybe Mom will stay sober and finally be happy, and we'll get the mom we've always wanted."

"Yeah, maybe." I could hear the skepticism in her voice.

If Mom could be happy, then all of us would be happy. We had wished for her sobriety and happiness for so long. It seemed at times it would elude her and our family forever.

We arrived at the treatment facility and checked in with the nurse, who immediately confiscated the cake. "No outside food," she barked.

"Why? I just baked that at home for her. It's her birthday," I argued.

The nurse's voice softened a little. "We're not sure what's inside the cake, not that you girls would try to sneak drugs to your mother, but some do."

"Damn!" Karen said as we stared at each other, insulted by the idea.

The nurse led us down the corridor to her room. We passed posters on the wall with slogans that said KEEP COMING BACK and ONE DAY AT A TIME. We arrived at Mom's room and found her reading. She looked up from her book and rushed to embrace us. Her hug wasn't an airy hug like in years past. It was a real hug. Bodies touching and arms pulling us close. She wore her own clothes, a pair of stretchy blue pants and a red blouse, not some hospital uniform like in the mental health hospital. She smiled so big I was taken aback. I'd forgotten she had such beautiful teeth and such a gorgeous smile. Had I ever seen her smile like this? She looked perky and happy and had a glow on her skin I'd never seen before. Her eyes were clear and bright and had hope in them. Hope looked good on her, shiny and clean.

"Girls, it's so good to see you both. Where's Monica?" Mom brushed the hair away from Karen's eyes and looked at us adoringly. I hadn't seen my older sister for months, not since the previous summer when I'd gone to the hospital where she'd given birth to her son, Brent.

"Probably at home with Brent," I said, thinking of how orderly her life was—marrying her high school sweetheart and having a baby.

We sat in chairs at the foot of her bed. Another bed and desk filled the room, but no one else was present. I was glad for the privacy.

"Happy birthday, Mom," I said, and Karen launched into the story about the cake being confiscated. I let Karen take the lead. I was exhausted and could've used a beer and a thick line.

"How's this place? You look so good," Karen said. I nodded my agreement with as big a smile as I could muster.

"It's good here. I'm finding myself," Mom said with conviction. I believed her.

On the drive home, we marveled at how well Mom looked. I counted the minutes until I could chug a beer. When we arrived, though, I felt more desperate than I could handle and while Karen was in the bathroom downed a few tequila shots and took off without a word to be alone in my car at the beach.

Dad had been dead for nearly six years.

74

I slept in my car in front of Karen's house that night. A flock of seagulls gathered at the end of the street, and I stared at them, unable to make myself go inside. I glanced at myself in the rearview mirror. The *Challenger* explosion played in my mind again. Why did the explosion and Christa McAuliffe's face keep flashing before me?

Finally, I peeled myself out of the car and went inside, where I heard the shower running and smelled freshly brewed coffee. The television was on—*The Today Show* again. I saw the explosion in my head. I drained a beer from the fridge, then grabbed another, sat down on the wicker loveseat, and stared numbly at the news. Somewhere deep inside, a silent scream came: "I want my mommy!"

I wanted the mommy I had never had. I wanted her to make this all better. Couldn't she do this one thing for me? Couldn't she think of me for once? She had looked so good in the New Beginnings treatment program—hopeful and fresh again. I wanted to look like that, to feel like that inside.

"Leslie, is that you?" Karen yelled from the bathroom.

"Yes, it's me. I'm back." I hid the beer from her view.

"Where have you been? Geez, Leslie, when are you going to get your shit together?" The steam from the shower followed her into the small room of her studio apartment along with the smell of lilac shampoo. She wore a fuzzy yellow robe, and her hair was in a towel.

"I don't know."

She returned to the bathroom just a few steps away. "Well, you can't stay here. I love you, but I'm trying to do something with my life, and I don't appreciate you coming here like this after a bender." She peeked out at me with a mascara wand in her hand just as I finished taking a sip of beer. "God, Leslie, stop drinking beer in the morning. It's disgusting."

I stared at the TV, not wanting to look at her clean, perky face. She shuffled through the clothing in the hall closet. "I mean, what's up with you? Just stop partying, like I did."

"I don't know . . ." My voice trailed off.

She closed the bathroom door and I could hear the blow-dryer. A few years back, Karen and I had partied together. We'd go up to Hollywood, dance in the clubs, and drink until we could barely stand. But she'd stopped when it got in the way of her work or school.

She came out of the bathroom, dressed in a leather skirt, pantyhose, and bodysuit, looking bright, shiny, and sparkling new. She said more softly, kindly, "I really am sorry, Leslie, but I can't live like this. Please be gone by the time I get home from work."

Where will I go? I stared through her, my eyes losing focus, my mind flashing. The end was near. I could feel it coming, and it was terrifying. "Okay," I mumbled.

She grabbed her purse and left. I stared at the door, chewing on my lower lip. "I want my mommy," I whispered out loud to nobody. A ball of hurt welled up inside.

I hyperventilated just thinking about giving up coke and alcohol. How could I give them up? *I can't!* But I couldn't keep living this way. At twenty-five years old, I was out of options and my back was against the wall.

Sliding down to the floor, I grabbed the putrid yellow phone off the end table. It had white push buttons and a curly cord. I pulled it close to me, picked up the receiver, and pushed 4-1-1. The operator answered, and I got the number for New Beginnings in Century City.

I got another beer from the fridge, guzzled it, and then did a shot of tequila. I picked up the receiver again and dialed. A woman answered, "Good morning, New Beginnings. How can I help you?"

"Um, hello? My mother is staying there, getting sober, and I need help. I need to get sober. Can I come and be with my mom there?" I sniveled, cried, and hiccuped as I said the words.

"Oh, I'm sorry. Who is your mother?"

"Paula Johansen." I twirled the phone cord around my finger.

"Oh, right, Paula is doing very well here. What's your name?"

Through tears and a lump in my throat, I blubbered out, "Leslie Johansen, I'm her middle daughter."

"Oh, that's nice. It sounds like you're in bad shape, and I'm sorry to tell you this, Leslie, but we don't admit immediate family members into the same inpatient treatment program at the same time."

I closed my eyes. "Really?"

"Yeah, I'm sorry. But there's another New Beginnings in Lakewood. Would you like to go there?"

"I don't know. Can I talk to my mom?" Tears were rolling off my face and my nose was stuffed up.

"No, I'm sorry. She's in a therapy session now and we don't allow calls anyway. I can have the admitting nurse in Lakewood call you if you're interested in getting sober. Do you have insurance?"

"Yes, I have COBRA from my last employer." I sniffed hard, pulling my purse near me while digging for the Dristan. I gave her Karen's phone number and hung up, leaning against the wicker loveseat. A gigantic pain filled up my chest and tears fell. The phone rang, startling me. "Hello?"

"Hi, is Leslie there?"

"Yes, who is this?"

She introduced herself as Annette at New Beginnings in Lakewood. "I hear today is your day to get sober."

I wiped the tears away from my face. "Hi," I said tentatively.

"Well, are you ready to get sober? I understand your mom is at our Century City location. Is that right?"

"Yes, that's right. She's been there for twelve days and she's doing great."

"Okay, well, why don't you come here? Are you sober? Can you drive?"

"Yes, I'm sober," I lied.

"Okay, pack a bag and come here now." She gave me the address and hung up.

An inkling of hope was born in that quiet moment. I did what I was told, grabbing my duffel bag of clothes, bathroom supplies, and two beers for the road. I got in my car and drove to Lakewood. I stopped to pee at a Taco Bell, snorting up the last of my cocaine on the top of the toilet bowl. I guzzled my last beer as I pulled into the parking lot of New Beginnings and met Annette at the front door.

Epilogue
2025

Since meeting Annette at the doors of New Beginnings on February 20, 1986, I have been clean and sober in the program of Alcoholics Anonymous. A life-changing spiritual experience visited me while attending an AA panel about two weeks into the twenty-eight-day program. The panel consisted of four or five people, but it was a man in his early thirties with a calm yet assured energy and the woman who sat next to him on the panel who stopped me cold. After the man shared his story, and then the woman shared her story, he casually and discreetly grabbed and kissed the woman's hand. She leaned into him, and they glowed in their sobriety and happiness.

It was a revelation to me. They were a sober, dating couple on a panel in a hospital program, sharing their experience, strength, and hope! They sparkled. Time seemed to split apart as the panel took questions, and the room froze. Was there a light from heaven? I'm not sure, but maybe. They spoke directly to me, and I knew I would have a happy, fulfilled life if I followed the sober path. I was 100 percent sure of it, down in the soul of my being. The light of hope filled me up inside and hasn't left to this day. That night, I found God, who I choose to call Love.

After the meeting, I returned to my room and wrote down all my hopes and dreams, energized like never before. Sometime early in the morning, one of the hard-assed nurses, a big Black woman who was the essence of "tough love," came into my room and found me writing. She called herself Aunt Jemima, which sounds terrible today. She said, "What are you doing, Leslie? It's time to sleep."

I looked up and said, "I found God. God is Love. And I found myself. I am going to stay sober for the rest of my life." Aunt Jemima's tough-love persona evaporated. Her face softened, and her eyes danced. She gathered me up in her enormous arms and held me to her ample bosom, surrounding me in her warmth and love. I closed my eyes and took it in. I loved her.

Karen and Monica visited me on family days. John Moravek, the Century 21 Legal Department sailor who had fired me, visited and said he was proud of me. Like a surrogate father, he took me under his wing and encouraged me along during my first tenuous years of sobriety. Sadly, he passed suddenly of a heart attack in 1995. At his funeral, I told the crowd how he had fired me and saved my life.

When I left New Beginnings, I had a cavernous hole inside and would have it for years, but it slowly filled in as I did my work. I attended ninety meetings in ninety days, found a sponsor and a therapist, and worked the AA steps like my life depended on it (because it did). It's been the hardest thing I've ever done.

I found work at a law firm in Century City and commuted back and forth for years, making enough money to buy my first ever brand-new car (1988 VW Jetta with a sunroof) at two years of sobriety. Also, at two years sober, I quietly took an English class at the local junior college, not sure I was smart enough to be in college. After all, it had taken me four tries to get my high school degree and I wondered if Dad could be right about my stupidity. I showed up to every class, did every assignment, and got my first ever A. I kept taking classes and after two more years was voted "The Most Outstanding English Student," which came with a partial scholarship. I transferred to UCLA and finished my degree in English literature two years after that.

Making my father proud was something I'd wanted my entire life, but it didn't matter now. I was proud of myself and proved I wasn't stupid after all and could accomplish whatever I set my mind to.

Making sense of what happened to me in the first twenty-five years of my life has been a lifelong pursuit. It's confusing to worship a father you hate and be manipulated and forsaken by your mother. I worked through Laura Davis and Ellen Bass's book *The Courage to Heal* while also working on the AA steps. I attended anger management classes through the National Council on Alcoholism, and I started seeing a woman therapist. I would be in therapy for the next forty years uncovering and healing from my childhood. When I wrote my first Fourth Step, I had anxiety attacks and cried for months, but I wrote down all my toxic, dark secrets. When I finally did the Fifth Step, I went through a box of Kleenex as my sponsor listened to me read my Fourth. Afterward, I was so filled with light and hope I thought I might blow away in the wind. I felt like I had lost hundreds of pounds.

Since my mother and I were only ten days apart in our sobriety, I went to her house one day in my third year of sobriety, overcome with anxiety and grief about the sexual abuse I was working through. It was then that she told me that my father never thought incest was wrong. Stunned, I asked her what she did about it.

"Nothing," she said. "What could I do? He had all the power."

For me, this is complicated grief, and I have tried to work through it for fifty years. While I loved my father, I also hated him for abusing me and stealing my confidence. And while I loved my mother, I also hated her for forsaking me.

The hardest thing I've done lately has been to face myself in writing this memoir. It's been a lot like another Fourth Step. In AA, they say we will take many Fourth Steps throughout our lives, and it's true. This one has been the hardest.

I've written this memoir to heal at another level and to be part of the conversation happening in the world now from survivors of all kinds. For so many generations, family trauma has been passed down, whether it be sexual, mental, emotional, or physical, and nobody talked about it. I'm proud to say the family trauma ended in my family. I have worked hard not to make the same mistakes my parents made. It takes a whole reeducation of the brain and is forever ongoing.

The book is titled *Nineteen* because that's when I became autonomous and had to figure life out on my own. It was the year all the air was sucked out of my life when my father died.

Thanks for reading.

An update on the family: Monica died in 2016 of an opioid overdose and cirrhosis of the liver. She was haunted by the relationship she never had with her biological father. She never met him and never healed from the betrayal of all that our mom and dad did to her.

Karen is married, has three children, and lives in Northern California.

Mom died in 2021 at age eighty-one from kidney failure. I promised her I would not publish another memoir until after she died. I kept my promise. My husband, David, and I took care of her for the last twenty years of her life. She retired from nursing after her final stay in a psychiatric institution in 1993. We bought her a mobile home near us in 1995 and supported her. She struggled with bipolar for the rest of her life, going on and off her medications at will. She manipulated, cajoled, took advantage of, and used me up until I almost gave up on her before she died. But I stayed with her until the bitter end.

I've been married to the same loving, kind, and generous man for thirty-five years. We have the dream that has always lived in my heart: a family of our own with two beautiful children. I am bursting with pride at the life we've created.

The primal need for parental love is a basic yearning. Wading through the minefield I grew up in has taken my entire life. I have found peace and acceptance, and for that, I'm grateful.

Acknowledgments

Thank you, the indomitable Brooke Warner, for being my publisher, writing coach, friend, and for always believing in me. You are a warrior, and I admire you greatly. Your wisdom and guidance have meant the world to me as I travel this road as an author. I am lucky and grateful that our paths crossed over a decade ago.

Without the kind and loving Judy Reeves, I could get nothing done in my writing life. You have always supported me, so my deepest thanks for being such a wise and generous mentor, coach, and editor of my work and for your patience and unwavering belief that I could finish this project, even when I disappeared for long stretches without warning.

Thanks to Suzy Vitello for helping to sharpen and focus my story. Also, thanks to Julie Metz and She Writes Press for the book's incredible cover and outstanding design. Thank you to my hardworking and enthusiastic publicist, Crystal Patriarche, Tabitha Bailey and Hanna Lindsley, and the entire BookSparks team, who have represented me for over a decade. Thank you to Lauren Wise Wait for being the best project manager and associate publisher any author could ask for. I feel much gratitude to Shannon Green for jumping in to expertly help bring my book over the finish line.

To my loving husband, David, who is my biggest supporter and was the first person to encourage me to write this memoir, thank you,

Honey. And to my sweet daughter, Marina, who serves as my social media manager and head cheerleader in all my writing endeavors, thank you, Sweetheart, for all your hard work. Thanks to my son, Dylan, for the original music in my book trailer, and audiobook and for always believing in me as I walked this challenging road.

To my "almost" stepmother, Elisabeth Brolin Clark, thank you for supporting my journey in writing this book and repeatedly sharing the details of the plane crash. Your survival these last forty-five years is a testament to your strength and character. I'm sorry for being a bratty teenager to you during the years covered in this book.

I am immensely grateful to my therapist for the past twenty-five years of life-changing work we've done together.

I'm also grateful to my dear friends Anita Knowles and Janis Siems for your support and willingness to listen to me talk about my process. And to Lisa Moravek, who has unconditionally supported my journey since we reunited, I am thankful for your support. The reunion with old friends Ron Johnson, Beth and Phil Neis, and Cher Ford have enriched my life. Thanks for your friendship, reading my pages, and supporting my journey. Raine will always live in love in my heart. Please email. I'm most appreciative to Carole and Winston Bumpus for the safe haven of their beach cottage on the Central Coast of California to write. I walk taller having you all in my life.

I am immensely grateful for my She Writes Press sister authors. Being part of a community of women writers has meant the world to me and dovetails into my spirit and vision for my life. Your sisterhood has made me greater than I could be on my own.

About the Author

photo courtesy of Leslie Johansen Nack

Leslie Johansen Nack's debut, *Fourteen: A Daughter's Memoir of Adventure, Sailing, and Survival*, received five indie awards. Her historical fiction novel *The Blue Butterfly: A Novel of Marion Davies*, has won six indie awards, including the 2023 IBPA Benjamin Franklin Gold in Historical Fiction. She has a degree in English literature from UCLA and is a member of The Authors' Guild, The Historical Novel Society and the National Memoir Association. She lives outside Seattle with her husband. You can find out more about Leslie on www.lesliejohansennack.com.

Looking for your next great read?

We can help!

Visit www.shewritespress.com/next-read
or scan the QR code below for a list
of our recommended titles.

She Writes Press is an award-winning
independent publishing company founded to
serve women writers everywhere.